Child Rearing and Personality Development in the Philippines

CHILD REARING AND PERSONALITY DEVELOPMENT IN THE PHILIPPINES

*George M. Guthrie and
Pepita Jimenez Jacobs*

THE PENNSYLVANIA STATE UNIVERSITY PRESS

UNIVERSITY PARK AND LONDON / 1966

preface

A psychologist interested in the phenomena of human personality often longs for the opportunity to know how different the behavior of an individual would have been if antecedent conditions had been different. He also asks whether the common characteristics of those whom he studies are the product of a common experience or the manifestations of all human beings everywhere. We owe to the anthropologists the belief that human behavior is modifiable almost without limit. However, we do not have the degree of control over human subjects necessary to vary many of the factors which we consider of greatest importance in determining adult personality. Different societies, however, do provide some of the variations whose effects we might like to examine. It was a desire to examine different conditions of personality development which prompted George M. Guthrie to seek a Fulbright appointment in Southeast Asia.

Guthrie spent the year from June 1959 to June 1960 on a Fulbright Research Award at the Philippine Normal College in Manila. It was his purpose to help the Child Study Center there develop a program of research on Filipino children. Shortly after his arrival he began to work with Pepita Jimenez Jacobs who was a staff member of the Center. Except for one year at an American university where she earned a masters degree, she had spent her life in the Philippines. She grew up in a large Philippine family in a community in Bataan on the shores of Manila Bay. Her curiosities were about her own people. She was most dissatisfied because American books, theories, and concepts had prompted Filipino teachers to think of Philippine children as American children, at least in those moments when they took literally much that they read. She was anxious to develop a knowledge of her own group based on studies of Philippine children. Mrs. Jacobs later became a graduate student at The Pennsylvania State University where she completed her doctorate in 1964.

This report of cross-cultural research is in several senses a bicultural product. The authors have attempted to combine the questions and observations of a newcomer with the insights of a member of the society. The product reflects its dual origin particularly in the chapters which report the feelings and experiences within a Filipino family. We have striven for continuity of style, but many pages will reveal differences in modes of thinking not only in the ideas but in the style of presentation. With the same intent, we have cited many of our respondents without converting their statements into idiomatic English. In some instances we have used Philippine terms when they cannot be translated adequately by English terms. Pronunciation follows the rules of the Spanish who set down Philippine dialects in Western script.

The authors are grateful for cooperation and assistance from many sides. The United States Education Foundation in the Philippines, known there as the Fulbright Office and directed by Dr. Jesus Martinez, was most helpful. Dr. Emiliano C. Ramirez, President of the Philippine Normal College, and members of his faculty made our data collection possible by their lively interest and helpful suggestions. Dr. Emilio Edualino gained the cooperation of his student teachers as interviewers. The Child Study Center, directed by Mrs. Adelaida Diyco, provided stenographic and clerical help, and materials and space. Several hundred Philippine Normal College students collected data for us, thirty in particular donated much time to the project. Hundreds of Philippine mothers talked for hours about thousands of Philippine children. If anyone declined our request for help, he did it with such consummate Philippine interpersonal skill that we were unaware of his refusal.

The analysis of the interviews was made possible by grants from the College of Education of The Pennsylvania State University. The Department of Psychology of Penn State aided in the preparation of the report in many ways. Indeed, the cooperation of colleagues made possible the sabbatical leave out of which this research has emerged. In addition we wish to thank Joan Hemman and Mary Ann Lloyd who helped with many aspects of the analysis and writing. Finally, our gratitude to Katherine Ratcliffe, Ruth Barks, and Ingeborg Van De Venter for their good nature and excellent typing.

G. M. G.
P. J. J.

University Park, Pennsylvania
January, 1966

contents

chapter 1

INTRODUCTION

The Philippines offers an almost ideal situation for the study of patterns of child rearing and of personality development. Filipinos have many children, they watch them carefully, and they love to talk about them. It is in many senses a society which takes great pride in its children, and there is at the same time a tradition of hospitality and openness to visitors and strangers which makes it possible to seek information freely and to expect remarkably frank and complete answers.

Although the country was ruled by the Spaniards for three hundred years and by the United States for another forty, the Filipino way of life has remained largely unchanged, particularly within the family system. The Spaniards brought with them the Roman Catholic religion, but pre-Christian beliefs and practices still figure prominently in the lives of many children. The Americans brought the English language into the country, but Philippine dialects are still spoken in the homes, and Filipinos still think of their children in terms of ideas best expressed in their own language. Theirs is a way of life to which a veneer of the West has been added in the cities, but at the core it remains Filipino and, in a larger sense, Malay. Thus it provides an accessible pattern of living which can be contrasted with another culture in such a way as to reveal many of the dynamic processes of both. For with different premises about the nature of children and with different ideals for adults, the Filipinos present a culture which has much of intrinsic interest and which permits a study of alternatives to the conditions in which babies become children and children become adults in the West.

Our Purposes

This research report seeks to present a description of the behavior and expectations of Philippine parents toward their children, a comparison of these findings with data from other cultures, particularly American, and a point of view in interpreting the role of childhood experience in the determination of adult behavior. A description of aspects of another society enables us to understand better the range of behavior possible and calls into question or confirms the universality of some of the descriptions of sequences of development which we have come to accept from observations of our own society.

The comparison of cultures offered us the opportunity to ask such specific questions as whether Philippine mothers were more permissive than American mothers and whether a certain pattern of childhood experience was inevitably followed by a given adult pattern. Once beyond the most superficial considerations, however, we found that this process of comparison presents some very real difficulties. The first efforts in the study led to the conclusion that a comprehensive point-by-point comparison of Philippine and American practices was not possible because parents in the two societies did not use parallel constructs in thinking about children. We would not find it particularly meaningful to match the adjustment patterns of an upper-class housewife and a lower-class male adolescent in American society. Their worlds are too different. Their experiences do not have many areas in common where comparisons are possible. So it is with children from two different cultures; their lives develop around different foci of interest and stress. In one society obedience and respect are critical areas of conflict and concern; in another society there is a premium on modesty. Depending on their definition of a child and of childhood, parents are concerned with different aspects of a child's development. Using different linguistic systems, mothers conceptualize their responsibilities differently, so differently that a good parent in one society may not be a good parent at all in another.

Our point of view grew out of our early efforts in this study and from a theoretical bias about personality theories. Briefly, we feel that it will be more fruitful to look at the problem of personality formation using the concepts of Sullivan's interpersonal theory rather than classical Freudian concepts. This preference developed because Freudian theory has too many biological and cultural universals which do not survive when they are examined in the light of data obtained in markedly different societies, whereas interpersonal theory enhances the likelihood of seeing and interpreting culturally determined patterns.

Theoretical Framework

No research treatise has been necessary to establish that there is a continuity in the personality pattern of an individual from childhood to adulthood. The means by which similarity in diverse situations is maintained is not readily explained by concepts ordinarily employed in psychological research. We deny that explanations in terms of an individual's innate nature or temperament are satisfactory, but we are not very convincing in alternative explanations. By and large we would insist that the mechanisms of recognizable similarity in personality are learned rather than innate but learned in such a manner as to resist marked modification by new learning.

Almost all of the theorizing and research in the domain of personality theory has been done with, or influenced greatly by studies of, disturbed persons. This has led to excessive attention to the discontinuities and failures of adult behavior and to their antecedents in childhood. The concepts which have evolved have been most useful in ordering events in pathology of individuals. Their predictive and descriptive utility outside of this domain remains questionable. The extrapolation of these concepts from psychopathology to account for differences between cultures is even more tenuous. It may be useful to examine certain events or crises in the childhood of a patient and to deduce the likelihood of certain sequelae in adult behavior. This is an empirical matter and can be checked for accuracy. Even if it is confirmed that an alcoholic who has suffered severe oral deprivation in childhood is less likely to respond to psychotherapy, it does not follow without separate confirmation that everyone in the same society who has experienced oral deprivation during childhood will later become alcoholic. It is also certain that other alcoholics can easily be found in the same society who give little evidence of early oral deprivation. With this level of uncertainty within a single society, it would be a dubious procedure to argue that any society which enjoys a great deal of drinking or for which alcohol is a problem has this characteristic because it has a certain pattern of breast-feeding and weaning. Extrapolating from couch to culture gives an interpreter a feeling that he has accounted for his observations. There is, however, a need to keep score on these explanations because the same childhood experiences can be followed by very different adult behavior. We know this now in the case of individuals, and we would very likely find it true of societies if we examined data with this question in mind.

A number of conceptual systems have been offered to account for the continuity of behavior from childhood to adulthood and to relate the phenomena of the adult to experiences in childhood. These have been developed in the study of individuals in clinical settings and have been extended to whole cultures with child-rearing practices being related to national character.

The Conceptual System of Kardiner

The most significant attempt to develop a genetic theory of national character is that of Kardiner and his collaborating anthropologists, Linton, DuBois, and West (1945). Drawing on psychoanalytic formulations, Kardiner developed a system which he termed "psychodynamic analysis." According to his system each child undergoes a certain set of experiences at the hands of significant adults. These more or less sanctioned patterns of behavior by adults toward children are the *primary institutions* which give rise to the *projective systems* of the child. Projective systems, which are unconscious, are the modes of interpreting the world which the child carries through life. These in turn give rise to the *secondary institutions*, particularly folklore and religion, which are manifestations of the operations of the unconscious projective systems or ways of interpreting the world. Secondary institutions are fixed modes of thought or behavior which are shared and communicable and result in personal or group disturbance if violated. Kardiner acknowledged that the key situations in childhood which influence personality formation, i.e., the primary institutions, differ from one society to another. The constellation of events which makes up a primary institution for one society is not necessarily universal. He acknowledged also that most attention has been directed to the primary institutions which in American society appear to give rise to neuroses. He dealt also with the question of whether secondary institutions, the product of projective systems, are permanent or subject to change. He concluded that they are not necessarily fixed, "if other factors are introduced into a child's life to counteract them."

Kardiner's formulation is an application of traditional psychoanalytic theory to the problem of explaining differences between groups. His concepts of primary institutions or child-rearing practices, projective systems or unconscious modes of thought, and secondary institutions or adult belief systems are an ingenious union of psychiatric and sociological concepts. There is in his theory an emphasis on the role of unconscious determinants of adult behavior and on the prepotency of early childhood experiences as sources of unconscious determinants. It is never clear how much subsequent events overcome the effects of certain primary institutions. The tendency is clear, however, to look for the major sources of variance of adult behavior in early childhood experiences rather than in the contemporary situation. For instance Kardiner (1945, pp. 29–30) says, "The more the ethnographer tells us about the traits of these people, the greater the number of institutions that we can place as derivatives of this basic personality structure. For example, we hear that the people discussed above have no interest in the arts and their skills rate very low. We also hear that they surrender easily to illness. These traits fall easily into place once we know the basic personality structure; but these particular traits *could not be predicted*." If we require only the condition of explanation, we have a theory which may be built of such vague constructs that in explaining data it may be accounting for very little. Kardiner expressed the hope that the theory built around the concept of basic personality structure would have some predictive utility if comparative studies could be carried out on fifty different cultures.

There are, however, several shortcomings in the psychoanalytic formulations of the relationship between childhood experiences and the behavior patterns of adults in a society:

1. Psychoanalytic concepts focus attention on those elements in middle-class Western families which are of primary etiological significance in the neuroses of middle-class Westerners who seek psychoanalytic help.

2. The roles of subsequent events and of contemporary determinants are minimized or ignored.

3. It has not been proven that the antecedents of individual psychopathology, Western style, are the significant determinants of shared belief systems and patterns of interpersonal relationships in either the Western or the non-Western world.

4. A vigorous application of the law of parsimony would result in explaining many aspects of behavior as the result of well-understood learning processes without having to invoke concepts of projective systems.

The Conceptual System of Whiting and Child

Whiting and Child (1953) have attempted to interpret the relationship between events in childhood and adult behavior patterns using the concepts of the Hullian learning theory. The *habit* and *habit potential* of Hull are changed to *custom* and *custom potential* of a typical member of a society. Thus, as a result of certain customs observed by parents in their activities with young children, the children acquire potentials for the expression of certain behavior as adults. Psychoanalytic theory provides the basis on which estimates are made of the domains in adult behavior in which the custom potential acquired in childhood would be manifested. For example, anxiety aroused by severe weaning experiences should lead in adulthood to explanations of illness in terms of something one has taken in through the mouth. Using data from seventy-five societies, Whiting and Child evaluated the relationship between certain events in childhood and certain belief systems in adulthood. The results were usually in the positive direction but, as in much correlational research, most of the variance was not accounted for.

Inasmuch as the childhood experiences examined are those emphasized by Freudian theory and the predictions made have a similar theoretical background, the Whiting and Child research is an empirical test of Freudian theory. The results suggest that there are many other sources of variance in addition to the childhood experiences examined. Their data show that socialization practices in the oral, anal, sexual, dependence, and aggression domains of a child's life are apparently independent of one another. That is, knowing that a society is quite severe with respect to training in the realm of dependency does not enable us to predict that it will also be severe with respect to aggression. This is in accord with the Freudian theory that difficulties or fixations are specific to certain of the organism's activities. But although they are based on the same Freudian theory, predictions of specific consequences in adulthood produced by fixations in childhood are not given much support by the findings of Whiting and Child.

Partly as a result of his experience using uneven ethnographic data from the Human Relations Area Files, Whiting and his collaborators developed a standardized system for participant observation (Whiting, 1953). The conceptual system delineated and the variables chosen for observation represent a shift away from a strictly Freudian viewpoint toward the theory of personality formulated by Murray (1938). Studies of six societies using this formulation have recently been published under the editorship of B. B. Whiting (1963). Aside from the fact that the Whiting Field Manual was developed for participant observation techniques rather than single interview contacts, there are at least two subtle ways which may be worth pointing out in which this formulation differs from our own methods in orientation to cross-cultural research. Whiting contends (1953, p. 2), "Another view—the one which we take here—is that although whole cultures (or whole individuals) are indeed unique, the component attributes, if properly selected and defined, are not. . . . Societies may be compared with respect to their common attributes without decrying their individuality." Our experience in this research has led us to the position that there are very few attributes which are common. Behavior which is superficially similar often turns out, upon closer examination, to occur within a context of meaning and purpose which is very different, at least in the two cultures with which we are familiar (Guthrie, 1966).

A second difference in emphasis lies in the amount of variance in adult behavior which we would attribute to socialization experiences in childhood. We are convinced that it is most parsimonious to account for as much behavior as possible in terms of the present situation of the individual. Since we have noted a wide range of socialization practices within a single society without a correspondingly wide range in adult belief systems, we are inclined to relate belief systems to the individual's reference group rather than to his childhood experiences. Evidence to support one emphasis over another is difficult to specify because the pattern of relationships between antecedent and consequent variables is exceedingly complex. Suffice it to say at this point that we place less emphasis on what has been called childhood determinism than does Whiting.

It is our contention that, given a certain pattern of childhood experiences, there are a large number of possible adult belief systems that individuals may hold. The explanation adopted will be influenced more by the prevailing opinion of significant others at the time the belief is acquired than by any other factor. The resistance of these views to change is probably a function of the fact that they are learned at an early age and/or are consensually validated by the group, rather than evidence of their being an expression of unconscious forces acquired in early childhood.

A Conceptual System Based on Interpersonal Theory

There are, however, alternative formulations of the process of personality development. These involve different models with different sets of concepts. Attention can be directed to different aspects of the process so that persons with different points of view will often not be concerned with the same data. Although offering an alternative formulation is a difficult task in the domain of personality development because Freudian theory has so preempted the field, we can gain a different perspective by following the formulations of G. H. Mead and especially of Sullivan and other socially oriented theorists.

It is not as simple a matter to offer a resume of Sullivan as it is to offer an outline of Freudian theory. Sullivan was not a system builder, actually most of what has been published under his name appeared after his death and was assembled by his colleagues. This has culminated in the recent publication of his collected works (1964). Probably his most eloquent expositor is Mullahy (1948, pp. 279–315). Sullivan is usually grouped with Horney and Fromm and other Neo-Freudians whose theories have been influenced by evidence from other social sciences.

Sullivan called his formulation the theory of interpersonal relations. He emphasized that, given a biological substrate, human beings are the product of their relationships with significant others. In place of Freud's single instinctual source of motivation, Sullivan suggested that individuals seek the goals of satisfaction and security. The former refers primarily to the reduction of tissue needs while the latter has to do with a feeling of belonging. Anxiety which arises when this latter need is frustrated, is the result of loss of contact with others, of a feeling of alienation and of being disapproved. The individual develops a good many "security operations," ways of relating to others which are designed to reduce disruptions in interpersonal relations. Sullivan suggests that the child tends to emphasize those aspects of himself which are pleasing to significant adults. In focusing on those performances which bring favor or disfavor, the self is developed as a "system of reflected appraisals." His emphasis is on understanding personality as the product of learning in contact with other people. This is in marked contrast to the Freudian view of personality as the system of resolutions of basic instinctual conflicts at certain crucial stages of development.

In our research we have been greatly influenced by Sullivan's system. As we see it, a child is born in a society with an established pattern of role relationships. There is a range in behavior that may be expected between various pairs of persons depending on sex, age, importance, and a host of other factors. Each individual develops a concept of himself as a result of his early relationships, a concept with both verbal and preverbal components, and one which becomes increasingly difficult to change as more and more learning takes place. This self concept gives continuity to a given individual's behavior patterns, for it serves as a sort of reference point in his decisions. It is learned at the hands of significant other people, usually parents and older siblings, and it leads to predictability within the family since the self is a system of reflected appraisals. It will vary, of course, from one family to another and will be different depending on the sex, age, appearance, and other factors in the subject. Personality develops within the matrix of the interpersonal experiences of an individual. He becomes in part what others expect of him and in part a compromise between their expectations and his own capacities. Personality patterns are learned, and since the demands of different cultures are different, so are the personalities which emerge as responses to those demands.

There is a good deal more accord in the folklore and supernatural beliefs of a group than in the specific details of their childhood experiences. Individual personality differences are much greater than differences in adult belief systems. We can account for a shared folklore in terms of communication in this domain throughout both childhood and adulthood. Myths and legends are learned from older persons; there seems to be little need to invoke a complicated set of projective systems based on early childhood experiences. Our emphasis then would be on current motivation, the present determinants of behavior. There is in this system no assertion that present patterns must be congruent with earlier patterns; rather the child changes as his prescribed roles change, sometimes gradually, sometimes abruptly.

Role definitions change with age, particularly over the years up to adulthood. With the changes in the shared expectations of his society which are directed toward a child, the child's behavior also changes. Behavior modifications can be abrupt and dramatic as in the case of those societies in which *rites de passage* are observed, or they can show a slower rate of change with wider individual differences. Children can go from dependence to independence, albeit painfully, if a society so defines an expected role shift. Aggression can be expressed up to a certain age and then sharply curtailed. It is our contention that changes of this sort, which probably take place in the transition from childhood to adulthood in every society, are a product of changes in role prescriptions. The new behavior is a fulfillment of shared expectations rather than an expression of earlier childhood experiences. The power of shared expectations is dramatically demonstrated in the case of those who feel they have fallen under the power of someone practicing witch-craft. It is also seen in instances of marked behavior changes among those who have violated taboos and been exposed. These examples illustrate our contention that it may be more productive to pay attention to contemporaneous motivation, the expectations of the present, than to earlier experiences in the Freudian genetic sense. This does not deny the therapeutic efficacy in individual cases of examining early childhood experiences to modify determinants of adult neurotic behavior, although a good many therapists might question the procedure on other grounds. We do assert that in the interests of parsimony we should seek to account for as much behavior as possible as a product of present influences on the individual. From this point of view it is necessary to pay attention to the way individuals relate to one another in all ages and stations and to avoid concentrating solely on the early mother-child interaction. We feel that, in seeking to account for personality organization and personality changes, it is more productive to consider role definitions which are shared and communicated than to utilize concepts of projective systems and related instinctual and acquired unconscious processes and forces.

The opposition of our point of view to that of Kardiner is parallel in many ways to the nature-nurture controversy and could be tested by evidence that would parallel the studies of identical twins raised in differing environments. The potency of early childhood experience versus later role expectations as determinants of behavior could be evaluated if we could observe children from one pattern of childhood experiences placed in two different sets of expectations for a number of years. No such study is known, but the anecdotal evidence from immigrant families suggests that young adults who move into a new culture can become rather completely assimilated without having shared in the childhood experiences of the new culture.

There are two important corollaries to the adoption of this point of view. Since interpersonal theory is culturally rather than instinctually oriented, it provides concepts which point to and emphasize differences between cultures. Interpersonal theories reiterate the role of environmental factors, and it is the environmental factors which concern us most in cross-cultural studies. The second corollary is more subtle. With differing value systems and differing approved patterns of interpersonal relationships, we can look for different personality dynamics, different areas of conflict, different adjustive mechanisms, in short, different personalities. Where the demands and expectations of two societies are not the same we should not expect the same personality processes, for personality refers in part at least to the habitual solutions individuals use to meet the demands they face. For example, the handling of sexual urges is extensively regulated in Western society. Personality patterns, in part at least, are the mechanisms individuals have developed to cope with demands in this conflictual realm. In another society the handling of anger and irritation may be much more emphasized than in the West. As a result the adjustive processes which we call personality will be organized quite differently and the participants in the society will seem quite different, as in fact they are. An interpersonal orientation thus gives us the concepts needed for an understanding of differences and offers the possibility of identifying other conflict areas that would be virtually denied by a more instinctual theory with its emphasis on physiological universals.

Problems of Comparisons across Cultures

A number of problems come to the fore when we attempt to compare two or more cultures, problems that are not recognized as long as we confine our attention to the one culture in which our conceptual system was derived. The pattern of events and concerns to which we must direct our attention are not the same from culture to culture. Applying Western-based concepts to a non-Western society we look for crucial events related to bowel training, sex differentiation, autoeroticism, and possibly handling of sibling rivalry. These events and interactions occur everywhere, but their significance in the life of a child may be quite different. In no sense can they be considered crucial personality-determining foci in the lives of all children everywhere. In another society parental attention may be concentrated on the inculcation of respect patterns, on the development of sensitivity for others' feelings, and on sharing habits where food is scarce. The significant formative events can lie in quite a different realm of a child's experience in different cultures.

This is in essence an adaptation of Whorf's hypothesis (1956) of linguistic relativism to the area of personality formation. Whorf asserted that an individual with linguistic system A actually experiences reality differently than does a person from linguistic system

B, because different concepts of the two linguistic systems draw attention to different aspects of reality. Our contention is that personalities, as configurations of reactions developed through experience, are quite different in pattern where the significant childhood experiences have been different. In more Sullivanian terms, since different cultures provide different threats and anxiety sources, the security operations which individuals develop will differ in configuration as well as in degree. These in turn will be reinforced by the linguistic patterns of the specific culture which will not only point out dangerous areas but will also tend to label appropriate security steps. For example, respect toward elders may be an area of anxiety in a society. Violation leads to severe disapproval. *Disrespectful* will become synonymous with a severe threat, and *respectful* will become a much sought characterization. In Western society *sissy* and *manly* have comparable roles. Extending our consideration, we find that the word which we have translated *disrespectful* will really mean something a little different, including not knowing one's place, presuming, lacking shame, and possessed of a scheming attitude. A member of the culture concerned could feel as distressed being called *disrespectful* as would an American male being called *effeminate*.

The conceptual system we have tried to use suggested not only an appropriate method of research but also pointed to areas of fruitful inquiry. Since it emphasizes the importance of role models and the expectations of significant others, we felt it important to concentrate on the attitudes and reports of mothers. And since we were dealing with the central importance of relationships between people, we concentrated our attention on those activities in which the child was with his mother or with significant older persons. At this stage of our knowledge the interview method seemed most appropriate. Written questionnaires were precluded by language and literacy deficiencies, and participant observation techniques would have restricted us to a very small number of children. We do not learn all there is to know about the processes of personality patterning in children from the information a mother gives an interviewer; but it is indispensable to know how she feels, what she says she does, and her reasons for doing so. With these purposes in mind we developed an interview designed to enable us to describe mother-child relationships, to compare these with equivalent data on another society, and to evaluate the usefulness of interpersonal theory in the study of child rearing and personality development.

chapter 2

CULTURAL VARIATIONS IN PARENTAL EXPECTATIONS

Having explained our adoption of the interpersonal or Sullivanian point of view, we intend now to examine reports of child rearing from a number of societies in order to develop this point of view, paying particular attention to the relationship between parents' ideas of the nature of children on the one hand and the sequence of child-rearing practices they follow on the other. This is not a test of the efficacy of the conceptual system as opposed to more traditional Freudian theories; it is, rather, an attempt to explore some of the range of views which may be found and to determine the child-rearing behavior that is associated with different definitions of the nature of the state of childhood. It is also designed to develop a perspective on our Philippine findings which will be reported in subsequent chapters. We have chosen to pay particular attention to the shared views of a society concerning the nature of a child, the shared expectations about crucial periods of change in a child's capacities, the role of the family structure, and the differences in treatment accorded to male or female children which may follow from different roles of men and women in adulthood.

The Definition of a Child and Its Effect on Child-Rearing Practices

Every society has a shared set of notions about a child, his nature, his potentialities, and his expected rate of maturation. The entire pattern of child-rearing practices and attitudes developed by the society is more or less congruent with this definition. A mother's emotional relationship with her child, her nurturance, discipline, and instruction are to a great degree influenced by the society's role expectations of the child at a given age.

An examination of a number of societies shows a highly consistent relationship between the definition of a child at various stages of development and the corresponding child-rearing practices of the adult members of the society. We shall try to demonstrate this relationship by considering a number of societies in which we can trace the marked coherence between the concept of the child and the child-rearing practices.

Non-Responsibility and Permissiveness

In the Philippine *barrio* studied by Nydegger (1963) it was shown that in this society a baby is considered to be a capricious, "senseless" being who matures in a leisurely and very individualistic manner. (We shall use the word "senseless" in this chapter in spite of its evaluative overtones. We mean a very limited capacity to learn.) Since it is useless to try to accelerate him, he is not encouraged to walk or talk, although the early achiever is greatly admired. Expectations are raised as the child matures, but these are always kept below the child's potential. Consequently the child is removed from danger rather than instructed to avoid it, and all problems are met indirectly by distracting and pacifying the child.

This sense of leisurely maturation influences all of the mother's actions in feeding, toilet training, modesty training, and even weaning. From the age of four months onward foods to supplement the mother's milk are gradually added to the diet, so that by the age of two the child begins to feed himself and at three eats regular adult food. Toilet training is equally as casual. At about one and a half years, when the child can walk, he is directed to the corner to relieve himself and later to the outhouse. Nydegger observed that control is obtained with no apparent resistance. Modesty training is similarly casual. Once toilet-trained, the boys are given short pants and the girls properly covered by their caretakers.

By definition the child begins to gain "sense" at four and by six can profit by instruction, training, and coaxing. However, discipline at this age includes only mild scolding and teasing, with a slap only if there is a clear violation of a prohibition. When the child is considered ready, he is sent to school, which symbolizes that he has reached a new maturation level. Here he is never pushed and is expected to give an adequate performance, not to excel. As he becomes older, he gains increasing responsibility and participation in family and kin affairs as a reward and as a social necessity. With the completion of sixth grade, childhood comes to an end.

We find a somewhat different pattern in the Okinawan village of Taira, studied by Maretzki (1963). Here an infant is a "helpless, pitiable treasure, incapable of knowing, understanding or learning" until he reaches six years of age. His antics are the misbehavior of a willful, capricious god, totally unpredictable and uncontrollable. Since he is godlike, he does not know better, and vice versa. Once the child reaches first grade, he is expected to begin to be more adult and responsible, much as is the Philippine child. However, in the meantime, this concept of the godlike fosters extreme indulgence, protection, and nurturance of young babies. The entire family goes out of its way to protect and indulge the infant. He is breast-fed any time, pacified, and kept quiet and comfortable for the first months. Until the period of weaning, all changes are gradual—as with the slow introduction of solid foods and the tranquil disregard of elimination.

When the little god turns five, he faces new independence and responsibility along with the expectation that he will prepare for the first grade. This brings a dramatic change in status. After a brief period of reward for responsible behavior, the child graduates to "sensible" status and is punished, though inconsistently, for omissions as well as commissions.

In Java, Geertz (1961) found a similar continuity of behavior patterns based on a definition of the child. The baby is seen as fragile and vulnerable to the sudden shock of a startling or emotional experience, which would lower his defenses and allow evil spirits to enter and cause illness. The child is consequently handled in a "relaxed, supportive, gentle and unemotional way" through infancy, weaning, feeding, toilet training, and sex and modesty training, until five or six when he is expected to become truly Javanese by learning proper respect and emotional control.

Minturn and Hitchcock (1963) in their study of the Rajputs of Kalapur, India, similarly found the child defined as pure and holy, susceptible to supernatural dangers, and, having committed no sin, unable to distinguish between good and evil. However, since in this extended family situation the child is just another infant, one incarnation of an individual, babies are not objects of interest or anxiety. Instead of the actively indulgent patterns of the societies thus far considered, the practices of Rajput adults are aimed at the cessation of a response, not at stimulation. All children are considered alike, not as independent individuals.

Except for rough treatment in bathing, the infant's life is free from stress and from deliberate creative stimulation. Usually no one pays any attention to the child, although adults respond promptly to its cries unless they are involved in other tasks. For the first two years the child is an observer, never alone, never the center of attention. This passive interaction continues throughout childhood. Children are nursed on demand. When the infant urinates, he is casually held away. When bowel movements are anticipated, the child is held over the courtyard drain; otherwise the mother wipes up the feces and cleans the baby with a slight show of disgust. The child is not encouraged to walk early because he will be a nuisance. When the child can speak, he is considered able to respond to directions and may be punished for failure. However, he is still considered too small to learn from verbal instruction and thus is taught through observation and imitation. During the years from infancy to school age there is a gradual transition from observer to participant depending on the family need for help. The primary emphasis is on obedience and passivity.

From four to six the child begins to take on adult responsibilities and standards. Boys spend more time with the men in their activities, and the girls stay home with mother. Chores and duties become regular. Parents become impatient, scold, and judge the child harshly by adult standards. The child lacks self-reliance, but he envies and desires the adult position and consequently seeks to achieve it.

The people of Tepoztlan, the village in Mexico studied by Lewis (1960), in a manner similar to the Rajputs of Kalapur attempt to limit and protect rather than stimulate the child. Although child-rearing practices do center around making the child less troublesome, he is indulged as a means of making him easy to control. As in the Indian society, the child is not hurried in his development. However, from five to twelve severe discipline is used to teach and control the child.

Romney's (1963) study of the Mixtecans of Juxtalahuaca, Mexico, indicates four very definite and distinct stages in the development of the child: the infant without awareness and ability to reason, the weanling entering early childhood aware of himself as an individual but still unable to reason, the five- or six-year-old shouldering the responsibilities and activity of late childhood with a capacity to reason, and the twelve-year-old as he enters youth and becomes actively aware of sex. This study will be considered later in detail in regard to the society's role expectations of the child at different ages as they affect the child himself. It suffices to say here that the actions of the adult toward the child are consistently influenced by the definition of the child at various ages. Each of the societies which we have noted so far appears to be permissive and indulgent. They do not hold the young child responsible for what he does. Since they feel that the child is largely incapable of learning, they make little attempt to teach him until he has reached an age, often about six, at which he is considered capable of learning and of improving as a result of punishment. Let us turn now to societies which are more demanding of their children and examine the relationship between the definition of the child and child-rearing practices.

Responsibility and Higher Expectations

Among the Gusii of Nyansongo in Kenya, studied by the Levines (1963), the infant is defined as fragile and susceptible to malevolent influences. Every effort is made to satisfy its needs and insure its survival. However, this concept changes drastically between weaning and initiation into adulthood. During this interval when the child is considered capable of being trained, he holds the most inferior status in the community and is ordered about and punished by everyone older than he. The helpless infant becomes the lowly, unruly servant who must be forced into the mold of adulthood through heavy duties and punishment.

Between the second and third year the child faces a series of drastic changes—weaning, birth of a sibling, responsibility and aggression training, and toilet training—which prepare him for his new role of responsibility and low status in the community. Weaning is postponed until the child can walk and take care of himself somewhat and usually occurs within two months after the mother finds herself pregnant again so that there will be no competition between the older child and the infant. Feeling that severity induces a faster and smoother transition, mothers use a bitter substance on their breasts and punishments such as slapping or burning with caustic juice rather than emotional comfort in weaning. The birth of a new baby is very disturbing to the child following so closely the loss of this physical relationship and dependency. The mother interprets the cries of the child as a death wish for the new infant and severely canes and punishes him to control his aggressive and dependent manifestations. Likewise "crying for nothing" is punished by severe beatings. Shortly after the new birth the older child is taught to relieve himself in the fields, and after a short learning period any infractions of the rule lead to caning.

Accompanying the change in the child's relationship with his mother is a more general change in his relationship with the entire community. Until initiation into adulthood (at eight or nine for girls and between ten and twelve for boys) the child is called "uncircumcised boy" or "uncircumcised girl," a term connoting inferior status. He is obliged to obey everyone and has few rights and privileges that must be respected by elders. Adults see the child as foreshadowing the man and, in attempting to curb his impulsive acts, use heavy physical punishment to teach correct behavior. Yet the mother's responsibility for the child's health and behavior breeds a strong though inconspicuous emotional attachment between mother and child. Levine observes that the mother, overburdened with an agricultural and domestic workload, must delegate care to siblings and reduce the maternal role to the bare essentials. Consequently most mothers will use any device to stop crying and trivial demands when they are busy but, inconsistently, will indulge the child when time permits.

In Gusii society, where the child is expected to take on heavy responsibilities at an early age, obedience, rather than enterprise or initiative, is considered the key to success. Beginning with the birth of a sibling, duties and errands mount steadily throughout childhood. An adult will never get something himself if he can order a child to do it. Similarly, older siblings demand services and distribute punishments. Although chores are not strictly sex-typed for the uncircumcised child, boys begin herding animals while very young while three-year-old girls carry small pans of water on their heads and at five serve as caretakers. Children may help their mother in the fields at three and by six or seven do extensive hoeing and other domestic and agricultural chores, so that by the age of initiation the child has already shouldered heavy economic responsibilities in the community.

Superficially there seems to be a relationship between the economic need of these people and the severe patterns of treatment of the child. However, it is difficult to determine whether this need is merely a rationalization on the part of the parent or is indeed more real and pressing than the need in the other societies we have considered. In numerous societies with pressing economic problems—the Philippines, Okinawa, Java, India, and Mexico—we have observed no excessive demands upon the children for economic contributions to the society. An evaluation of the Gusii on the basis of all the societies we have considered indicates that economic need itself is not enough impetus for such expectations of the child and that it is the definition of the child in this society which forces him into the harness of responsibility at such an early age.

Children in the matrilineal society of Jamaica (Clarke, 1957) also have very definite responsibilities and chores around the home and may be severely punished for shirking them. However, in this case, because many homes are fatherless, the children and mother cooperate in domestic duties in constant companionship and interdependence necessitated by the family structure of the society. We will study this problem in greater detail in another section of this chapter.

Conflicting Definitions and Ambivalent Training

Having discussed several societies with harmonious definitions of the preschool child, we should consider one which sees the child as angelic but at the same time as basically evil to determine how these opposing concepts influence the child-rearing patterns. In the Puerto Rican village studied by Landy (1959) the child is seen as a plaything, lacking in ability to think or to act independently. Curiously enough while the child is regarded as an innocent angel, it is also believed that the male is born with *malicias* (vices or bad habits with a connotation of craving to violate sexual taboos) and that the girl is born defenseless and corruptible. This basic contradiction may explain the inconsistent child-rearing patterns and the ambivalence and capriciousness of parents who assume that as long as the child is not in trouble, they do not have to actively guide him. Because of this contradiction in expectations, parents vacillate between extreme indulgence and extreme restrictions. When the infant cries, a majority of the mothers are highly responsive. The child is breast-fed on demand but is not forced to eat. There is no common weaning pattern. As might be expected in this instance, the weaning is either gradual or abrupt with scant middle ground and is completed as early as seven months or as late as seven years. When food is available, the child may eat all that he can, but at the same time he is saddled with strict table etiquette which may or may not be enforced depending on the whim of the parent.

Toilet training, too, is characterized by extremes. Mothers do not feel that the child can train himself, nor do they feel that control comes with maturation. Usually they become very active and emotional about the problem, holding the child over the pot and spanking or scolding him in irritation when he does not respond. Bed-wetting, so calmly accepted and ignored in the Okinawan society, results in cuffing, spanking, and scolding. Masturbation, sex play, aggression, and violation of cleanliness taboos are all severely punished. Parents do not permit children, especially girls, to stray far from home, in order to prevent potential mischief and stop them from learning bad things from other children.

Landy also reports that obedience is highly important but involves a conflict with the masculine ideal of aggressiveness where mother and son are involved. Rewards are infrequent and unsystematic, in part because parents fear that a child will become swelled with praise and lose respect. Children are not relied on to get things done since a child is considered unable to reason and unwilling to listen. More than half of the children are not given regular chores to perform although later tasks and duties increase sharply and become a burden. These are assigned merely as duties and do not engender initiative and independence. Although a mother does much to foster the strongest kind of dependency, the resultant behavior irritates her, and as the child grows older, she becomes less and less responsive.

It is not surprising, that along with the inconsistency and ambivalence which Landy notes in the Puerto Rican village he also reports that half of the parents whom he interviewed demonstrated rejecting attitudes toward children in general. This is in marked contrast to the other societies which we have noted in which there were marked differences in overt behavior but still strong evidence of the acceptance of children.

Stages of Defined Transition in Childhood

In our consideration of continuity in the definition of the child as related to child-rearing practices in various societies, we have seen not only the development of a consistent pattern of treatment for the child but also definite transition points at which a child's role in society is redefined. For instance, after the age of six or seven in a majority of these societies the child ceases to be considered "senseless" or without judgment and is given definite tasks and responsibilities. These transitions indicate that the parents and the society define the child as having certain characteristics and abilities at a certain age, and that they expect, and usually obtain, marked changes in behavior at certain relatively fixed points in the child's life. We shall examine in detail one society in which these transitions are strikingly clear and then refer to several of the cultures that we have already cited.

Among the Mixtecans of Juxtalahuaca, Mexico, studied by Romney (1963), childhood is divided into a series of obvious stages. The "senseless" *infant* gains awareness at the time of weaning when he enters *early childhood,* a stage which lasts until he cuts permanent teeth. *Late childhood* begins with the sixth or seventh year when the child slowly gains the capacity to reason. *Youth* begins at age twelve or thirteen when the child becomes actively aware of sex. A child who dies before he reaches this age becomes an angel because he is not responsible for his status in the next world. In spite of these definite stages in childhood, transitions are smooth and flexible with the exception of weaning and the change from early to late childhood.

Until the age of two the child is considered to be like an animal—without awareness or ability to reason. Awareness is developed gradually but the ability to reason is not acquired until about age seven. Realizing that character is in part learned, the parents believe they are capable of shaping the development of the child, especially between the ages of six and twelve. In the period of early childhood the child is capable of learning by repetition but is not considered capable of learning by reason. Since he cannot recognize right from wrong, he is not considered responsible for his behavior.

At five or six the Mixtecan enters late childhood and suddenly finds that he is expected to be able to reason and to learn from teaching. New parental expectations at this stage bring a drastic change in the activities of the child and an increasing demand for responsibility accompanied by a withdrawal of nurturance. The child's concept of himself reflects the new status accorded him by parents and community. The transition to a responsible role is smooth. Wanting to be older and identifying with the roles he must assume, the child discharges his tasks without a fuss and quickly changes from a passive to an active role in the community. Although strict obedience and mastery of skills are not expected until later, the new duties are associated with new techniques of discipline and punishment which replace the early childhood rewards and nurturance. Since the child can understand, nurturance is not considered appropriate. Slowly over a period of two or three years the roles of the male and female are differentiated and the child becomes subject mainly to the parent of the same sex. Thus begins identification by sex which leads to the period of youth.

In a society in which the stages of transition are very distinct we can see how the child and the parent react and conform to the role expectations of a given age. Looking back to some of the societies previously studied we can see similar relationships.

In the Philippines in a characteristically gradual pattern the child changes between the ages of four and six from a "senseless," capricious infant into an individual who can be taught. The infant is not expected to learn feeding, toilet habits, and modesty, and consequently socialization practices are casual and indulgent. Even the weanling is indulged in his emotional upheaval, quickly becoming involved with his peer group and kin as a substitute for maternal nurturance and taking on a few chores as a means of slowly integrating into the community. By six the child is expected to learn through instruction and reasoning, but consistent with the pattern of indulgence, he is never pushed.

In Okinawa the child is indulged as a capricious, helpless god until the age of six and then having reached the age of reason, is expected to behave and perform as an adult after a short period of training and reward. The preschool child is defined as "senseless" and uncontrollable and consequently is surrounded by an atmosphere of permissiveness which fosters casual social training and indulgence. As he reaches kindergarten, the child is faced with a constant but gentle pressure to learn proper social patterns but does not face a dramatic change until he reaches first grade. At that point he suddenly finds his kindergarten activities ridiculed by adults who expect him to learn new skills and obedience because he has now gained "sense." After a short period of reward he graduates to the status of a responsible individual in the community.

A parallel situation occurs in India where the pure, susceptible, innocent child is kept from stress and deliberate stimulation until between four and six when he begins to take on adult responsibilities and is judged by adult standards. In his early years he is raised with as little conflict as possible since he is too "senseless" to be of any help and would only get in the way. Weaning, too, is casual and apparently causes little upset. However, as the child begins to gain the ability to reason at four, he is given an increasing number of chores and responsibilities and is expected to meet the adult standards which he is so eager to achieve.

Among the Gusii of Kenya, contrary to the practice of other societies we have considered, the "senseless," fragile infant is suddenly jolted from his secure position between the ages of two and three and is delegated to an inferior, servant status in the community until initiation into adulthood in the later preteen years. Until then he is deprecated as an "uncircumcised" child and is heavily punished for childish behavior and misdemeanors. At the age of three he begins to shoulder some of the adult workload, and by six or seven he does many heavy tasks in the community.

In Puerto Rican society as reported by Landy (1959), it is not possible to trace the transition in role expectations at different stages of development because the conflict in definition of the child makes rearing patterns and expectations unpredictable and conflicting. However, in each of the other cultures noted the transition from one stage to another is determined by the society's expectations of the child based on its concept of his mental capacities at a given time. In each of these societies the actions of the child and his reactions to his environment are largely determined by the cultural expectations for the child at that age. We have seen in Mexico, the Philippines, Okinawa, India, and Kenya that the behavior of a child at any stage in his development is an expression of the role expectations of his society though he may be capricious, "senseless," or mature. Furthermore, rather sudden changes in role behavior can be produced by changes in expectations.

Family Structure

A most important factor in child rearing is family structure. Since it is beyond our purposes to attempt a comparison of basic family structures and relationships in different societies, we shall restrict ourselves to the description of a few home situations. An examination of the family in three societies, India, Jamaica, and China, will illustrate the role of this basic unit in child rearing.

Among the Rajputs of India, studied by Minturn and Hitchcock (1963), the patrilineal extended family is valued highly and primary emphasis is on its solidarity and unity. The nuclear conjugal family relationship is ideally kept subservient, and a man will side with his brothers or his mother against his wife. The stress is on the male line of descent. In the sample consisting of Hindus and a few Muslims used by Minturn and Hitchcock, women are of inferior status and must observe *purdah*. Men and women live in separate quarters; the women and children center their activities in the courtyard, and the men and adolescent boys center theirs on the separate men's house platform. The wives of brothers usually share the courtyard along with their young children, unmarried daughters, son's wives, and son's children—two or three generations related in the male line living together. The average number of women and children per courtyard in these extended families is seven; three adult women on the average feed five or six men and adolescent boys. Although arguments between wives may necessitate setting up a separate hearth, the basic patterns of authority, property allocation, and economic cooperation of the extended family are never broken. The rank of the husband determines the rank of the wife. Often closely related families of the same lineage live in one area, although they may or may not be closely knit. This extended family situation has several important effects on the child-rearing patterns which we have previously noted: for the first two years the child is a passive observer, free from stress, given little affection or attention as an individual, but surrounded by kin and secure in his environment.

With many women and older children in the courtyard, the child has many caretakers and need not depend entirely on his mother for nurturance and care. Although the mother is the primary caretaker responsible for feeding, dressing, and washing, if she is on good terms with other women of the courtyard, they will help with her children when she is busy, even offering the child a milkless breast as a pacifier. If nothing is effective, the child is assumed to be hungry, and someone takes over the work of the mother so that she can feed him. When the child becomes more mobile, he is turned over to a child caretaker. The role of men in the care of the young child is negligible except for occasional discipline. In spite of helping in caretaking, a woman will never interfere with or punish another's child if the mother has seen the misbehavior; although, depending on her personality, the grandmother may intercede and demand lenience.

As a secure member of a group, the child learns little self-reliance or individuality. His sensitivity to group approval is manifested in parental sanctioning techniques, i.e., a mother may say "What will so and so think!" or a father may publicly announce his displeasure in his son on the men's platform. Sometimes all the mothers will refuse to speak to a child implying group, as well as individual, sanction.

In later childhood the child is suddenly expected to meet the standards of his adult relations in his chores and behavior. By six the child's care is delegated to the parent of the same sex. The boys are exposed to stricter discipline and masculine values and learn the family loyalties and hatreds. Children perform chores regularly and are eager to attain the coveted status of adulthood. However, parents judge their child's work in comparison with adult performance and are impatient with ineptness while learning. Thus children are not notably self-reliant or conscientious.

The patrilineal extended family system influences the development of the child by making him an object of little affection with many caretakers, giving him a strong sense of group membership and need for group acceptance, and demanding adult behavior and competence from him in later childhood. Now let us consider the effect on a child of a matrilineal society with an insecure family structure.

Among the Jamaicans studied by Clarke (1957) the relevant kin are invariably on the maternal side, and the grandmother's household is often associated with the family land and line of inheritance. Parenthood is the hallmark of adulthood and normal, healthy living, but men are satisfied with the proof of their virility and do not necessarily accept the obligations and duties of parenthood. Children are "woman's business," and a man who does not provide for them meets no public censure. Types of unions include marriage among the few financially able; concubinage, which tests compatibility and in which the woman helps work; lowly housekeeping, which usually terminates when a child arrives; and a matrilocal arrangement on the woman's land which she may terminate if her husband proves unfaithful or inconsiderate. Except for marriage these relationships are seldom stable. Children by other mates are seldom taken into a new relationship but are farmed out to maternal relations if the mother is financially unable to support them. Most men acknowledge their responsibility for maintaining children by women with whom they have cohabited for any length of time, but upon separation their assistance becomes sporadic because of financial insecurity. Poor relief often helps keep mother and children together.

Only 58 per cent of the children in Clarke's study lived with both parents, and these early and most impressionable years coincide with the time of greatest parental strain and tension. The mother is the main caretaker of the children. However, the grandmother always accepts responsibility for the first child and may collect other legitimate and illegitimate kin in her home. A woman may build her own house on family land as a means of caring for her children. The instability of family relationships has important effects on the development of the child and on child-rearing practices. The child may accept any one of a number of women as his mother. He may learn to call his grandmother "mom" and, copying his mother's brothers and sisters, call his mother by a pet name. Suckling may be the only act establishing the maternal relationship. After weaning the mother may seldom see the child and may be replaced by a sister caretaker.

Attitudes and mother-child relationships in the simple family households based on marriage and purposive concubinage are different from those which develop in casual housekeeping and fatherless family homes. In the latter the mother-child relationship evolves into protective interdependence which smothers self-reliance and initiative. A majority of the children in lower-class working homes live during the formative years under the threat of a disruption of family life. Although this is not a unique individual experience in their culture, it has a profound effect on the relationship between parent and child. The child, seeing his mother turned out for another woman and faced with paternal indifference if not harshness and outright neglect, consciously or unconsciously learns to depend on his mother for permanence and security. Even when the father is with the family, the mother is the principal teacher and disciplinarian, and mother and child cooperate in home duties with constant companionship and interdependence. The girl identifies herself with her mother, while the boy begins to build up a type of behavior which according to Clarke might be described as "husband substitute." The authority of the mother and the duty of the child is never questioned because of the intimacy and stability of this one dependable relationship in the child's life. As a result of the intensity of this relationship, going to school is a major crisis to the child because it forces a break in his companionship with his mother and puts her authority in conflict with that of the school.

The mother depends on the child to do household tasks before he goes to school or in lieu of school, yet the teacher flogs him if he is late or absent. The mother's authority is challenged by those who have undisputed control over the child most of the day, and the child is forced into the traumatic situation of choosing to obey his mother or the teacher.

Finally, the boy never learns a different father role, and the cycle is repeated since neither society nor experience teaches him the meaning of paternal responsibility. One feature of the strong mother-son relationship is that the persistence of the son's dependence into adulthood results in failure to achieve personal independence or to develop satisfactory relationships with others including his mates.

Vividly contrasting with the maternally oriented society of Jamaica are the Chinese studied by Hsu (1948) before the Communist takeover, in which the father-son role is the basic relationship, and all other family relationships are regarded as extensions subordinate and supplementary to it. The father-son relationship is based on mutual duties. The father must raise his son in the tradition of his ancestors to perform his duties properly in both the material and spiritual worlds; the son must honor and obey his father and after his death carry out the proper rituals related to the spirit of his dead father. The mother-son relationship, similar to the paternal one but with less authority, is based as much on biological ties as on the extensions of the system. The husband-wife relationship is subordinate to the parent-son relationship. The principles underlying this patrilineal kinship system are lineage, generation, sex, and seniority. These are preserved through the stringent social patterns which permeate Chinese life. For example, the living quarters are set up on the basis of social correctness rather than in consideration of personal preference, comfort, or hygiene. A number of closely related nuclear families (brothers and their old parents) often live together in one home occupying separate sections of it. The parents live in the wing of the eldest son. Some rooms are overcrowded, while large areas may be unoccupied. Members of each individual family occupy rooms in the same wing or two adjacent wings. Although form calls for obedience to all older relations, the father often resents the interference of other relatives. Only the parents have real authority over the child, and the interference of grandparents may lead to increased inconsistency in punishment.

Aside from this socially exacting kinship system, there is another set of ties with the spiritual world of the ancestors which overshadows many aspects of Chinese life. The ancestors are the source and basis of socialization of the younger generation. The family is considered a continuation of past generations and a preparation for coming descendants and lives in accordance with the ancestors' wishes and for their glory. Happy ancestors imply prosperous descendants and vice versa.

Rather than allow differences in temperament among children, adults encourage children to conform to the common ancestral traditions. Education aims to mold the child into the pattern of his parents, grandparents, and ancestors and prepares him to assume the traditional, prescribed roles as soon as possible by training him for his livelihood, social adequacy, and ritual appropriateness. Consequently the child develops little individuality or independence.

In learning to conform to the ancestral pattern the child is encouraged to act as an adult. Childish acts are tolerated but not encouraged, and since parents are proud of the mature child, there is no concept of helping the child play as a child. Most children quickly become acquainted with the family business and learn to please the spirits by witnessing the rituals. Girls are given chores earlier than boys and care for siblings, wash clothes, harvest, and cook at six or seven while boys of twelve and thirteen still roam around. The adult male and his sons are unalterably bound together. The father is anxious to have his sons measure up to envisioned heights almost at birth. Thus no part of the adult world except sex is closed to the child, and no part of the child's world is his own. The child is praised verbally or by the spirits at a seance for skill in trade, social and filial acts, ritual generosity, and individual achievement, just as an adult is.

The Chinese society based on paternal and ancestral authority thus has three major effects on child-rearing practices. The child grows up in a world based on authority and competition for ancestral glory; he is encouraged to mold himself in the ancestral patterns rather than to develop independence and individuality; he is encouraged to dispense with his childish play at an early age and act as an adult, carrying on his material and spiritual duties.

Each of the three societies which we have observed in regard to family structure has its own kinship system and relationships which defy definition in the kinship terms of another society. How can we compare the role of kin in child development in India, Jamaica, and China when the relationships in one society cannot be expressed in terms of those of another? How can we measure the relationships when in the case of China a whole spiritual world of ancestors is involved? How can we begin to determine the differences, when kin may serve as surrogate mothers in some societies? Obviously comparison is highly complex. We must content ourselves for the moment with observations of the effects of the family structure on the child-rearing practices in each society as a separate unit. We have found that the pattern of child-rearing practices is indeed influenced by the family structure and relationships in each of these societies.

Differential Treatment of the Sexes

We have argued that the definition of the child and the concept of his place in society at a given age is the basis of consistency in child-rearing practices. However, in many societies two children of the same culture and even the same family may grow up in emotional environments and social relationships entirely foreign to each other based on sex differences. Differential treatment of the sexes is an important variable in any study of child-rearing practices. We shall examine the importance of sex discrimination in six societies: in Kenya and Mexico where sex does not determine acceptance, in China and India where the female holds inferior status and hence is attended more carelessly and harshly, and in the matrifocal societies of Java and Jamaica.

Among the Gusii of Kenya studied by Levine (1963) children of both sexes are highly valued because the male has a permanent stake in the homestead and the female brings cattle as bridewealth at her marriage. Both boys and girls are treated alike except that modesty is stressed earlier for girls. Girls are also considered more reponsible than boys, show more initiative in chores, and have heavy work loads by six or seven. Girls are said to grow up more quickly and are initiated into adulthood and the full work load at eight or nine while boys are not initiated until ten or twelve. In adulthood childhood equality is lost, and the woman's only means of achieving status and prestige is through bearing children. The woman has few protected rights, and the husband may always withdraw his favor or take a second wife.

Among the Mexicans studied by Romney (1963), where exploitation of one sex by another is atypical, the family acts as a cooperative unit in all situations, and even when a man has public duties, his wife shares them with him. The family ideal is to have many children of both sexes because it is inevitable and because the family needs their economic contributions. It follows that the father prefers sons to help him, and the mother prefers daughters. The family with children of only one sex receives sympathy. The father spends little time with female children and interacts intensively only with his sons over twelve who join him to work in the fields. In the early childhood period of no responsibility, Romney observed no sex differences in treatment or in the development of behavior systems except that the nurturant response of girls is greater and increases with age. Socialization of sex behavior is handled casually, and clear-cut differences do not appear until the age of five or six when the child begins to take an active part in society as a member of the labor supply in sex-differentiated tasks, a process which occurs gradually over the course of two or three years. Mothers make constant demands on girls who are trained earlier and have more frequent and time-consuming duties such as caring for siblings, carrying water, running errands, tending the fire, caring for animals, cleaning, and washing clothes. Boys at the same time begin gathering firewood, running errands, and taking food to their working fathers. At the age of twelve they shoulder an adult work load when they join their fathers and brothers in the fields.

In these two societies sex typing of interpersonal relationships and roles in the society is delayed until late childhood, and child rearing in general is not influenced by discrimination on the basis of sex. Thus the male and the female develop in a similar emotional and instructional environment during the crucial early years. On the other hand, among the Chinese before the Communist takeover (Hsu, 1948), we find the female child entering a world in which women have inferior status and female infanticide is common. From the first, parents show greater indulgence and preference for boys. The male child may be carried on his mother's back for two or three years, the female for a much shorter period. Every effort is made to cure the sick child, but the effort for the male is considerably more than for the female. At the age of four or five discrimination manifests itself in the increasing work load for the female child. By the age of six or seven daughters care for younger siblings, clean, wash clothes, and soon learn to help harvest and cook. By twelve or thirteen they carry a considerable portion of their mother's burden while boys of that age still roam about freely. Although the father is the final authority, the mother disciplines both sexes until the age of ten. Then the father begins to discipline the male but has little control over the female. Since the caretaking is delegated to the parent of the same sex, the mother disciplines girls more severely than boys.

The female in the adult world occupies a subservient position. She carries all the uncleanness associated with sex and childbirth and is excluded from the spiritual and ancestral system of rewards. She holds a subordinate position in the extensions of the father-son identity system which forms the basis of the Chinese social structure. She can only look forward to old age when she will be honored and revered as her son's mother in a relationship similar to that of the father and son although with less authority.

In India among the Rajputs studied by Minturn and Hitchcock (1963), the prevailing preference for sons in a culture where female infanticide was banned at the turn of the century is still reflected in the fact that almost twice as many female children as males die because of lack of prompt and prolonged medical care. Two-thirds of the living children are males. The vast difference in the worth of the female and male child is evident from infancy. The midwife is paid twice as much for delivering a boy, and only sons are given elaborate birth ceremonies. However, most couples prefer to have at least one daughter because giving a daughter in marriage is a virtuous Hindu act.

Up to the age of four or five children wear the same clothes, although girls are not protected from the cold with warm garments as are boys. In dictating chores, however, the mother is especially lenient with her daughter, making duties irregular and brief because a girl is considered a guest in her own house and will soon have to work hard for her husband's family. Mothers also express a sentimentality for girls not expressed for boys. Care gradually falls to the parent of the same sex, and boys occasionally sleep in the men's quarters to which they will move permanently at the age of twelve. Girls are gradually expelled from the men's platform where they play in early childhood. A mother may continue to discipline her sons but ineffectively because the sons, now aware of the low status of their mother, become rude and unmanageable. In the men's world boys are exposed to stricter discipline and masculine values. While daughters soon marry and leave the village, sons remain and hence must be taught the patterns of loyalty and hatred which define their social group. The child now has regular chores, although the extent of his work depends on the size of the family for girls and the size and wealth of the family for boys.

In the Indian and Chinese societies where the male elements are the core of the family structure, the female is in an inferior role, and every aspect of her early training and the atmosphere surrounding her are affected by her lower status and value. The question is, in a matrifocal society, where the woman forms the basic kinship unit and is the core of family structure, is the opposite implied?

Among the studies reviewed there are a number of matrifocal societies, but none of these manifests discrimination on the basis of sex. The Javanese society studied by Geertz (1961) is matrifocal, consisting of a solid core of women with a loose periphery of men which is unstable because of the high divorce rate. In spite of familial dominance by women there is no discrimination. In fact girls get less attention in early years than boys. Girls receive modesty training earlier and are given regular chores such as shopping, selling goods, and household duties, while boys run comparatively free. Girls are kept at home and are relatively isolated because sociability interferes with chores, while boys, who as adults are not so important to the family unit, are free from domestic obligations.

Among the Jamaicans studied by Clarke (1957), where the relevant kin are invariably on the maternal side and the basis of inheritance is often matrilineal, the sexes are also treated equally. The children of both sexes help with domestic chores and the instability of family life fosters mutual dependency between mother and child, the only permanent ties in the family structure.

An Overview

In our analysis of various cultures in this chapter we have tried to show how a society's definition of the nature of a child has a great deal to do with the kinds of relationships that develop between parents and children and between children and all other individuals. We have cited several societies in some detail in order to develop a perspective for examining Filipino children. We have noted that the set stages of transition in a society, the family structure, and the sex of a child have much to do with the development of a child, but by and large it is the attitudes of people—the parents, siblings, kin, and neighbors—that are crucial rather than the handling of certain specific transitions such as weaning or toilet training. We could have isolated one aspect of the child-rearing pattern and then tried to show the relationship between this event and the adult personality. However, the pattern of parental attitudes and expectations toward children are the factors which produce continuity in the experiences of the child. Children become in large part what parents expect them to become. Parents have a more or less shared set of ideas of the nature of a child at a given age. These are communicated to the child as they guide the parents' treatment of the child. It is not a simple matter to prove that parental expectations are more significant than parental handling of certain crucial development stages such as weaning or toilet training; it is simply our unsupported contention at this stage that this is the more fruitful way to approach the study of parent-child relationships and of personality formation.

chapter 3

A BRIEF LOOK
AT THE PHILIPPINES

A glimpse at the Philippines, designed to give the reader some feeling for the social and physical environment of the country, would seem desirable before we present the results of our research. The greatest danger we face is oversimplification. Filipinos are very different from one another, the more so as one gets to know them. Eighty different dialect groups reflect the fact that there are differences from one island to another. Recognizing the uniqueness of each individual, we can still offer certain generalizations which will provide a context for our report.

Geography

The Philippines is a chain of islands just north of the equator, stretching from close to Formosa to within sight of Borneo. It is a southern extension of the islands of volcanic origin which include Japan. The islands run in a north-south direction and frequently have a mountain ridge in the center rising to four thousand feet or more. Almost all of the people live on the narrow coastal plains which surround most of the islands. Since they are in the tropics the major differences in temperature are a function of altitude rather than of latitude or season.

The Filipinos are descended from the same racial origins as the Indonesians, the people of Malaya, and the Thais. Although their prehistory is not well known, it is almost certain that some of their ancestors migrated down the Malay peninsula into Sumatra and Java and then north by way of the islands of Borneo and the Celebes. There is evidence that others migrated directly across the East China Sea. The languages of Malaya, Indonesia, the

Philippines, and many adjacent areas are similar and are referred to as the Malayan portion of the Malayo-Polynesian language system. There have been several waves of migration into the Philippines which have apparently had the effect of driving earlier inhabitants into less desirable mountain areas. At the present time the least accessible mountain regions of the Philippines are inhabited by Negritos, black pygmy descendants of peoples who are believed to have lived in much of this part of Asia prior to the arrival of the Malays. The present inhabitants of the lowland Philippines are descended from groups who probably arrived in the Philippines about two thousand years ago.

In the processes of migration these peoples became separated into smaller groups and in their isolation developed different dialects. In addition to the more than eighty dialects in the Philippines there are over two hundred in Indonesia. These languages were readily transcribed in the Roman alphabet by early Western missionaries and governors. Today, earlier forms of Malay writing are rarely found. The multitude of dialects, however, has impeded the educational and cultural development of the Philippines. To overcome this there has been a serious attempt to develop the use of a national language, which, as has happened in several other Asian countries, varies only slightly from the dialect of the capital city. In the Philippines the people of Manila, the capital, and of the surrounding area of the large island of Luzon speak Tagalog from which the national language, Pilipino, has been developed. It was in this area that our research was carried out.

History

The Spaniards arrived in the Philippines in 1521 and had more or less completed their conquest of the islands by the end of that century. For the following three hundred years their reign and influence were largely undisturbed. Because of the treaty of Tordesillas the Spaniards concentrated on their holdings in America. The Philippines was governed through Mexico, contact being maintained by the annual galleon which sailed from Acapulco to Manila. There was little wealth in the Philippines to benefit the Spaniards, but they accrued great riches from the trade with China which passed through Manila. Similarly, while Spanish priests worked diligently converting almost the whole population to the Roman Catholic faith, they kept one eye on China and longed for the day when they could work in that richer land. When the United States seized the Philippines in 1898 and suppressed the subsequent struggle for independence, they found an almost feudal system operated by the Church. America's rationalizations were not too different from those of Spain. It was their God-given responsibility to educate the people and incidentally to use the Philippines as an area for expansion of America's trade with Asia. Forty-four years of American occupation saw expanded programs of health, welfare, and education, but the Philippine economy developed around the American market for sugar, coconut oil, and manila hemp. Independence came in 1946, about a year after the last Japanese were driven out of the Philippines. Thus, after four hundred years the Filipinos could call their country their own although it was still severely damaged by some of the most destructive fighting of World War II.

Two other influences should be mentioned. From India across South Asia and into Java came the Hindu religion which is practiced in Bali to this day. But most Indian influences became fused with indigenous practices, and their manifestations in the Malay world, particularly the Philippines, are difficult to discern. For more than a thousand years Chinese junks have traded with the west coast of Luzon and Mindoro. Brass gongs and porcelain burial jars remain as silent testimony to this trade. Living evidence are thousands of Chinese who now reside in the cities and towns and millions of Filipinos with Chinese ancestors. The Chinese have migrated in large numbers to all of the countries of Southeast Asia where they control much of the wholesale and retail trade. The ruling class of each of these countries has a high percentage of Chinese ancestry, much higher than that of the rank and file. But the Chinese language and Chinese religions have not achieved a proportionate manifestation in the mainstream of Philippine culture. With Spanish, Indian, Chinese, and American influences exerted on them the Filipinos have preserved to a remarkable degree the Malay way of life. They are more like their Indonesian cousins from whom they have been more or less separated for two thousand years than like their more recent Spanish and American conquerors or their Chinese neighbors who have flowed in a small but steady stream across the seven hundred miles of the China Sea.

Climate

The Philippines is part of Monsoon Asia with tropical temperatures and seasonally heavy rainfall. In the region of our study the temperature rarely goes above 100°F and rarely below 70°F. By the standards of a temperate climate there is little variation from month to month and also little from the hottest part of the day to the coolest part of the night. The monsoon winds bring heavy rainfall from May to October. There is very little rain from January to March.

The temperature pattern determines clothing, housing, and food supplies. People of tropical areas are influenced in their selection of clothes by considerations of modesty and the need for protection from the sun, not by the need to keep warm. Housing is designed to protect them from heavy rainfall and from intense heat. Food supplies become available throughout the year, so there is less need for extensive storage of food than is the case in temperate climates. Each of these factors has had a profound impact on the style of living which has evolved in the tropics.

Persons from temperate climates are sometimes led to interpret life in the tropics as simple and leisurely. A closer study of man in a tropical environment suggests that his life has its hardships and complexities too. The lazy, carefree native gathering coconuts is no more representative of life in the tropics than is a Boy Scout hike representative of living in a temperate forested area.

Since a supply of food is almost continually available, there is less incentive to modify nature and wring from her more than she freely gives. Accordingly crop yields are low. There has not developed in equatorial areas the belief that man must struggle with, and modify, his environment. On the contrary, accommodations are made to what are considered the imperatives of nature, and a fatalistic view of life, which accepts things as they are rather than fights to change them, is common. This is exemplified by the hillside farmer who burns off the brush, raises crops for a couple of seasons, and then moves to another part of the hillside when his patch has eroded and lost its fertility. Because of this attitude there has developed virtually no pattern of conservation or long range investment for improving resources.

Housing is not designed to give each family member very much privacy. The whole family characteristically sleeps in one room, often under the same mosquito net. This has given rise to another misconception that persons who live near the equator are not as inhibited in matters of sexual relationships as those who live in colder climates. A number of movies and novels tend to spread this view. This is a mistaken idea. In tropical areas there are many taboos, some different from ours, surrounding sexual behavior. Western morality as exemplified in movies is quite immoral by the standards of many non-Western peoples. Even though adult persons of the same family may sleep in the same room, they may never expose themselves to one another. They develop considerable skill in changing their clothes and in bathing, retaining great modesty all the while. Indeed, Western bathing suits are found offensive by many persons who live in areas where clothing is not needed for warmth at all.

In the Philippines men who can afford to do so dress in Western style. The farmers often wear shorts and a shirt, particularly while working in the fields. Women wear Western dresses with longer skirts than are usually the fashion from Paris, avoiding low necklines and sleeveless designs. Children may go naked until six, but after that they wear at least shirts or a simple dress. Women, who are very modest about the cut of their dress, breast-feed their babies quite openly on buses and in the markets. This is not defined as immodest except by those from the cities who have fallen under Western influence. Similar patterns of modesty prevail even in non-Christian areas of the islands, except that some women in these areas do not feel obliged to cover their breasts.

The Locus of Our Research

The data for this report were collected from mothers who lived in the *poblaciones* (towns) and *barrios* (villages) within a fifty mile radius of Manila on the large island of Luzon. This is an area of relatively level countryside only slightly above sea level. For the most part one crop of rice is grown each year, a crop which depends on the monsoon rains since there is not an extensive irrigation system. One half or more of the farmers are tenants with farms of from two to ten acres. Farming is carried on with locally made hand implements or plows. The only source of power is the carabao or water buffalo. Incomes are low, with few in excess of one hundred dollars, or four hundred pesos, a year.

Those who live in the towns are tradespeople, government employees, teachers, craftsmen, fishermen, laborers, and a small number of landlords. Their income and educational level are usually higher than are those of the rice farmers. The lines of demarcation between town and countryside are blurred by the fact that relationships by blood and marriage are very common between semi-urban and rural groups. Contacts with Manila are also common and easy because there is an extensive network of roads throughout much of Luzon and a well-developed bus service. Movement toward the larger cities, particularly Manila, has been increasing markedly, for urban residence has higher status and there is a labor surplus in the rural areas. Education is valued among other reasons because it facilitates the rural to urban transition.

Our interviewers, who were student teachers on practice teaching assignments, came from similar backgrounds and from essentially the same geographic area as the respondents. They did not ordinarily have their internship experience in their home municipality. The culture gap between them and the mothers whom they interviewed was minimal.

About half of the interviews were conducted and recorded in Tagalog, and many more were at least partially carried out in Tagalog but written in English.

Social Science Research in the Philippines

Although the Philippines was under the control of the United States for the first forty years of this century, it has not proven an attractive area of research for many American scholars, and scholarly interest seems to have declined over the period of American possession. The earliest reports on the Filipinos were, of course, not made by social scientists, but are nevertheless the product of shrewd observation often influenced by moralistic evaluations.

The most comprehensive work on the Philippines is Blair and Robertson's fifty-four volume translation of reports, principally in Spanish, covering the period of 1493 to 1898 (1903). A great many of these reports are by missionaries and other people of the Church. Two fascinating descriptions written in the last century of Spanish rule are provided by a Frenchman, Gironiere (1854), and an Englishman, Foreman (1890).

Early in the American period H. Otley Beyer went to the Philippines and in the next sixty years became the dean of social scientists in that country. His interests range from ethnography to archaeology, and his collection of writings and artifacts dwarfs others in the Philippines. Beyer's work is scattered in journals, and a major portion of it in a great many unpublished volumes is in the Museum of Ethnology and Ethnography in Manila, where he is now curator. Other early anthropologists included Barton (1930), Cole (1945), Keesing (1962), Lambrecht (1932), and Vanoverbergh (1932). These men concentrated on the non-Christian areas of the Philippines, particularly the Mountain Province of Luzon, and largely ignored the more populous, advanced, Christian lowland areas. More recent anthropological interest, such as the work of Lynch (1959), Hart (1955), Fox (1953), Kaut (1961), and Stoodley (1957), has been concerned primarily with lowland Filipinos, although Eggan (1954), Scott (1958), and Conklin (1957) continue the interest in the Mountain Province. In addition sociologists Hollnsteiner (1962), Coller (1960), Pal (1963), and Hunt (1954) have begun to study social structure in the Philippine lowland groups. Most Filipino social scientists are members of college and university faculties where their responsibilities are so demanding that they have little time for research. Significant contributions have been made, however, by Oracion (1952), Pal (1963), Tangco (1951), Hollnsteiner (1962), and many others who have just begun to report their research.

One of the first psychologists to work in the Philippines was A. V. Hartendorp who went from the United States in 1917 with the intent of giving intelligence tests to isolated groups. Since he was employed as a teacher, he was sent to lowland areas and had little contact with the isolated groups. He did do some testing, reported by Carreon (1926), on Philippine school teachers. Hartendorp remained in the Philippines, established a literary journal which was destroyed by the war, and is now executive secretary of the American Chamber of Commerce in the Philippines. In more recent years Stewart went to the Philippines to give tests in that culture. However, his book (1958) is more a travelogue than a research report.

Relatively little research has been done on Filipino children. Pecson's annotated bibliography (1962) of research done in the Philippines lists only four studies concerned with socialization, none particularly relevant to our research. There are, however, four later studies which have been published since our data were collected. Nydegger (1963), participating in Whiting's coordinated study of child rearing in six cultures, lived in an Ilocano *barrio* in northern Luzon and, using anthropological techniques of participant observation, developed an extensive description of child rearing in one rural community. Although his results are somewhat different from ours, this may be largely a function of real differences between his Ilocano parents and our Tagalog parents. Nurge (1965), using similar anthropological methods, lived in a *barrio* on Leyte, an island south of Luzon. Her concern was primarily with dyadic relationships within the family. Her results spell out in great detail the obligations and attitudes that exist between various pairs of people in the Philippine extended family. Abasolo-Domingo (1961) lived in a Tagalog *barrio* on the outskirts of Manila, where she used both participant observation and psychological techniques of doll play and projective tests. She found low and insignificant correlations between the children's doll play and TAT data on the one hand and her ratings on the behavior of the mother on the other. Her observations show no marked disagreement with our data even though they were collected by a somewhat different procedure. Each of these three researchers was guided by Whiting's field guide (1953) and concerned himself with at least some of the systems of behavior, such as aggression, nurturance, dependency, and achievement, which Whiting described.

In a report prepared for a regional conference (SWA, 1958) interviewers for the Social Welfare Administration reported data on two *barrios* near Manila. The report is difficult to evaluate, but it reports child-rearing patterns under more urban living conditions than the other studies mentioned and is for that reason not directly comparable.

Solis has offered a guide to teachers and parents, *Understanding the Filipino Child* (1957), but it is not the purpose of her book to report empirical research. More recently she has been responsible for the establishment of a National Center for Child Study to coordinate the work of Child Study Centers which have existed for a number of years at regional normal schools.

The unfortunate result of the dearth of research on the personality development of Filipino children is a strong tendency to utilize principles and procedures developed in other cultures in Philippine educational and clinical settings. A number of incongruities and conflicts emerge which have been explored in part (Guthrie,

1961). But while the inappropriateness of non-Philippine child-care procedures may be readily discovered, there remains the question of the appropriateness or applicability of many concepts and models found useful with children in another society. All research in the Philippines in this area of interest is pervaded by concepts of Western origin. How different would the concepts have been if they had been developed on Filipino children?

The Philippine Family

An understanding of the family system of the Philippines is essential to a comprehension of the society. The equality of men and women is an ancient Malay tradition which has withstood Muslim influences in Indonesia and Spanish Catholic traditions in the Philippines. An interesting manifestation of this equality is shown in the Tagalog dialect where one word, *siya,* is used for "he" and "she." Tagalogs do not differentiate male and female in conversation, thus reducing the likelihood of making one or the other superior. Conversely they have two words for "we," *tayo* and *kami.* The former includes the listener, the latter excludes the listener, an opportunity to emphasize the closeness of relationship. These personal pronouns express an important aspect of the society. It follows, then, that kinship through the mother is as important to the child as through the father. There are many examples of the equality of women. The parents of the bridegroom traditionally pay for the wedding ceremonies and also provide gifts for the newlyweds and for the bride's family. Inheritance traditions call for equal division between daughters and sons. In the age-authority hierarchy in the nuclear family each child is expected to show some respect and obedience to older siblings regardless of sex. Finally, women play prominent and powerful roles in Philippine business and government.

Relationships many times removed are remembered carefully with the result that each child has many relatives and virtually doubles this number when he marries. He is responsible for helping all of his relatives and can in turn look to them for help when he needs it. In addition to relatives by blood and marriage each Filipino gains relatives through various ceremonies. For instance he assumes a responsibility toward the sponsors of his child at baptism or marriage. By giving and receiving favors he extends even further the extent of the group to whom he has obligations and to whom he can look for assistance. This bilateral, extended kinship means that each individual is part of an enormous network of persons, and we can understand him only as we see him in the matrix of relationships in which he makes almost every decision. One is tempted to draw an analogy to the tropical forest where a vast variety of biotic relationships exists with many plants drawing from or giving to other plants some of the conditions essential to life. There is a sort of relatedness which supports a complicated and beautiful growth, but a relatedness from which an individual plant cannot be separated. So it is in the human family here, each person living for, and with the aid of, many others.

Within this social system each individual must be alert to the concerns of others. The geographic and social closeness of relationships requires each person to learn very early in life that he must be vigilant to the temperament of others and seek above all to minimize stresses. This is achieved through observation of patterns of deference, reciprocal obligations, and hospitality. Filipinos place great emphasis on politeness, on concern for others' feelings, and on humility. Favors are neither extended nor received without full cognizance that a new relationship is thus established and that favors in one form or another shall be returned. Finally, sharing one's food is the most decisive way of making another person feel important. This triad of characteristics, humility, politeness, and concern for others' feelings, appears in many aspects of the lives of Filipinos. It is a solution to the need for a pattern of living congenial to the physical demands of the environment.

That portion of the Philippines with which we are dealing has a great many of the characteristics of a peasant society. Most of the features of personalized relationships and reluctance to change associated with a traditional or sacred society are readily apparent. The tropical environment, the Malay family system, the Spanish influence epitomized in what Lynch has called folk catholicism, the destruction of war, and now the Western media of communication with Western ideas have produced a society which has borrowed much. But beneath the additions it remains uniquely Filipino.

chapter 4

THE INTERVIEW
AND INTERVIEWERS

We undertook this research with the intention of producing a report which would parallel that of Sears, Maccoby, and Levin (1957) on child rearing in New England. Since they provided the interview schedule in their report, our first move was to use that schedule without modification. It was immediately apparent that some of their questions were inappropriate in the Philippines and that the whole focus of the interview reflected its American origin. With Philippine families in mind we had to inquire in greater detail about the role of relatives. Environmental demands introduced new hazards and removed others. The circumstances of birth in the home in a traditional setting gave rise to a host of beliefs and practices in the Philippines not found in the bacteriologically and socially more aseptic American hospital delivery room. To be most productive the interview schedule had to ask Filipino-oriented questions in a Filipino way.

Since the problems of cross-cultural comparisons are mentioned frequently in this report, it may be desirable at this point to make clearer some of the differences in the interviewing situation in the Philippines. Philippine social patterns are characterized by a good deal of deference and indirection, and interviewers must be much less pointed initially and must keep in mind respect patterns which are related to age. An interviewer must be most cautious in asking questions dealing with topics which are only discussed within the family. An interviewer must also expect a good deal of vagueness if he presses for exact dates and quantities. A rural Philippine mother is not accustomed to an outsider's asking personal questions in a matter-of-fact manner. Accordingly an interviewer must be prepared to spend a good deal of time establishing confidence and good feeling.

Just as the situation requires special attention, so do certain episodes and factors in the life of the Filipino child. For instance, many Philippine mothers take quite seriously the possiblity of influencing their unborn child by their own activities, thoughts, and diet. Many adults beside the parents are responsive to the baby's needs and interests. The Philippine mother has her own ideal of a good child and her own hopes for the kind of adult the child will become. Her present aims and her hopes for the future guide her relationship with the child. When her values differ from those of a Western mother, her pattern of child rearing may also differ. Faced on the one hand with the desire to obtain data which would permit comparisons with American research and on the other with the desire to see Philippine child rearing as the Filipinos see it, we had to compromise between the requirements of comparability and the requirements of meaningfulness to Philippine mothers.

Development of the Interview

In order to obtain data as comparable as possible with the Sears report, we sought information concerning pregnancy and delivery, feeding, cleanliness practices, dependency, sex roles, aggression, and obedience and punishment. These data parallel chapters two through eight in the Sears report. In addition we sought information concerning the child's fears and the parents' values and hopes.

The earliest forms of the interview were developed in Tagalog, the dialect of the Manila area, and then in English. Using both languages we were reducing the likelihood that matters of importance to either culture would be missed. The first complete draft of the interview schedule had sixty-three questions which were developed after discussion among the authors and their colleagues. Subsequent revisions were made to clarify questions and to cover areas which had been missed.

Selection and Training of Interviewers

All interviewing in this research was done by seniors at the Philippine Normal College who were in the internship phase of their four-year teacher education program. This phase involved supervised practice teaching in schools in the cities and towns outside of, but within a hundred kilometer radius of, Manila. As part of their training the students were expected to visit homes in order to have direct contact with parents. In order to evaluate the provisional interview schedule, approximately two hundred practice teachers were asked to do two interviews each and submit their verbatim records upon return to the campus. Two two-hour sessions were held with these students prior to their departure to explain the research and the interview procedure. A recorded interview was played, and some role-playing techniques were used. These students submitted more than three hundred interview records. Examination of the protocols and reports of the students led to revision of the schedule to clarify questions and to include areas which had been omitted. The final form is shown in the Appendix on pages 209–219.

The following term a new group of students going on practice teaching assignments were asked to participate. There was an eager, almost unanimous, favorable response. All students were again asked to interview two mothers. Thirty women students who were deemed the ablest and most reliable by members of the faculty were asked to interview ten mothers each. The data used in this report were obtained from the interviews of these thirty selected students. The authors met the students in a total of seven one-hour sessions before the interviewers left the college. There was an additional two-hour individual contact when they returned for conferences in the middle of their off-campus assignment. By the end of the term we had 279 usable interviews. One interviewer's protocols were lost and an additional eleven interviews were not completed. The interviewers served without compensation. They gave evidence of responding favorably to our appeal that they help collect information which might lead to a better understanding of Filipino children.

The Final Form of the Interview

Although we were obliged to abandon use of Sears' interview in unmodified form, we did organize our interview to cover the same topics, adding sections dealing with children's fears and with parents' ideals. Parallel forms were developed in English and Tagalog.

Interviewers could use either form and could record answers in either language. The interviews, as we received them, were about equally divided. There were instances in which both English and Tagalog were used in the same report.

The final interview and principal source of the information reported here consisted of ten parts plus a series of questions designed to permit direct comparisons with data reported by Sears et al. The introductory section sought specific information about the family situation—age, occupation, and education of father and mother; the children in the family; other adults in the home and their relationship to the child.

The second part was concerned with the mother's pregnancy and the birth of the child. We asked how many children she hoped for and what she thought those who could not have children should do. We were interested in her experiences during pregnancy, her cravings and aversions, and her feelings about maternal impressions or her ability to influence the nature of her unborn child. Since it is a matter of concern to Filipinos, we asked what steps and beliefs had been observed in connection with the disposal of the placenta. We failed to include questions about the postnatal care of the mother. This has been described by Nydegger (1963) for another Philippine group in the Ilocos region of Northern Luzon.

Questions on feeding dealt with the choice of breast or bottle, the duration of nursing, reasons for preference, and the age of weaning. We were also concerned with the relationship that prevailed between mother and child. Finally, we followed the introduction of nutritive supplements and the development of self-feeding skills.

The section labeled "Dependency," for want of a better term, inquired into the extent of the child's communication with the mother, and the mother's response when the child came home crying from play. It concerned also the child's play group, the child's help-seeking, his overt displays of affection, and the response of the one to whom the display was directed. We inquired concerning the mother's differential response to each of her children and the extent to which she felt or showed favoritism for any of them. Finally, we were interested in the incidence of bickering and jealousies among siblings, the mother's response to the child's demands to go with her, and the child's special areas of sensitivity.

Family demands for obedience and sanctions used on the child constituted the fifth section. Questions included frequency of disobedience and punishment, methods of punishment, and the extent to which the child was allowed to reason or explain himself. Since many people are involved with a Filipino child, we listed the ones to whom the child owed obedience, the consequences of his failure to obey, the various people who usually disciplined the child, and his differential response to these agents. In addition, we asked which of the child's traits the mother liked least and what she usually did when the child displayed this trait.

The section on cleanliness training concerned the child's use of diapers and clothes, his tendency to litter the house or make it dirty and disorderly through his play, his toilet training, and the incidence of bed-wetting. In connection with bed-wetting we inquired into the sleeping arrangements of the family.

Four main questions were asked concerning curiosity about the body and modesty. One question inquired if the child ever asked where he or a younger child in the family had come from, and we asked the mother how and when she herself found out. Another asked how the mother handled questions about differences between boys and girls. The third category dealt with bathing and changing: whether the child did these by himself or was helped, and the physical arrangements the family used for these activities. The fourth question inquired into words the mother prohibited the child from using.

The section on aggression delved into circumstances that angered the child or hurt his feelings and the mother's way of telling that the child was angered. We also asked about the people who often became objects of the child's anger, the child's temper tantrums, the child's involvement in quarrels and fights, the child's teasing and his reaction to teasing, and matters about which he was sensitive and about which he bragged.

The five questions we asked about fears were added in the final interview schedule. This was after our attention was called to the very common technique of discipline of evoking the child's fear so that he would obey a rule or a prohibition. The questions included recall of the child's early and present fears, how the mother or someone else frightened him into obeying, what he did when he was frightened, the stories that frightened him most, and, in order to uncover a possible trace of this technique in the mother's early life, what she recalled that frightened her as a child.

The last section of the interview looked into special concerns of the mother as she went about her task of child rearing. What was the mother most careful about concerning the health of her child? What precautions did she take? What about the child did she enjoy most? What were her dreams for him? We included questions on how the mother compared the way in which she was rearing her children with her parents' methods of rearing her and with other people's methods. For a final look at the mother's definition of her values for her children we asked, "How would you like your children to be different from other children?"

We then selected seventeen tables from the Sears report and repeated the questions on which the tables were based. The interviewers were instructed to record the mother's answers and to rate the mother's responses using the categories which we had taken from the Sears tables. Since this was the first time the majority of the mothers had thought about some of these matters, we feel that we at least have the advantage of spontaneity in their answers. Their responses spring from a traditional system of beliefs which is less open to question than ideas arising out of firsthand experience or derived from the expressions of experts.

The interview schedule was long, for it actually had more than the seventy-two main questions. Many interviews took longer than the projected two hours. Fortunately the mother looked on it as a social visit, a chance to talk to an interested person about her child and about her convictions as a mother without the reservation that would have been present if it were the child's school teacher or someone else of authority. Instead it was a student who had come to learn and to ask her about raising children.

Treatment of the Interviews

Based on a study of 40 of the 279 protocols a coding system of 138 items was developed. We found we could achieve our purposes using a maximum of eight categories for any item; a ninth was reserved for responses which were not taken care of in the first eight, and a zero category was used when the necessary information was missing.

To test reliability fifteen interviews were recoded by the same coder at least five months after the initial coding. Mean percentage agreement for all fifteen pairs of codes was 89 per cent; the range was 83 per cent to 94 per cent. We had expected a lower agreement because we knew that for many of our items the categories were not mutually exclusive.

The tabulations from all interviews and from the accompanying rating scales borrowed from the Sears study were condensed to 279 code sheets and punched. In this way we obtained the count and corresponding percentage for each category for all 119 items and the 19 additional rating items from the coding. We used a computer program in which the responses in the zero or no-information category were omitted and the percentage for each category was derived from the total number of responses with information. In addition, counts and corresponding percentages were obtained for each item category for each of three groups of mothers as defined in the following paragraphs.

Choosing Our Sample of Subjects and Informants

Since the greater part of the child population goes to public schools, we decided to use first-grade children for our subjects and to ask their mothers to oblige as our informants. The normal age at which children enter first grade is seven. A few manage to get in earlier, and those who do not quite make it at seven enter school a little older.

We actually dealt with the problem of sampling only with our final group of thirty interviewers. Each of them borrowed the class roll of the first-grade teacher in her training school, identified numbers 1, 3, 5, 7, and 9 from the list of boys and numbers 2, 4, 6, 8, and 10 from the list of girls, and arranged interviews with the mothers of these children. If for any reason interviews with these mothers could not be arranged, the interviewers could draw names from a specified list of alternate numbers and arrange to interview the mothers of these children.

Thus the 279 mothers who comprise our sample of informants are mothers of first-grade children whose ages varied from five to nine—148 boys and 131 girls. Their homes are in the provinces of Rizal, Cavite, Laguna, Batangas, and Bulacan, all on Luzon and adjacent to Manila. The mothers' ages ranged from twenty to over fifty, with almost 55 per cent falling between thirty and thirty-nine years. We classified the mothers into three groups according to the amount of education they reported. The first group consisted of 169 mothers (61 per cent of the whole group) who had some, or a complete, elementary education but no more. The second group was made up of fifty-six mothers (20 per cent) who had some, or a complete, high school education, and fifty-two mothers (19 per cent) fell in the third group with education beyond high school, almost all of whom had college certificates. We shall frequently refer to them as the first, or least educated, group; the second, or middle, group; and the third, or most educated, group.

Socio-economic status is an elusive variable to measure, particularly in the Philippines where its components have not yet been studied by a Warner or a Hollingshead. For the purpose we had in mind, classifying by education seemed most pertinent, since in the Philippines at least, if not elsewhere, education is the chief agent of culture change. We wanted to find out if the mother's education made any difference in her attitudes and in the techniques of child rearing she practiced.

The mothers' occupational status was also of interest to us. We wanted to know how many of these mothers were full-time homemakers; how many were at home but were engaged in other occupations like tending a very small store, taking in sewing for the neighborhood or outside laundry; how many were out of the home part of the time vending fish or farm produce in market stalls; and how many were employed full-time in schools or in offices. We present the information here for the subgroups instead of for the total group because of the pronounced differences between the first two groups and the third group of mothers. In the least educated group 73 per cent were full-time homemakers, in the second group 80 per cent, and in the most educated group only 23 per cent. No one fell in the second category of "in the house but occupied" in the most educated group, but 13 per cent did in the first group and 7 per cent in the second group. "Employed part-time" categorized 11 per cent of the first group, 9 per cent of the second group, and 6 per cent of the third group. The biggest difference, however, is in the "employed full-time" category—3 per cent in the first group, 4 per cent in the second group, and 71 per cent in the third and most educated group.

A description of the fathers of the subjects should be considered even though we were not concerned with them in this study. Their ages ranged from twenty to over fifty, 52 per cent falling between thirty and thirty-nine, 34 per cent between forty and forty-nine,

7 per cent over fifty and only 5 per cent between twenty and twenty-nine. Only six of our mothers (slightly over 2 per cent) were widows. The schooling of the husbands compared with their wives is also of interest. Sixty-five per cent of the husbands of the mothers in the first group had no education beyond elementary school. Twenty-seven per cent had started or completed high school, 3 per cent had some college, and 5 per cent were college graduates. Of the husbands of mothers in the second group 53 per cent were on an approximately equal educational level with their wives, 9 per cent had some college, and 27 per cent had college certificates. Only about 11 per cent had only elementary school, a level a little lower than that of their wives. Seventy-four per cent of the husbands of the mothers in the third group had started or completed college, 24 per cent had started or completed high school, and one was an elementary school graduate. The general picture is of a husband with an education slightly higher than, or equal to, that of his wife.

The occupational status of the husbands as differentially distributed in the three subgroups further qualifies the child-rearing situation in which we find our subjects and informants. Seventy per cent of the fathers in the least educated group were laborers, farmers, fishermen, drivers and mechanics, and stall keepers; 28 per cent were in business, with the army, with the government, or in private professions; and 2 per cent were unemployed. In the second group 39 per cent were laborers, farmers, and the like; and 61 per cent were in business or professional activities. Only seven fathers (14 per cent) in the third group were laborers or employed as mechanics. One was a farmer. Eighty-four per cent were businessmen, army men, government employees, and professionals. The general picture that we draw is one of a stable income for the majority in the second and third groups and a very limited income for the majority in the group with the least education.

The size and composition of the families from which our subjects come is also well worth considering. Fewer than half had adults other than the father and mother living with the family, 39 per cent had one or two additional adults. Ten per cent had more than two, usually relatives or in a number of instances paid household help. Children in the family ranged from one (2.5 per cent) to eight or more (15 per cent) with the median falling at five. Fourteen per cent of our subjects had an eldest sibling over twenty years old, 20 per cent had one in the fifteen to twenty age range. Sixty-eight of our subjects (25 per cent) were eldest children, forty-eight (17 per cent) were youngest children, and only seven were only children. Eighty-two (30 per cent) of the families our subjects represent had babies a year old or younger at the time of the interview, and 81 per cent had children in the preschool age level and younger.

Our Interviewers' Comments on Child-Rearing Practices

After some of the interviews, our interviewers commented on the family and the parent-child relationships. Their comments spring from deep personal convictions on the proper methods of raising children but are influenced also by a desire to say what they feel is expected of them. Consequently they reflect Philippine ideals in child rearing with some superimposition of ideas from Western textbooks. Comments on the desirable qualities of mothers are presented below:

> The mother knows how to temper her affections with proper discipline. That is why Florante can't find occasion to be spoiled or to abuse.
>
> She is a strict but democratic mother. She is consistent in what she says.
>
> Renato's mother is an ideal one, being a teacher and financially well-off. She is democratic, tolerant, and understanding. She manages her home in spite of the fact that she stays the whole day in the school teaching. She never gets a maid who is uneducated. She has favoritism but never shows it. She has foresight for her children. She avoids giving corporal punishment. She always uses a positive approach.

A consistent, affectionate mother who does not show favoritism and who tempers her affection with proper discipline appears to be the ideal among these young women. The concern and emphasis on minimizing favoritism is evident in the following comments of these Filipinos on the problems of the eldest, youngest, and only child:

> D., being an only child, is loved by both her parents too much. I am afraid she will become a spoiled child. She gets everything she likes and I think bribing her to follow her parents is not a good practice. Her mother and father shower her with the love and affection so badly needed by a child.

The mother seemed to have a little knowledge about child care. She is kind and loving to her children. However, the way she treats her children is not just and fair because she always asks her ten-year-old Lita to do the baby sitting. She's unfair in such a way that Lita has not time or only a short time to play.

The fact that Feliza is the youngest in the family does not justify the parents in treating her more favorably than they do with the two other children. There is so much toleration and pamperings practiced at home that Feliza gets used to this and expects it even when she is no longer at home. She expects her playmates to obey her will or desire just as she expects her folks at home to do.

Being the youngest in the family, this boy was spoiled.

Although she says she does not believe in favoritism, I could sense that she favors Francisco more than the other children. She reasons to give him more attention because he is very weak. Thus the child is very dependent on the mother.

From these comments it is evident that a common but undesirable element in the Philippine family structure, as far as our interviewers were concerned, is spoiling the only or youngest child and overburdening the oldest daughter. The interviewers fear that pampering in childhood will make the child unable to develop the finesse and ability to give and take in crucial interpersonal relationships and will make him overly dependent on his parents. Yet while criticizing overindulgence, they emphasize the concept of the child's need for love and affection which permeates the parent-child relationship in the Philippines.

The bulk of the remaining comments are criticisms of neglect and lack of affection and the use of punishment and rewards.

The mother is neglecting her child. She does not give much attention to her child's needs. Instead she lets her maid do her own job in rearing the children.

The moment I first saw the mother I knew that she didn't spare the rod. Maria is very quiet and shy. The mother ought to be a little sympathetic to her children. Although they have a big house and completely modern facilities, this is not the foremost duty of the parents. They should first love and protect their children.

The child is of a secretive type. He does not tell everything to the mother. The mother often has to ask him what he likes or what bothers him. He is also not very affectionate, especially to the father. The parents should have shown more affection to this child so that he would be closer to them or encourage him to tell them every problem he has.

The parents resort to corporal punishment and scolding him. They often give him money to get him to obey his elders. He should be made to obey through proper motivation, not by rewards nor by punishment.

Mrs. B. proves to be a good disciplinarian. She punishes her children whenever they are at fault. She doesn't show any favoritism. However, the father counterchecks this, because when the children are punished they go to him, and he makes them stop crying by promising them chocolates or new dresses. Thus the children are exposed to both extremes. I think the children will continue groping in the dark unless the father changes his attitude a little to meet that of the mother.

The parents, who are educated, know the proper approach in dealing with the child. Only they also resort to corporal punishment. The child often uses embarrassing words. This should not be encouraged.

The mother does not have a schedule when feeding her child, which is not a good practice. The child is given extrinsic motivation, I think, because whenever she cries if she is teased, the mother gives her something to make her stop. This is not good, because the child will always look for that as she grows old.

The recurrent theme in these comments is that a child must have love and affection to develop properly and that giving these is a parent's first duty to the child. The interviewers seem to have correlated wealth and conveniences with the affection-starved home. Whether or not this relationship is significant is beyond the scope of our report. Conversely, no one in the Philippines sees poverty as a cause of unhappy, poorly raised children.

The other major concern is the proper use of rewards and punishment. Overstrictness and corporal punishment are condemned although actually used by 58 per cent of the mothers interviewed. Bribing, used by 24 per cent, is also condemned because it is believed to give the child false motivation which will be reflected in later life. Inconsistency in punishing is seen as confusing the child and disrupting his sense of right and wrong.

The comments of the interviewers give a striking emphasis to the primary importance of love and affection in the Philippine home. They indicate the interviewers' preoccupation with equal and consistent treatment for each child in the family. Finally, our interviewers disapprove of physical punishment and of bribery if either is used excessively. We would conclude that, whatever the effect of non-Philippine ideas in their education, these interviewers still see the ideal child as respectful and obedient, but they are quite sure that punishment and/or bribery are not the best methods of bringing about the desired result.

In the chapters that follow we have interpreted the results of our interviews but have resisted the temptation to present a percentage-by-percentage discussion. We have also included many brief direct quotations in order to convey as accurately as possible some of the attitudes and opinions of our respondents. These excerpts from interviews also emphasize the range of opinions within the group. Since one of the authors is a product of the environment under study, we have drawn on her experience for interpretive and background comments in many of the chapters which follow.

chapter 5

A CHILD'S BIRTH INTO
A FAMILY

The Philippines is a child-oriented society. Children are eagerly desired since they are seen as assets to a family. Their companionship is sought by parents and older siblings, and by older relatives and neighbors as well. At every age a portion of family life revolves around the child providing him with many roles ranging from a passive recipient of the attention which is showered upon him to a responsible caretaker of younger siblings, from an entertainer of parents and older siblings to the ever necessary water-carrier. There are few adult activities from which a child is excluded. He accompanies his mother to market, his older sister to school, his older brother when courting, and his father to the fields. The Philippine family creates many places for children within its activities and often creates many children to fill these places.

In the Philippines having children is a central purpose of marriage. Failure to have children is a matter of grave concern to both husband and wife, even to relatives and neighbors. Since children are so important to a marriage, we asked each mother how many children she had hoped to have when she got married. The following responses give some impression of the point of view expressed by many mothers to this question:

I thought I would have as many as I can have!

It is not mine to say; it is God's will.

I didn't know then. The children just kept coming, and I'm happy about that.

We wanted many and God did grant us that. Now we realize it is difficult to raise that many on the little we have.

We didn't think about how many children we were going to have. But I believed that the more children you have, the more you are blessed.

This persistent theme recurs throughout: "Children are a gift from God." They are an indication that the large family is "in God's grace" or "blessed." Thus there is no real planning as to family size, nor any real attempt at spacing. Some mothers said they had a certain number in mind or an ideal set—"two boys, two girls, perhaps" or "boy, girl, boy and so on, alternately"—but the number of children they have bears no relation to what they thought they wanted. One mother of ten said she originally wanted about four but added, "I'm glad I had more!"

Childless Couples

A couple not able to have children is considered unfortunate. "They simply are not fated to have them" is often the explanation given. Special devotions to patron saints are believed effective. Couples who cannot have children are advised to dance in front of the church in the town of Obando, an activity of possible pre-Christian origin, and make pilgrimages to the Virgin of Antipolo. Some couples spend most of their childbearing years praying for children, never losing hope that some time the gift they ask for will be given them.

The possibility of physiological reasons for failure to have children is not unknown. "They should have themselves checked by a physician" was not an unusual answer, "Whatever is wrong might be corrected and they might still have children," or also, "There are specialists on that these days." There seems to be no dichotomy between recourse to prayer and seeking help from a physician. A doctor's guidance, supported by prayer, may result in the wanted child unless this is contrary to fate.

In such cases a couple may adopt a niece or nephew, or orphans. Blood relationship is a stressed consideration in adopting children, because the Filipinos believe the child will eventually return to his natural parents. Even when the adoption circumstances preclude the child's knowing the identity of his original parents, the "blood leap" is supposed to be so strong that the child will know his parents if they meet, and the adopting parents sooner or later will lose their child.

> Childless couples can adopt children if they are resigned to let the child return to his parents. This can't be helped.
>
> They should adopt children of close relatives.

Orphans are not considered a risk, particularly when they do not have any close relatives to "draw them back." Nieces and nephews will naturally visit their parents, and they are expected to continue loving their parents, but sharing one's child with one's brother or sister is much different from sharing him with someone who is no relation.

The Trials of Pregnancy

Pregnancy is a stressful condition for a Philippine mother filled as it is with nausea, cravings, and aversions. She loses a good many meals; she turns against foods which she has previously liked; and she longs for foods which she has not previously sought, often foods which are not available. Beyond this she experiences changes in her moods which cause her to long to see and be with certain people or which cause her to hate those whom she can usually tolerate. Odors may acquire a new importance. Each of these experiences is considered important for the influence it may have on the child to be born. What a mother feels or craves, likes or dislikes, may modify the physical characteristics or temperament of the child. It should be noted that these symptoms occur in a society where there is a strong approval for wanting children. Evidence of this sort may lead us to reevaluate theories that attribute nausea of pregnancy to the pregnant woman's rejection of her condition. Some of the responses which mothers offered included:

> Chestnuts! I developed a craving for them at midnight and had my husband take a trip to Manila to get me some right then.
>
> I asked for a papaya fruit that grew in the neighbor's yard. I would not accept one bought in the market.
>
> Just the sight of the food I wanted was enough. I needed to see them every day, not necessarily eat them. If they were not there, I was ill-tempered and uneasy.
>
> There were quite a lot I craved. We are poor, and somehow I managed to control myself. I knew I had all these children and had to be thrifty.
>
> I craved a lot of special food, and we are poor. But I had to have them as I'd be ill until I got them.
>
> My husband also craved the things I craved.
>
> I liked apple and squid.

I craved particularly turnips. The father would bring home turnips. He had no difficulty with me except the times he did not bring home turnips.

I hated anything that smelled good.

These fancies and whims of the mother are actually part of a whole set of beliefs. What the mother likes or dislikes, anything to which the mother attaches strong feeling, will have some bearing on the foetus. *"Kanino ka ipinaglihi?"* or *"Saan ka ipinaglihi?"* (Who or what were you conceived from?) is the usual question asked when one is curious about certain characteristics or dispositions of a person and how he came to have them. The following excerpts illustrate these beliefs:

A beautiful fiesta queen I stared and stared at—I kept seeing her face even after I had gone back home. I was pregnant with M. then, probably the reason why I have such a pretty child.

My husband irritated me so much, especially when he smiled. If you look at Junior, he looks exactly like his Dad.

Took quite a liking to one of my girl pupils, would pinch her in one of these moments. My boy is a little sissyish; may have been because of that. (From a teacher)

Our neighbor! Why would I say that I did not "conceive M. after him" as he has taken after him in everything, even in his ways!

He is overactive. When I was pregnant I took quite a liking to the *dalag* [climbing perch, a very active fish].

I am not especially fond of circus shows, stunts, and things like that. But when I was carrying him I took such a liking for them. My son is quite a climber.

I liked *balut* [hard boiled duck egg] a lot then, especially the embryo part. Notice how hairy his arms and legs are!

Loved chocolate candy and *pili* nuts. This is why Tessie is somewhat dark.

I craved young coconut. Pedro is fairer than my other children.

Took after a pink *pomelo* [grapefruit]. Notice how he's fair and rosy, in contrast to his brothers and sisters who are all dark.

Red apples. Mario's cheeks are rosy like a girl's.

I can't remember any whim, but she has a birthmark on her cheek and my mother-in-law says it's some pork I didn't get to have when I was pregnant with her.

A birthmark on her right thigh shaped like a tiny jackfruit, which I craved when I was conceiving.

I liked eating *aligi* [red crab fat], and Patricio has a red spot right on top of his head for it.

I don't know why I craved green mangoes that were a little crushed when I could have had good green mangoes anytime. Rosie has a harelip because of that.

I liked looking at beautiful ladies but I don't think that made any difference for her.

I liked ice cream so much and hated foul odors. She has a very sensitive sense of smell.

I hated my husband sometimes. I used to quarrel with him. The child resembles his father, even in his habits.

The Husband's Role during Pregnancy

The husband's indulgence of these whims, some of which are very unreasonable, is deemed an expression not only of his responsibility for his wife but also of a father's concern for his unborn child. The child's characteristics—his appearance, talents and abilities, even interests—are believed to depend on indulgences given the wife during this period.

Six instances were reported in which the husband suffered drowsiness or nausea associated with his wife's pregnancy. One mother said she was fine during her pregnancy but her husband "had nausea in the mornings. He even had to stop smoking and could only resume it after our boy was born." Another husband "craved ice cream and was sleepy all the time."

In spite of problems during pregnancy the mother is seldom severely incapacitated, and the household routine is never disrupted. A mother is rarely out of circulation for the entire nine months. In most instances her indisposition starts at about the third month and ends by the fifth or sixth month. Even then she is usually indisposed only at certain times during the day. The father, grandmother, or an aunt takes over the management role when the mother is unable to go about the chores, or at least they make these chores lighter for her.

Childbirth

Delivery still most frequently takes place in the home, the existence of provincial hospitals notwithstanding. Seventy-five per cent of our mothers delivered their babies at home, and of those who delivered in hospitals, two consented to go there only after there were complications in the delivery. The general trend does not hold for the group of mothers with the most education, almost two-thirds of whom delivered in hospitals.

Of the group in our sample who reported giving birth at home, almost two-thirds were attended by a licensed midwife, a nurse, or a physician, and only about a third by the traditional *hilot*. Two mothers reported unattended deliveries—one before she could get to the hospital and another before the midwife had time to get to the home. There were a number of cases in which the *hilot*, faced with unfamiliar complications, agreed that the family call for more competent assistance. Some mothers who had been assisted in their delivery by a nurse or doctor still made use of the services of the *hilot* for prenatal and postnatal care. Faith remains strong in the traditional practices of massaging the mother, heat treatments, and herb baths, aimed at helping the mother recover from the system displacements and injuries that went with the pregnancy and birth process.

Following is a typical picture of this important event in the family: The mother starts feeling labor pains and, largely for moral support, calls for her mother or someone with whom she has some dependency relationship. The father is of course present, but he is helpless in his state of concern unless specifically instructed. He, or the errand-running member of the family, goes to the midwife, doctor, nurse, *hilot*, or whoever has rendered prenatal services and is therefore expected to assist in the delivery. The wife is urged to walk about the house to ease the delivery. Meanwhile the husband boils the water to dip the attendant's things in, gets the delivery mat or bed ready in a room or draped section of the house, and, when the attendant is the traditional old woman of the village (the *hilot*), gathers the herbs she will need for the delivery. The husband either stays with the wife throughout or is told by the older women to leave. The children are hushed out of the house with "Mother is giving birth to a baby, and you'll see him soon." Usually they are given chores to keep them occupied while waiting. Some children, both the very young and the older ones, cry or are apprehensive about their mother's suffering or fear she may die and leave them orphans, but they all are aware of the event at the birth of each new sibling, know that it happens, and accept it as a part of life.

The mother bears the pain stoically or cries out and sighs with relief when the baby utters its first cry, then asks, "What is it?" She is told to rest but admonished not to sleep ("She may forget to breathe") while the attendant cleans the baby, cuts the umbilical cord, wraps him in soft baby garments, and gives him a thumb-size roll of cloth dipped in *tiki-tiki* (commercial vitamin supplement) or *ampalaya* juice (bitter melon) to suck while she attends to the mother. The juice or the first suckling of the infant is intended to induce elimination and thereby cleanse the baby's system.

After the placenta is expelled, the mother is cleaned, swathed, changed, and given hot soup for nourishment. The other children quietly take a look at the "new one," being careful not to disturb their mother.

The erstwhile youngest is surprisingly secure in his displacement despite being teased that he is no longer loved. The father, aided by some member of the family, washes out the articles used in the delivery and takes care of disposing of the placenta—an important aspect of the belief system surrounding birth.

The mothers' own recollections on giving birth and their feelings about it indicate the range of variations to the pattern. The following are remarks on childbirth from the mothers in our sample:

She was born in our house. The midwife attended me. I had no difficulties inasmuch as she was the fifth child. But I had trouble with my first-born.

I really had difficulty, probably because he was my first.

It was difficult, but that was because I was afraid. I was happy when he finally came.

I can't remember having any difficulty, and that may be because I was used to it already. (From a mother of ten)

I almost died. They had to get a doctor. She was so big!

The child came even before my husband returned with the midwife. I simply picked him up and held him until they got there.

It was a forceps delivery. Dry labor. I suffered for two days.

They made me sleep. I did not feel it. (Very rare)

A doctor and a midwife stayed with me. Labor lasted a whole day. The child was delivered with one foot first. He was breathless for a few seconds.

It was difficult, but I was happy. He was my first boy, after three girls.

I give birth very easily. It runs in the family.

J.'s head was covered with a cellophane-like membrane. The *hilot* said that this is a sign that J. will get rich when he grows up, but only after much suffering.

I was uneasy. My *lola* [grandmother], my mother-in-law, and the nurse attended me. It was difficult.

My husband was changing his clothes to take me to the hospital when J. came with a lusty cry.

His head was too big. I became unconscious and when I came to, he was out.

These comments indicate that childbirth is not an easy event devoid of any suffering for the mother. What is noteworthy is the attitude that suffering is an inevitable part of it as are difficulties during pregnancy. The discomfort, the pain are all part of the mother's role, the means by which she fulfills her responsibility for bringing life into the world and by which she pays her debt to her own mother for suffering when she herself was born.

Parenthood and Old Beliefs

A sense of responsibility for this new life is evident in the concern about the mother's cravings and fancies during pregnancy, the things she is advised to like or avoid for the sake of her unborn child, and the seriousness with which her whims are indulged. The idea that what the parents do could affect the nature of the child later, the kind of person he will eventually become, continues after the child is born. How the placenta is disposed of, what kind of godparent is chosen for the child, and the mother's disposition during the nursing period are believed to affect the personality of the child and are matters that entail much care and deliberation.

Translations directly from the mothers' accounts can give only a limited picture of the variety and richness of the values and parental expectations reflected in the placenta disposal practices:

Wash the placenta carefully, salt it, and put in a clean coconut shell. Bury it, but not too deep so it won't take long for the child to learn to speak straight.

It must be buried underneath the stairs or some part of the house so the child won't be a vagabond and so he won't be careless and a spendthrift.

Bury it deep enough to keep animals from dragging it out, or the child will stray from home when he grows up.

We gave it to our laundrywoman who threw it in the stream. What the connection was with my child I didn't know, but my mother suggested this would make a traveler of him.

Down the river went the placenta together with some written notes so the child will be a quick learner.

I remember the *hilot* cutting a piece of it, broiling it, and mixing this in what I had to drink. They said it was to keep my child from being sickly.

We threw it down the river so our child would be able to stand the cold when he grew up.

Bury it in a coconut shell covered with the top part—the one side with holes in it—so the child won't catch cold very easily.

They say if we bury the placenta under a rain spout, the child will not fear water. My husband wrapped the placenta with a little garlic and vinegar in newspaper so our child will be dainty and intelligent.

If you wash everything clean before it is buried, the child will always be clean when he grows up. Lina is so clean and dainty, hates dirt of any kind.

My husband buried them under the trees. We just think this is better than having it lying around.

If the placenta is not carefully buried and it happens to be dragged out by dogs and pigs, the child will be a crier and this will be quite a bother.

Bury a pencil, a page from a song album, and paper so the child will be intelligent, and interested in music.

Whoever is laundering the things used in the delivery should not speak even when spoken to, or the child will grow up talkative.

In burying the placenta, one should not look at other things or the child will be cross-eyed.

If buried too deep, it will take long for the child to grow teeth.

She is such a good child. They buried the placenta directly under that part of the house where the shrine is.

We have information on beliefs and practices concerning the disposal of the placenta for about four-fifths of our sample. In our most educated group 40 per cent used hospital delivery as the reason for not having any thoughts in this regard, but only 10 per cent of the mothers in the other two groups gave that reason. More than two-thirds of the least educated group said they believed that the practices have their traditional meanings, and only about a third said they were only following a custom or that burying was the practical way to dispose of the placenta. There are major group differences in admitting meanings to the practices, or even in admitting the practices, but where the beliefs were expressed, they provide some insight into the expectations for their children of many Filipino parents.

We should, in passing, mention a constellation of beliefs about pregnant women. Since we did not include a question on the subject in our interview, our information is not well documented. In the Philippines, as in many parts of the world, a pregnant woman is a sort of supernatural lightning rod. The object of attention of many evil spirits, she must observe special precautions for her own protection. As we have mentioned in a previous report (Guthrie, 1961, pp. 47–58), the *aswang* or vampire is a particular hazard. Even at the time of delivery, strange animals such as dogs are driven away for fear that they may be the embodiment of a malevolent agent. Everywhere pregnancy is seen as a dangerous time in the life of a woman; in the Philippines increased dangers are attributed in the traditional belief pattern to the system of supernatural agents believed to cause illness and misfortune.

The Joy of Parenthood and a Large Family

When having five or more children is the rule rather than the exception, it occurs to us to ask, "Why?" First, what is there about having children that would make parents plan for only one or two? In the middle-class American family a child, from conception to graduation from college, is admittedly an economic drain—doctor bills for prenatal and postnatal care, clothing, house space, food. The mere thought of providing these for one or two is forbidding, and how much more so for six or more! The demands that child rearing places on the mother's time, her activities, her fulfillment as an individual and as a wife are also considerations. And then, with the mission successful, the young adult moves on to create a life separate from his parents.

These deterrents to the natural course of family growth are not so imperative in Philippine rural culture. The cost of traditional prenatal care, delivery, and postnatal care is within the means of the nuclear family unit, or at least within reach of resources of the larger extended family. Since it is warm all year, clothing is not a major budget consideration. The climate, too, and a different set of expectations of privacy make house space for more than two children no problem. The extended family connections make education of the children an attainable goal. The family seeks resources outside itself for the first few children, and the older children then help with the younger ones.

Nor is child rearing the exacting and all-consuming task that it may be to mothers in another culture. The large family, or at the start the extended family, provides a built-in baby-sitting service. Older children help mind their younger siblings; unmarried aunts and uncles lend a hand too. Children do not necessarily tie the mother to the home. Few adult pursuits outside the home exclude children. Nor is there any concern about shielding children from adult activities. There are no absolute rights or wrongs; behavior is appropriate or not according to one's age. There is such a consensus about appropriate behavior within the circle in which the family moves that admonitions and instruction come from all quarters. The mother can thus take her children with her and still enjoy herself, or she can leave them to the care of the rest of the family.

Thus, since the disadvantages of large families are few and bearable, the Filipino parents can continue the tradition. To have children or not to have them, to have them now or to wait, to have many or only a few are not alternatives that they face or matters they think of and plan for.

Children are an extension of their parents, the means by which parents realize or fulfill themselves beyond the possibilities to which their own time limits them. Their value as a measure of the family's state of grace, an indication that the parents lead good lives, cannot be overemphasized. Expressions like, "My child's cooing takes away the ache of my back muscles at day's end," "Great is the joy of watching them smiling in their sleep," "Their laughter makes up for all the pain and trouble they cause," "They are my staff in my old age," and "They certainly fill my hours" reflect the Filipino mother's and father's attitudes about parenthood. They accept it; having children and raising children means harder work but also gives a continuing purpose and a richer meaning to married life.

In this society where relatives assume many responsibilities for one another and where kinship ties are of the highest importance, it is not surprising that there is much interest in each newborn baby. When a man's wealth is in part the number of his relatives, there is an eager acceptance of large families. While many births were once offset by high infant mortality rates, this same frequency now is resulting in many more living children. It should be noted nevertheless that the infant mortality rate in the Philippines is still very high in the rural areas and in all but the wealthier families in the cities. At this point there is little interest in the rural Philippines in reducing the size of the family. The population of the Philippines is among the most rapidly rising in the world. Most of the beliefs and values we have cited will probably maintain the present population explosion in the rural areas.

Comparison with the Findings of Sears, Maccoby, and Levin

At the end of each chapter we shall try to present a comparison of our findings with those of Sears, Maccoby, and Levin (1957). This is a chapter in which comparison must be very broad. American mothers take little stock in maternal impressions. The American research team did not inquire about nausea during pregnancy. Hospital delivery is seen as an impersonal, medical event carried out aseptically and anonymously with relatives, friends, and children excluded. In a sense drugs sometimes exclude even the mother from an awareness of the delivery. A hospital attendant disposes of the placenta as he would any other human tissue. The American child starts life removed from his family, while the Filipino infant arrives in his family home surrounded by relatives.

The issues considered by American mothers regarding the size of their families are different from those of the Philippine mothers. Women in the United States, whatever their religious beliefs, have at least some feeling that they can plan or avoid pregnancy. Almost all of them hope for a certain spacing of their children. A pregnancy may mean a prolonged interruption of any employment they have held outside the home. They decide when they want children and how many, although their desires may not always be realized.

The contrast in the Philippines is great. Children are eagerly wanted and in large numbers. It seems that the only planning a majority of our respondents did was for more. During pregnancy the Philippine mother observes a number of practices and dietary rules designed to influence her unborn child. Delivery becomes an event of which the whole family is aware, a sort of token of the extent to which the new individual will become a part of the larger social unit. Whereas the American mother weighs the pleasure of the new addition against the inconvenience and curtailment of her other activities, the Philippine mother and the whole family with her sees the new baby, the first or the sixth, as a blessing to the home, a sign of God's will, and a source of pleasure to all.

chapter 6

FEEDING THE BABY

Of all activities between mother and child, none is the occasion for more prolonged, intimate contact than nursing and feeding. In this relationship a mother can communicate many things to the child, and the child acquires many ideas about the kind of treatment he can expect from the world. Harlow's work (1959) has emphasized that the overall physical contact elements in the interaction may be equally as significant as those related specifically to the mouth. We shall examine the relationships that develop between mother and child with particular attention to the total situation of a mother feeding her child rather than solely with whether or not the child is breast-fed and with the severity of the weaning experience. This will involve an examination also of the introduction of solid foods and the child's food preferences. In the Philippines all of these events belong together. The mother's process of lactation does not assume the emotion-loaded role that happens so frequently in Western breast-conscious societies.

Breast- or Bottle-Feeding

Just as she expects to have children, the Filipino mother generally expects to nurse her child when it comes. A woman suckling her infant is the Filipino's favorite picture of motherhood. She does not have to make a big decision to prepare herself emotionally for breast-feeding. Babies are nourished this way all around her, and she herself was breast-fed unless serious circumstances prevented her mother from doing so. This view is evident in the casualness with which the Filipino mother goes about suckling her child. She does it in front of company. She uses the breast to quiet her child in any gathering, in church, in the market, or even in a packed bus. Of course, especially with new mothers, nursing is executed with different degrees of shyness and *delicadeza;* but they learn early that this aspect of motherhood is no cause for embarrassment. Almost 90 per cent of the mothers reported having breast-fed their children, 61 per cent without recourse to a bottle, 21 per cent using a bottle as a supplement, and 6 per cent turning to bottle-feeding later for some reason. Only slightly more than 10 per cent did not breast-feed—they did not have any milk or they worked or in two cases the child had difficulty sucking. Most of the working mothers managed to continue breast-feeding, at least at night, even if their children used a bottle in the daytime. Wet-nursing, which occurred only once in our sample, is resorted to rarely when a mother who cannot nurse allows her child to be nursed by a relative or a neighbor whose child is almost the same age. The age requirement is necessitated by the belief that the mother's milk adapts itself to the baby's changing needs, so that a mother with an eight-month-old baby would not have milk suitable for a newborn.

When asked how they would have fed their children if they had had a choice, the mothers reiterated their preference for breast-feeding, although a few conceded that the bottle does free the mother for other activities. A few favored mixed-feeding for various reasons. Mothers who bottle-fed believed it was good discipline for a child. Of the mothers who favored breast-feeding, more than 36 per cent believed that the mother's milk is more nutritious, 15 per cent thought it was safer ("certain to be clean," "pure," "sanitary"), 11 per cent cited the added expense of buying milk, and 12 per cent did not want the extra burden of preparing the formula. About 10 per cent added that breast-feeding the child strengthens the mother-child attachment.

Essentially the claims for mother's milk assert: "It is nature's food for babies. It has what the baby needs in just the right proportions, the right temperature, the right consistency." From the mothers, we got the following comments:

> Mother's milk has all that she needs, and there is less danger of infection too. (From a teacher who had to bottle-feed her baby.)
> Breast-feeding is economical. We wouldn't have the money to buy milk.
> I don't have to get up at midnight to prepare his milk. Besides, children get stomach upsets from different kinds of milk.
> My breast-fed children are healthier, and bigger!
> The child loves her mother more when she's breast-fed.

> I work, so he did not completely nurse from me. But I wish he had, because all the necessary nutrients are in mother's milk. (From a nurse.)
>
> If the mother is healthy, her milk is always best for the child.
>
> No better way for a baby to feel that mother loves her. I also feel I am doing right by my child in breast-feeding her.
>
> They're more often sickly when they're bottle-fed. Germs can easily come with careless handling, and any mistake in preparing the formula can cause upset.

From these comments it is evident that the nursing mother is concerned that the child get milk that is best for him. The precautions she observes to insure this include making sure her breasts are clean before she nurses, eating the right foods, and avoiding certain types of food believed to be harmful. Food such as watermelon, turnips, and ice cream, are "cold" and therefore make the milk unsuitable and cause a stomach upset in the infant. Sour food such as green mangoes, tamarind, and so forth cause the baby's stomach to sour and make him prone to vomiting. One woman mentioned eggplants and *upo*, a kind of gourd, as something else to avoid; she called them "itch" foods. "Heavy" foods such as the *saba* variety of bananas and "sticky rice" are to be avoided also, but these affect the mother and only indirectly the child.

There were however a few mothers, usually in the most educated group, who either minimized the advantages of breast-feeding or stated a preference for bottle-feeding. Some of their remarks were:

> I'd rather he was completely bottle-fed so that I can go about my work.
>
> I should think they are all the same. One can add all sorts to the formula to get it more like mother's milk. Babies can get used to the bottle after a while.

A mother, of course, should not nurse when she has beriberi, a condition of serious thiamine deficiency, when she is ill, when she is emotionally upset, or when she is exhausted from heavy work. The Philippine expression, "The child sucks it from the mother," implies that a condition transfers itself to the child through the milk. Others maintain that the condition of the milk is affected by the state of the mother—something parallel to "milk from contented cows." Although all mothers are preoccupied with the delicate digestive system of the infant which is sensitive to the slightest changes in the mother's milk, some also suggest that the mother's disposition during the nursing period, her emotional state, can influence patterning of the child's temperament—a happy mother insuring a cheerful child, an unhappy mother causing a sullen and ill-tempered child. The mother stops nursing the child when she becomes pregnant, again lest her milk make the child sickly.

A mother's ability to nurse is said to come naturally, and thus if a mother is healthy she should be able to nurse. However, the Filipinos realize that certain external aids are necessary to insure a steady and abundant supply of milk. Eggs, milk, fruits, *mongo* (a kind of legume), and yellow and green vegetables are frequently prescribed. Plenty of liquids, both at mealtime and between meals are also necessary. A good mother consumes vast quantities of broths from meat, chicken, shellfish, or fish, and special leafy vegetables, soups, tea, and coffee so that her milk supply will be plentiful.

Schedule or Demand

Frequency of feeding was a matter of concern to 50 per cent of the mothers. More than a third in each group of mothers reported some scheduling. Of those who followed a specific schedule, 10 per cent belonged to the least educated group, 20 per cent to the second group, and 40 per cent to the most educated group. Of those who reported no scheduling of any kind, the trend is reversed with 55 per cent in the first group, 42 per cent in the middle group, and 25 per cent in the third group.

I just know when he is hungry. I get a pain in my breasts and my milk starts to drip.

I fed him every time he cried. I knew he was hungry then.

It usually worked at four feedings a day but this was never at regular hours, especially when I had so much work around the house.

I fed him every three hours, but there were times when he had no appetite, so I'd wait until he cried and then I'd feed him.

I followed a schedule, but I never wakened him for feeding when he was asleep.

He was on a three hour schedule—doctor's advice!

The advice available to the mothers seemed to account largely for the differences in feeding schedules between the groups. More than 50 per cent of the mothers in the most educated group cited the doctor, nurse, or a book or article as the source of their ideas on scheduling in contrast to only 14 per cent in both the least educated and middle groups. Over 80 per cent of the mothers in the two less educated groups, as compared to 43 per cent in the most educated group, said they based their practices on their own opinions or on the advice of their mothers, in-laws, or neighbors.

Sensitive as the mothers were to their babies' crying, only a few babies (6 per cent) got the breast or bottle when their mothers felt they were not hungry. Mothers could sense, almost by some kind of built-in schedule system, whether the child was hungry, or whether he was wet or uncomfortable or had colic. Only about 20 per cent used pacifiers, usually a rubber nipple, because such objects are generally believed to deform the mouth (of special concern for girl babies) and because sucking nothing but air reportedly induces colic. A few mothers used in-between feedings of *calamansi* juice, a citrus fruit resembling a lime, or warm sweetened water in a bottle to calm and distract the child. In a majority of cases the mother or some other member of the family gave the child attention in various forms—picked him up, rocked him, lulled him to sleep, or amused him with talking or objects. Only about 10 per cent, actually 7 per cent of the least educated group and twice as many in the middle and third groups, believed that leaving the child alone would do him good, that crying is good exercise, or that picking him up at every squeal he makes would spoil him.

> He won't cry if there's nothing wrong. So I see to it that he's comfortable and free from bites of bedbugs or ants.
>
> If she cried and I felt she was not hungry, I would sing for her.
>
> I would take her in my arms and dance her around. She would usually stop.
>
> I either went and played with her awhile, or when I was busy, the older children talked with her or rocked her in her *duyan* [swing or cloth hammock].
>
> I gave her water and put her back in bed. I only used pacifiers when I went somewhere and had to leave her.
>
> I left him alone. To stop his crying I'd give him a rubber nipple.
>
> I let her cry and cry. I did not use any pacifiers.

She had a definite feeding schedule. But if at any time between feedings she cried, she needed affection or she probably was thirsty, or she was uncomfortable. I'd take her in my arms or give her water or try to massage her stomach.

Weaning the Child

One of the most frequently mentioned advantages of breast-feeding is, "I don't have to get up when he wakes up hungry at midnight," because almost all Filipino babies sleep with their mothers until they are weaned. When the mother finally decides to wean her child, he either sleeps alone or more frequently he sleeps with other members of the family. In this context weaning takes on a double meaning—cessation of breast-feeding and sleeping away from mother. The child is faced with prohibitions against seeking his mother's breast at night topped by the loss of the familiar warmth and cuddling he has always received from his mother.

The median age at weaning in our sample was about thirteen months; 49 per cent of the mothers weaned their babies during the first year, 30 per cent between thirteen and eighteen months, 16 per cent between nineteen and twenty-four months, and 6 per cent over two years. There were differences in the three groups of mothers in the age at which they weaned their babies. In the least educated group 58 per cent continued to breast-feed their children after they were a year old, 45 per cent did this in the middle group, while only 33 per cent in the most educated group nursed that long. In two extreme cases occurring in situations of only, or youngest, children in the middle group, weaning did not come until after four years. Weaning under six months of age (twenty cases, 7 per cent) occurred only under unavoidable circumstances because of the mother's illness and lack of milk. A few working mothers decided to wean their children to the bottle at the time they went back to work, but it should be recalled that quite a number continued to breast-feed at night even when their children were placed on the bottle in the daytime.

A mother usually weans her baby for a specific reason, not simply because at a certain age the child should be weaned. Only eleven mothers (4 per cent) gave the child's being too old to breast-feed as the reason for weaning. Fewer than 10 per cent weaned their children because they did not have any more milk, and only about 6 per cent used ill health as a reason. In the sample as a whole, forty-eight (20 per cent) of the mothers weaned their babies because of another pregnancy. However, there were large intergroup differences. Twenty-seven per cent of the least educated group, 14 per cent of the second group, and only 4 per cent of the most educated group gave pregnancy as a reason for cessation of breast-feeding. More than a third (eighty-eight mothers) stopped breast-feeding because their children could eat foods other than milk, and a little less than a sixth reported that the children weaned themselves. Fewer than 10 per cent gave interference with their other activities as a reason for weaning. This last reason was given twice as many times (17 per cent) in the most educated group as in the other two groups. Following are some representative answers to questions concerning the reasons for weaning and the age of the child at weaning:

> He was one and a half by then. I weaned him because I was pregnant again.

> She was only a little over a year. Another baby was on the way.

> He was four, and really quite big. I simply hid the bottle and kept all milk away from him.

> A year. I was working so I decided to wean him. I had no difficulty at all.

> I weaned him at eleven months because he had grown and could eat the other food very well. I had difficulty though, because I had a lot of milk and had to get rid of it.

> She was only a year old and was a hungry baby. I was growing thin, so I had one of her aunts sleep with her. She was given a bottle every time she cried.

> I stopped nursing her when she was only two weeks old. I was very sickly, and I felt the bottle would be better for her. It was easier to wean her from the bottle after that.

> I got him used to *calamansi* juice, soft rice, and soft-cooked eggs, so that when I finally weaned him at one and a half there was not much difficulty.

Mothers differ in their definitions of weaning. About 50 per cent of the mothers in the middle and most educated groups and a fourth in the first group considered it a simple shift from breast to bottle or from breast milk to regular foods. The more general notion of weaning appears to be the separation of the mother and the child until the child no longer asks to nurse. In order to achieve the separation, mothers resorted to making the breast or bottle dis-

tasteful to the child (30 per cent), had the child sleep beside someone else in the house, or sent him to a grandmother or a close aunt
(22 per cent). This process of keeping the mother and the child
apart until the child no longer asks to nurse from the mother appears to be the more general notion of weaning.

> I gave her the bottle when she asked to be fed. It was difficult
> because she would cry hard and long for the breast.

> Her father took care of her. I hid myself from her for three
> days and three nights. Those first three days were the most
> difficult; she just cried and cried and refused the bottle.

> I sent her to mother's and she stayed there for a week. She
> did not ask to nurse even once when she came back.

> She slept on her father's side instead of on mine. When she
> cried, he gave her the bottle.

> Every time she'd wake up crying to be fed, her father would
> rise and give her a glass of water or a biscuit.

> I applied indigo dye around my nipples. He thought they were
> dirty and he stopped.

> The ginger on my breast didn't taste too good. He cried at
> first. In a day he had learned.

> I put something bitter on the nipple of his bottle and told him
> it wasn't good, it wasn't sweet.

> I just gave him evaporated milk and KLIM [powdered milk]
> instead of nursing him.

> When he woke up at night and asked for food, I just got up
> and gave him soft-cooked rice softened still more in broth.

> I just told him, "You are big now and you mustn't suck any
> more." He listened and obeyed.

Examination of these statements reveals very few difficulties
experienced in connection with weaning. The most common problem
is the mother's pity for the child, particularly when it is her first
and weaning is attempted early. The mother's softness and indeci-
sion, resulting from her concern that she is being unjust and is hurting the child, is often behind unsuccessful first attempts at weaning.
We suspect that in our study weaning appears to be abrupt and
harsh because the second or third attempt, which is successful, is
reported.

Another difficulty that was mentioned, particularly when the
mothers weaned their children young, was the discomfort from un-
sucked milk which often caused fever. Very few mothers in our
sample complained of their babies' teeth or gave this as a reason

for finally deciding to wean, but direct experience with mothers nursing at the time would probably reveal a greater incidence of discomfort.

We obtained very few clear indications of when children were weaned from the bottle, especially when there was an early shift from breast to bottle. The mothers and even the interviewers understood weaning in the usual Filipino sense as separation from the mother in terms of feeding or the point when a mother could be away from the child without fearing that he would starve. Thus, even if breast-feeding was discontinued as early as the second week, the mother referred to this as weaning and the interviewers accepted it and made no further inquiries on the termination of bottle-feeding.

Feeding the Weanling

Since the baby's system is considered very delicate, much care goes into providing a smooth transition from milk to anything solid. Children are not generally given food that requires chewing until after they are a year old. In fact, a third of the mothers in the first group reported starting them on solid food at, or after, two years. This is not surprising, since mothers who let their children eat anything "hard on a baby's stomach" are labeled neglectful or too lazy to prepare the right food for their child. By "right food" mothers mean soft-cooked food, mashed potatoes or sweet potatoes, or mashed fruits. Rice should be soft-cooked, gruel or porridge-like, or, if it has been cooked for adults, it should be softened in broth or soup before being given to the child. Soft-boiled eggs, plain egg yolk if hard-boiled, or oatmeal are approved. Ice cream must be given at the right time of day, never in the morning. Meat or fish cut in very small pieces—"finger-picked" almost to grain size—may be given with rice. Mothers often stated the belief that children are not able to chew as well as adults. The following are some typical responses given by mothers when asked what they fed their children after weaning:

> I gave him rice as soon as he was weaned at two years of age. By then he could take part in regular family meals.
> He could have "soft drinks" [Coca-Cola or Tru-orange] and ice cream at one year old.
> We gave him coffee when he was a year, four months. He liked *calamansi* juice, too.

At three years we let him eat rice and bread.
He could have biscuits [cookies] then. They're easy enough to digest.
I gave her fruit at one year. At fifteen months I could feed her fish or meat with rice.

It is apparent from these quotations that the mothers were more concerned that the food be digestible than that it be nutritive. There are definite group differences here; the better educated groups try harder to get milk and fruit juices for their children while those in the least educated group are content that their children are getting something to eat. This explains the frequent occurrence of carbonated drinks and coffee (usually rice coffee with sugar and evaporated milk) in the reported postweaning diet. True, there is some vague notion of certain foods being more nutritious than others, but nutritious is a blanket term for good for the body. Milk is nutritious; oranges are too. The orange flavor in the carbonated drink is often taken as carrying the sustenance of the real orange.

H. Guthrie (1962) has presented a detailed report on the introduction of solid food to the Filipino child with an analysis of some of the nutritional problems which Philippine infant-feeding patterns may produce. Nutrition is a relatively new concern, and the average mother sees it in terms of specific deficiency conditions she has known or seen around her. Thus dietary supplements suggest the notion of medicine—a cure or a preventative—and the mother looks for the necessary vitamins and minerals in drugstore preparations she has heard about rather than in the food she feeds her family and her infant. *Tiki-tiki*, a rice bran extract, may be given very early in the child's life to prevent the dreaded beriberi, a serious, even fatal thiamine deficiency. Multi-vitamin preparations and cod-liver oil appeared frequently in the accounts of infant diets, and the daily doses were administered religiously. A number of mothers were administering Castoria as a diet supplement with the apparent understanding that anything from a bottle was good for the child. Originally some mothers would use supplements or medications on a nurse's or doctor's advice; then application of these remedies would spread from neighbor to neighbor.

Although it is beyond the scope of our research, it may be pointed out that children in this society depend for a much greater portion of their nourishment on their mother's milk than is true in societies where solid food is introduced earlier. Among the consequences of this pattern is the severe nutritional crisis frequently seen in a child whose mother suddenly stops nursing him. The result is that it is the toddler of three or four who is poorly nourished and not the suckling of twelve months. Mother's milk is certainly nutritionally more adequate than any available substitute, and under conditions of limited refrigeration and sanitation facilities it is certainly the safest food for the child. Nor should the fact that it is the least expensive be overlooked in the economy where this study was done. The pattern of prolonged breast-feeding has economic as well as social causes. The results so far as nutrition is concerned are beneficial. The effect on personality development is less certain.

Feeding Skills

The shift from sucking to other ways of feeding involves the learning of certain skills, and we assumed that if the child no longer took nourishment from the bottle he probably used a cup or spoon. When we consider the age at which a child begins to drink from a glass and to eat with a spoon, the late weaning and late introduction of solid foods comes into sharper relief. Only a fourth of the mothers in the first group started to feed their children with a spoon or from a cup before they were a year old. More than 40 per cent of the mothers in the middle and most educated groups started their children that early. The ages for eating solids or semi-solids and feeding with a spoon do not necessarily correspond because the system of finger-feeding is still used in rural areas.

Sooner or later the child learns to feed himself, but there appear to be no stage-linked expectations. Less than a fourth of our total sample reported that their children had started to feed themselves before the second year, and more than a fourth reported that they had not started until the third year. Some of the usual replies to our questions concerning training the child to feed himself and the age at which this training occurred were:

He did not start feeding himself until he was two. But he'd make a mess and not eat very much. I fed him still and he got more that way.

She learned to eat by herself at two. I'd let her eat with us at the table and she imitated our ways. She saw how her brothers and sisters were doing it.

He started feeding himself at four. He could eat with the family then.

The children probably could have learned these skills at an earlier age, but there was no demand for them to do so. Caring for the child is the mother's main concern and the concern of the other members of the family who are available to help. The important thing is that the child gets something to eat. If it is easier for somebody to help the child, is less mess, and takes less time, everybody is happier in the end. Why be concerned about the age at which he learns to take care of this himself? The Filipino mother knows that he will eventually learn. There is no hurry.

Feeding Difficulties

In answer to a question that covered the whole span of birth to the present in the life of six- or seven-year-old children, mothers generally gave no indication of any trouble with the feeding of their sons and daughters. Perhaps this was due to their concern that the child should like what he ate or to the absence of any conflict about what or how he ate. Only about 8 per cent of the children were reported as choosy and less than 3 per cent as having a poor appetite. The rest were labeled "good eaters," some of them with one or two aversions and no more. The parents' reactions to these aversions included preparing something else, letting the child go without it, letting him wait a while, and pressuring him to eat. In 55 per cent of the cases some form of aversion to food occurred, but only in 7 per cent was any pressure placed on the child to eat the food he was rejecting. Most of the mothers' comments on feeding difficulties are similar to those below:

> She liked everything.
> When she refused anything, like vegetables, eggs, or oranges, she'd be given other food, like bread and milk.
> He hated onions and tomatoes in his food, but he does not mind them any more.
> He hasn't forgotten his aversion for *ampalaya* [bitter melon]. I prepare something else for him when this comes in the day's menu.
> She wouldn't eat squid. It was the color of it. I just know and prepare something else for her beforehand.

At first I had difficulty. He won't eat eggs. I would give the other children eggs and not give him any, and this made him envious. Later on he asked for them. He would eat only the white and give away the yolk.

None of my children liked vegetables, but I did not force them. I didn't like them myself.

If he refused something, I didn't care. Somebody else ate it for him.

The child's experiences in feeding are congruent with his other experiences in many respects and are part of a larger complex of solicitude and indulgence. The mother takes primary responsibility for him and spreads this responsibility later after breast-feeding has terminated. Food remains an important element in the relationships of the individual throughout life. Offers of food are essential to almost every expression of hospitality. At the same time the individual Filipino, by Western standards, nibbles almost constantly. He rarely goes for more than an hour or two without eating something. One eats because one enjoys it; one gives food to children to bribe them; one gives food to other adults as a gesture of friendship. Children are not forced to eat something because it is good for them. Balanced interpersonal relationships are much more important than a balanced diet.

The more or less continuous association of the mother and the child both day and night, and the resulting mother-child relationship, has to be strained briefly at weaning when the child is physically separated for the first significant period both in the day and at night. Other familiar adults support the child during this period. The strained separation seems necessary because lactation does not stop spontaneously in the mother, an apparent manifestation of her pleasure in this role. The late introduction of solid foods may mean that weaning is a nutritional crisis. It is impossible to determine how much of the child's crying which may follow weaning for several days is due to the longing for the mother, and how much is due to hunger.

Comparison with the Findings of Sears, Maccoby, and Levin

This chapter permits many direct comparisons of Filipino and American customs and practices. Ninety per cent of the Philippine children in our study were breast-fed compared with only 40 per cent of the American in the Sears study. But the difference does not stop here. The median age for weaning in the Philippines was thirteen months, while only 1 per cent of American mothers nursed their babies for nine months or more. Forty-eight per cent of American mothers imposed no scheduling or at most vague scheduling of feeding, while 67 per cent of Filipino mothers were rated as equally permissive about feeding intervals. Weaning is difficult to define because it may refer to the termination of breast or bottle, a transfer from breast to bottle, or a physical separation from the mother. Differences in the age of beginning and ending weaning are not great between the two cultures. The difference is that weaning in the United States means giving up the bottle, in the Philippines it means giving up the breast. In the Philippines it also means the temporary loss of the close physical relationship, particularly at night, since the child has been sleeping with the mother since birth. Since cow's milk is available at a reasonable price in the United States but not the Philippines, we cannot attribute all of the differences in the mode of feeding to the culturally sanctioned preferences of the mothers.

With respect to feeding problems, the much later introduction of solid foods in the Philippines may account for the fact that only 20 per cent of Philippine children present some feeding difficulties while 45 per cent of American children do so according to the standards of the country.

The differences in feeding practices between the cultures are great, differences which are prompted by both preference and necessity. However, breast-feeding is hardly the matter of choice in the Philippines that it is in America because there are few satisfactory substitutes for mother's milk available for the Filipino child. Nursing her child is both a virtue and a necessity for the Filipina. It is an uncertain virtue and not a necessity for the American.

chapter 7

DEPENDENCY

Although all human infants arrive in the world in a state of utter helplessness, differences in the extent of reliance on others begin to appear in the earliest months. In some societies a child is given minimum attention; in others he is cared for much beyond the requirements of simple survival. In this chapter we are concerned with the configuration of attitudes of parents and of children which relate to the help and direction which children receive. We are concerned with who cares for the child and what feelings are involved for both the child and the one who helps him.

Dependency is an important concept in American psychology because it refers to an area of conflict which arises when children are encouraged to be self-reliant and assertive. These patterns necessitate a break with earlier habits of receiving help and support and of having little opportunity to make one's own decisions. For the American, the problem of dependency polarizes around the degree to which he can learn to make his own decisions, accept responsibility for his own acts, take his own risks, and accept his own gains and losses.

If we apply American concepts to the Philippines, we are obliged to conclude that the Filipino is very dependent. He is willing and eager to receive help from his relatives and friends. He does not particularly aspire to be on his own and often seeks the help and cooperation of others in activities which he could carry out himself. But American concepts break down at this point because dependency is not the problem for the Filipino that it is for the American. The concept of dependency with its connotation of conflict and feelings of inadequacy clouds rather than clarifies our understanding of a Filipino child's developing pattern of relationships with older people. We must consider rather the approved pattern of development for the Filipino child as it involves communication with, and help from, parents, siblings, and peers. The pattern is different, with different ideals, different goals, and a different prod-

uct in adulthood. Instead of dependency, we should consider closeness, cooperation, respect, and duty. Giving and receiving help are
important interpersonal encounters in the Philippines at all ages.
The Philippine ideal is not self-sufficiency and independence but
rather family-sufficiency and a refined sense of reciprocity.

Communication with Parents

In response to a question concerning how much the child talks with
his mother, we found that 51 per cent of mothers described their
children as very talkative, and only 10 per cent called their children
silent. This is in startling contrast to the experience of a visitor
who finds Philippine children shy and silent. The pattern appears
specific to the situation. Within the family the child is encouraged
to be talkative, expressive, open; in the presence of older visitors
he may be seen but not heard.

The child's talking within the family is encouraged for several
reasons. It proves the child is alert, and an alert and bright child
is a very good reflection on the parent. Also, in a family group
which seeks its everyday amusements within itself, the growing
prattle of the child is a welcome thing. The highest points in the
family life of a child are the times when he begins to utter a few
words, or what will later amount to words, and when he starts to
respond to the proddings of the older members of the family with
a repertoire of new skills, little tricks learned each day. *Sinungaling,*
or tricky, is the fond term for him at this stage. This enjoyment
of the child continues even when the mother has become distracted
by the birth of another baby. In spite of the new arrival, the father,
siblings, and relatives, and the mother too, still pay attention to
him. This *pagkasinungaling* (clowning) wears off with age and the
child develops interests in other things rather than being the center
of amusement for his family. It is as if he had played the role
enough and is off to more mature pursuits.

The child's talking serves still another purpose. The good
mother knows her children and is sensitive to their troubles, but
she cannot possibly know them by intuition. The child's running
to his mother, his confidences, and his help-seeking, all of which
she encourages, are expressions of closeness and of faith in her re-
sponsiveness as a mother. The child is not supposed to be secretive

but open and therefore predictable. There are times when he should be quiet, and he is taught to recognize these times, but otherwise his careful and detailed recounting of exploits, thoughts, and feelings are welcome. Thus, a child may be *tahimik* (respectfully quiet, not given to exhibitionism or loudness) but not *dungo* (quiet in a stupid sort of way). And he certainly should not be secretive, at least not within the family circle.

Only one parent, and that one from the most educated group, said she was too busy to listen to her child's talk. Others admitted they were busy sometimes, in which case they listened as long as they could or redirected the child to someone else. In a few cases of excessive talkers, the mother admitted to ignoring, or putting a stop to, the outflow. But in the majority of cases, "He tells me everything" is reported with much pride as proof of the closeness between mother and child.

> He persists in stories even when he is ignored or told to stop. This continues up to bedtime.

> Sometimes I would be so busy, but he'd be standing there, talking away. I would keep on working, nodding my head, answering "yes and yes" every now and then.

> Yes, he is very talkative. At night he used to tell me stories and everything that happened that whole day. Sometimes I'd enjoy them, but sometimes I'd get tired of it. Sometimes I'd shout at him, especially when I was very busy. I think he is very talkative to me and to his father.

> Yes, she tells me everything. I encourage her to do this so that she will not have to hide things from me later on.

> I encourage my child to talk with me so he won't turn to other people.

> I listen to her so I can correct her when she is thinking something wrong.

> I encourage her to tell me everything she wants. When I am so busy and can't stand her talk any more, I give her food so she'll stop talking or else I ask her to play outside.

> I encourage her to tell me all she wants to. I don't get bored or annoyed if she talks too much even when I am busy with my work.

We see another aspect of this relationship when the child comes home crying. Very few mothers ignore such an incident except those who think their children are crying too much. A few soothe the child with words or with offers of food so that he will stop crying.

About as many rebuke the child's crying. But almost 75 per cent of the mothers hold a minor court of inquiry, questioning the child and whoever is around as to what has happened and who was at fault. The child is usually punished when found at fault, but whether he was offended or offender he receives *advice*. This word appears again and again in the interviews. Advising is not a one or two sentence reprimand or admonition; it is, rather, a prolonged review of circumstances and a restatement of family expectations of what makes a good boy or girl. God's wrath, the family name, what people will think are all involved in these admonitions.

> When she comes home crying, I ask why she is crying. When I hear a report about her from her playmates or the neighbors, I advise her to be a good girl. I often tell her God loves all those girls and boys who are good.

> I ask her to relate to me what happened. I spank her if she is at fault.

> When he comes home crying, I ask him what happened. When I hear some report or complaint about him, I try to reconcile with the parents if it is serious. If he is at fault, I scold him.

> I ask him why. I just let it go and tell him never to play with them any more if he was in the right. At the same time I tell the parents of his playmates to keep their children from teasing him because he resents being teased.

The child is expected to accept reprimands without retort or murmur, without any signs of anger or resentment. Many adults report that they look back on these experiences with gratitude. The nature of the relationship is such that the child comes to see the parental monologue as an expression of the parent's love and concern. He is not permitted and does not permit himself to express resentment. On the contrary, one often hears the statement, "If it were not for my parents' advice when I was a child, I would not be what I am now."

This pattern of advising is continued well into adulthood. Older siblings, relatives, or friends may offer advice, may even give it without being asked. Concern appears to be sufficient occasion for advising. The recipient sees an earnest desire to help and reacts to the person with apparent gratitude. To reject the advice would produce a painful situation between the adviser and the one advised. Acceptance of the advice is a measure of how much one values the advice-giver. Implied criticism in the advice should not hurt if it is tempered by a tone of concern.

Siblings and Peers in the Child's World

In his relationship with other children we find further indications of the preferred pattern of development for the child. When one sees an older child saddled with his younger siblings or a younger child holding on to an older sibling, one wonders what opportunity there is left for peer relationships to emerge. The ideal pattern is one of looking after a younger sibling and looking up to an older one. The sibling cluster remains the important group even when the child relates to children outside of it. Age differences of up to three or four years between siblings do not matter, nor is it necessary that siblings be of the same sex to be close. Only a sibling too young to join in the games is a drag, but even then it is common to see a youngster in a game running to the finish line with a baby brother astride his hips.

Kababata, childhood friend, is a term one hears often when someone refers to playmates he grew up with. The most frequent choice for a playmate is one of the same age; he does not have to be of the same sex. The introduction of an outside playmate does not reduce the importance of the sibling group. Its boundaries are merely widened to admit the friend. If friends are older, they are looked up to for protection by the child's younger siblings. Parents recognize these friendships and encourage them when they consider their children's choice as suitable. Some advising goes into the choice of friends, usually regarding the other child's conduct, his words, his manners, and his cleanliness. Members of the nuclear and of the extended family provide most of the companionship the child receives. An outsider who is brought in as a friend is fitted into the age-determined family relationship and is responded to in many of the same ways as members of the family.

The Parents' View of Child's Play

Play is approved for the children because the children enjoy it. It is, in an informal sense, supervised by older siblings and by the older children in the neighborhood. Parents see it as an expression of childhood and, when time allows, they join in the games themselves at the child's level. They make little attempt to influence the children's play beyond keeping it within the limits of safety. When called on to help out, to lay out the posts and the beams for a play house, to provide materials for a play store, a miniature clay pot cook-out, or a mud bake, the father and mother usually participate without seeking to impose parental ideas on the children's game.

The child is also permitted to accompany his parent in many activities. A mother washes her clothes, and her little girl gets to wash the little things, her hands and arms deep in lather and soap bubbles. A father weeds the garden, and the little one trails behind him pulling weeds and seedlings. The relationship that is fostered is one of companionship with respect. Parents are human beings, bigger and older. They can get angry, but they can also show love. They encourage children to join in the activities of adults, and they, in turn, join the children in their play.

In a society in which rugged individualism is not particularly esteemed, this pattern of indulgence predisposes the child to expect support and companionship from his family. He is not pushed out; he can go out if he wants to, but he is welcome back if it does not work well. There is no coercion used on him to make or keep friends. It is not as important that he learn to take care of himself and protect his own rights as it is that he learn to show the proper respect for older members of the family and their teaching and do his part to maintain the good name of the family.

Children's play will inevitably involve conflict. When this leads to a fight in the neighborhood, mothers reported that they investigate the cause and then punish the child if necessary. This is accompanied by the usual advising, with all sorts of sanctions invoked to discourage the child from again getting involved. Fights are usually stopped; they are not ordinarily permitted to continue when an adult concerned about the children's upbringing is around. But at times fights do run their bloody course to the cheers and cries of children who relish the spectacle. They are watched and arbitrated by unrelated adults who gauge a boy's mettle by the offense or defense he puts up in a fight.

But fighting is not considered an inevitable matter in children's play. Fighting is not good; and if children continue to fight, they must be kept home. Eighty per cent of the mothers reported that children were called home when they quarreled with a neighbor's child. Better that the child come home to avoid a challenge than that he stay and get hurt or hurt someone else. Better to stay home and play alone than invite fighting by playing with quarrelsome playmates. This pattern of the avoidance of direct conflict is instilled early. A value more important than skill in defending oneself is skill in avoiding having to do it at all.

> When I hear a bad report about her from her playmates or from the neighbors, she is not allowed to play outside the house.
>
> When she has a fight, I tell her that she should not do it again or she will not have any friends.
>
> I always advise her to go home to avoid trouble because at times mothers have misunderstandings with other mothers just because of children.
>
> I advise him not to play with those boys. I also tell him to fight back, not to come home crying.
>
> I do not listen to him as long as he is not hurt himself. Children are really like that.
>
> I arrange with the neighbors so that there will be no hard feelings, especially if he is at fault. I scold him and try to advise him again and again.
>
> Whenever she is in trouble, she runs home quietly, but she does not ask for help. I don't punish her when she gets into a fight, but I advise her to stay away from those children.
>
> I talk with her first, and then I talk with the other child. Afterwards I take the other girl to her parents.
>
> She does come home crying sometimes. She is very affectionate, even with her playmates, but she is weak and has very shallow tear wells. She is not choosy with playmates, but she would rather play with bigger children who tend to protect her.
>
> I repeat this to her constantly—never to resist or fight back. She either should come to tell me or go to the other child's mother to ask her to stop.

It is not that being pushed about or a crybaby is considered a virtue, but a mother would rather see her child come home crying from having avoided a fight than see him with his nose bleeding. It is probably a different story with fathers, but we have no direct reports about that. "He can hold his own" or "He takes care of himself" implies skill in interpersonal relations, not self-assertiveness or a tendency to bully. A mother considers it a virtue that her child manage himself so that he is liked, and that he possess a certain blend of friendliness and childhood dignity.

The Child's Expressions of Affection

An aspect of the parent-child relationship that seems much like dependency but differs from it in a subtle way, shows in the child's expression of affection for his parents and elders. Half the parents characterized their children as *malambing na malambing* (very affectionate), while only 10 per cent said their children were not at all affectionate. Seven per cent said their children were affectionate toward them only to get things. But it is very apparent that affectionateness, like talkativeness, is expected and encouraged within the family circle. The absence of it is not decried, however; it is simply attributed to the child's natural temperament and accepted as that.

Children express their affection in a variety of ways. Younger children sit on a parent's lap, wrap their arms around his neck, kiss the parent on cheeks or forehead, stroke his arm, or ask for presents and money. A few snuggle up to mother at siesta time, and the youngest child especially is known to play with his mother's nipples to a late age. Most parents accept the attention of their children as a matter of course or are pleased by it. Fifteen per cent consider it a bother. One hears parents attempt to brush aside their children's demonstrations with *"malaki ka na"* (you are grown now), but it is probably safe to say that they would at least want one of their children to be this way.

> She is that way. There are times when she wants me to carry her, although she is too big now.
> He's not so expressive of his affections. He just shows it by helping me carry my things and being always obedient.
> He is very loving. He would always kiss our foreheads and is most especially loving to his father. When making a toy, for example, he would call for his father's help.
> I know it when she has something she wants me to get her. She'd kiss me and sit on my lap.

The Child's Sensitivities

Closely related to the child's display of affection is his susceptibility to hurt feelings. Almost 80 per cent of the mothers characterized their children as *tampuhin,* having a tendency to be sensitive and to express hurt quietly, a fourth of them very much so. Frustration or some perceived injustice or unfairness gives rise to a wide range of behavior from quiet acceptance to sulking, wheedling, and sometimes even tantrums. The term *tampo,* the noun for *tampuhin,* however, refers to the more quiet expression of these feelings, the gathering of a few tears in the eyes, avoiding contact with the parent or with whoever caused the hurt, refusal to eat or to come when called, all of them calculated to arouse sympathy but not loud or defiant enough to cause irritation. Invariably they have their effect because parents tend to feel sorry for the child, to soothe him and give him what he had been denied before. More than 50 per cent of the parents demonstrate this reaction of pacifying the child or trying to make amends. Only when the child becomes violent, or the *tampo* becomes too habitual, automatic, and hence unconvincing, does the parent react negatively.

> You never know when she'll get that way, but usually it is when she doesn't get what she wants or she's been yelled at.
> When she wants something and she is crossed, she just goes to a corner and cries.
> He refuses to come to the table, even when my voice shows I'm no longer angry.
> He sits down in a corner and doesn't respond when I talk to him.
> She cries or pouts or remains silent for hours.

Another aspect of this parent-child relationship is shown when the mother has to go out, and the child wants to go along. There are a variety of parental responses; the most common is to tell the child he cannot go and to leave him at home with someone who is close to him. Two interesting responses that mothers make include promising something to the child or fooling the child and departing without his knowledge. The promises are bribes to get the child to acquiesce, although in most cases they also serve as reassurance that the parent is coming back. In almost all of the responses it appears that the mother seeks to soften the blow. She does not want to leave the child in tears; she avoids an outright denial of a child's wish. She would like to humor the child by one method or another, so that even if he may not be happy at being left at home, at least he is not brokenhearted, even temporarily, nor does he create a scene. There is little inclination to force the child to accept the fact that the mother must sometimes leave, nor is there much inclination to let the child cry with the expectation that he will soon get over it. There will come a time when the child is old enough to realize this, but while it bothers him, why make an issue of it?

She listens to reason. She used to cry when I didn't take her with me. But I told her that children are not allowed where I work, and she's content staying with her aunt.

He knows he will get it when I promise to bring him back something. Now he no longer insists on coming along.

She insists on tagging along, and there are times when promises are not sufficient. I just take her along. But not when her father is there. One word, and she stays.

When I go somewhere, I leave her with her sisters. She is willing to be left alone. She doesn't insist on tagging along as long as she is given money.

I hide from her when I go or promise her a toy or money when I get back.

When I am going somewhere I don't show myself to her so she doesn't have any chance to ask to tag along.

The Child's Affection toward the Father and Other Family Members

The mothers were asked to comment on the child's attachment to the father and to other persons. Although the mother was closest to the child when he was an infant, other children and other activities may have intervened to cause the child to be closer to someone else. Most frequently the child turns to his father or to an older sibling if his mother has younger children or is otherwise occupied. The father is an easy source of money and does not feel particularly guilty about buying the child's affection. He is the one who most often relents and gives the child the few centavos he asks for. Sometimes a routine is established with the child greeting his father when he comes home, kissing his hand or tugging his shirttails, and receiving five centavos. This occurs in spite of the fact that the mother controls the family money.

He will go to his father when he starts to get sleepy and curl up on his lap. His father lets him and takes him to his bed when he finally falls asleep.

She goes to her father when she wants a new pair of shoes or a dress or candies. She is very close to her father because she knows she is his favorite.

She is very close to her father. She goes to her father when she wants something to eat, when her mother doesn't give her money.

In the extended family situation where relationships cut across household walls and follow lines of blood connections, a child's affection and attachment may be spread across many people. The father and mother do not feel that they must be first in a child's life. Love for parents is accorded a sort of instinctive status so that parents feel quite secure and are able to let others raise and care for their children if circumstances dictate. There is not the feeling that they have in any way lost their children or failed in their duty to them. A child is the child of his parents no matter who raised him, his grandparents, an aunt, or even a *yaya* (baby caretaker).

Sharing of Parental Affection

The possibility always arises that parents will feel closer to one child than to another. About a third of the mothers were quite willing to admit that they had favorites among their children. The children are usually aware of this and accept the fact. More than half of these mothers give a reason for favoring one over the other: the child is particularly good-natured or obedient, he is the only boy or she is the only girl, or she is the oldest and the most helpful. Most frequently the favorite is the youngest member of the family. The youngest child often experiences a prolonging of his childhood status and is the object of special attention, not only from his parents but from older siblings as well. Favors come in the form of affection, tolerance of the child's requests for help, new clothes, special treats. To a certain extent this is culturally sanctioned, and the other children in the family accept it.

> I do make an effort to treat my children equally. I remember how hard it was because my parents had favorites, and I resolved I wasn't going to be that way with my children.
>
> Yes, because he is the youngest and attention is showered upon him.
>
> I pay more attention to my younger one, and he sort of resents this.
>
> No, I don't have any favorites. They are all the same to me. I pay special attention to her only because she is the youngest.
>
> One can't help having favorites.
>
> They know which one is my pet and they also know why.

I love my children equally since there are only two of them. I love my oldest son by my first husband the most. My youngest feels this, so they often have a quarrel especially when I have given more food to the oldest or buy him new shoes or a shirt.

I treat my daughters and sons equally. I give them what they need. If one gets a pair of new shoes, all get new pairs eventually.

Sibling jealousy is hardly recognized as such by the mothers. There is a little bickering among siblings about who gets the biggest or the first share, who gets away with more things, or who gets the lightest spanking, but fewer than a third of the mothers reported any of these indications. The relationship among siblings, solicitude on the part of the older and dependency on the part of the younger, may acount for acceptance of any differential treatment observed; but it is also possible, especially where age differences among siblings are slight, that the parent's conviction, "They're all my children and therefore I love them all," is successfully communicated.

A Dependency Pattern within the Family

There are two sides to the child's dependency relationship with his mother: his seeking of nurturance, or simply his need for nurturance, and her response. At first the mother's nurturance came unasked; the very helplessness of the infant drew her near anticipating what she could do for him. The child soon learned to use signals to bring his mother or somebody else to him. These signals—crying, whimpering, cooing, kicking—were interpreted by the mother. If she judged them to mean hunger, the infant was fed; if she thought he was uncomfortable, he was checked, changed, taken up, and lulled to sleep. A pattern was formed of a need and the response to the need by the parent. Both child and mother developed perceptions and expectations, each of the other.

A child's needs change with age, but there is always somebody helping with things he cannot do or even with things he can do, such as bathing, changing his clothes, combing his hair, even washing him after his toilet routine. Each has to be done just right: he'd forget the back of his ears and the ring of oil and dirt around his neck; he'd burst the shoulder seams on his shirt if he did it himself; he wouldn't wash himself clean enough, and then he'd smell. There are things he is too young to do correctly by himself. There are people around to help him anyway, whose responsibility it is to take care of him. By the time he can finally do these things for himself, he will very likely be old enough to help somebody else with them.

There is no particular agreement on ages at which the child must do things for himself. Some children do things at four which others still have done for them at eight. The family situation has much to do with the level of the child's independence. When caretakers are available, the child seeks help or is given help. When there are none and there are early responsibilities, the child takes his share. He has a place in the family, a part in its activities, responsibility to some or all of its members. The family members have responsibilities too, some of which involve him whether he likes it or not. When he needs help, he feels very free to ask for it, and he does ask for help in a wide variety of situations.

> She comes to me when her sisters beat her or when she is not feeling well.
>
> He asks his older brother to explain his assignments to him.
>
> He can't tie his shoes or take a bath. I help him with these. (Seven-year-old)
>
> He asks for help only when he can't really do it—as when he can't lift a heavy pile or he is tired or he can't button his pants and his shirt.
>
> He starts things, like a toy cart, and sometimes he can't make the wheels. He asks his father to help him then.
>
> He only asks how to do the thing. He is told, and he does it himself.
>
> She asks to be helped all the time; even when things are within reach, she asks somebody to hand them to her. It's this way with all of them, their *lambing*. (Children ask that things be done for them so that the parent can feel needed.)

Fewer than 10 per cent of the mothers complained that their children sought help they did not need. About 15 per cent actually expressed some concern about their children's dependency, and almost an equal number proudly said their children did things themselves. More than half the mothers, however, took the child's asking for help as a matter of course. Seven of the mothers expressed concern that their children were too independent, that they asked to do things themselves or would not let others do things for them. Children learn that little acts of dependence please rather than irritate their elders. They can express their affection for a parent by letting the parent do things for them which both know the child can do himself. There are many manifestations of a pattern like this in adulthood in which many people prefer cooperative work to solitary efforts. Both he who helps and he who is helped derive a good feeling from the relationship. It is as if one operated from the premise, "I will make you feel good by letting you help me."

Thus there appears to be little value attached to early development of independence. As long as the family situation permits someone else to minister to his needs, a child has plenty of time to learn. The emphasis is not on his assuming responsibility for himself; it is on his assuming responsibility for others in the family according to his age and abilities. It is understood that he will not bother others for most of the things he can do himself. But there is the suggestion, implied in the remarks of the mothers, that the child's reaching out for help is a mark of a continuing attachment. The child seeks help even when he does not need it as a bid for affection and attention. If the mother is free, she indulges; if not, she thinks nothing of ignoring the child or reprimanding him or teasing him—"You've outgrown those tactics, child!" If the child rejects help that is proffered or help that is understood as available, the one who offered help is hurt, and the pattern of responsibility of one for another is disturbed.

This, then, is the situation in which the child develops; his needs are taken care of for as long as possible. He reaches out for help or for attention; and if he picks the right time, he gets it. If not, the situation is plain enough or he is made to understand. If someone in the family needs help and he is there, he is called on to help. He is not so much an individual as he is a part of a family whose older members are his support and whose younger members are his responsibility. Responsibilities are not pushed on him when he reaches a certain age. Instead he grows into them, gaining the necessary skills as he participates in the day to day activities of the family.

Comparison with the Findings of Sears, Maccoby, and Levin

This chapter makes it evident that dependency in the American sense cannot be applied to the Philippine situation. It is in this realm that we can make our clearest case for our assertion that psychodynamic principles are specific to the culture. The problem of dependency in the middle classes of Western society with their emphasis on independence and individual striving has received a great deal of psychiatric attention. As individuals, Westerners struggle with their dependent needs, develop ulcers, exaggerated reaction formations, and many other symptoms. The whole society encourages individual effort and honors individual accomplishment. The struggle for independence and freedom from the control of others can greatly influence the formation of personality patterns.

There is a marked contrast in the Philippines where family solidarity requires each individual to submerge his own personal interests for those of the larger group. From childhood he learns to enjoy being taken care of and realizes that he can make others happy by being dependent on them. There is no age when a child is expected to leave home nor an age when he is expected to become fully self-reliant. Even marriage means that each of the couple has a number of additional people from whom support will be forthcoming and help may be required. Achievements and failures are therefore family products. The society honors the family which achieves; it approves the individual who works within the family context and who experiences the interests of the family as his own.

To make the differentiation more clear we can compare the mothers in the sample of Sears et al. with the Philippine mothers in the handling of nurturant and succorant responses. Definitions of dependent behavior given by the American mothers include demanding attention, affection, and bodily contact; seeking reassurance; asking for help with things he can do himself; and constant talking as a means of gaining attention. The mother's ultimate aim in dealing with this dependency was to make the child fond of her but not passionately attached and to make him pleased with her attention but not demanding of it. The Philippine mother seldom has to cope with the problem of the overly possessive child because, when she is occupied, the child turns to the father or older siblings for attention. Nevertheless 50 per cent of the Philippine children were considered by their mothers to be very affectionate, a trait which is expected and encouraged in the family circle. Thirty-four per cent of the mothers were pleased about this, 47 per cent felt it was a matter of course, and 18 per cent felt it was a bother. Although Sears et al. did not measure the child's affectionateness, 53 per cent of the American mothers, in evaluating the amount of attention their kindergarteners wanted, said that their children wanted a little or some, 27 per cent wanted quite a bit, and 10 per cent wanted a great deal of attention. The Filipinas' reactions to the child's dependency behavior are as follows: 14 per cent were pleased about dependency, 16 per cent were concerned about dependency, 45 per cent took it as a matter of course; 1 per cent were pleased about the child's independence, 3 per cent were concerned about independence, 11 per cent took independence as a matter of course. Americans, on the other hand, when rated on a scale responded as follows: not at all permissive of dependency, 11 per cent; low permissiveness, 26 per cent; moderate permissiveness, 30 per cent; quite permissive, 19 per cent; and dependency accepted as all right, 11 per cent. Nearly 60 per cent of the Filipinas were pleased about dependency or took it as a matter of course, while only 30 per cent of the Americans were quite permissive of it or accepted it as all right.

Unfortunately these stark statistics do not present an accurate picture; for as we have seen, the differences in family structure and social interaction make it impossible to talk of dependency in one society in terms of that of another. The little Philippine toddler is encouraged to help his mother and father make a game out of their regular chores as part of a pattern of indulgence which predisposes the child to expect support and companionship in the family. It is important for him to channel his nurturant and succorant responses more into maintaining the delicate balance in family relationships than into becoming an independent adult devoid of strong family ties. In addition, the fact that the Filipino child is rarely, if ever, alone probably makes him look dependent. A more accurate interpretation might be that he has a low tolerance for solitude.

Since the American mother is the major influence in the child's early life she must gradually direct her child toward seeking attention and affection from his peers and from other adults and must teach him to express his attachments in the more subtle manner of the adult. The lack of emphasis on family and kin ties in American society makes it imperative that he learn to take care of his own interests since he cannot expect others to show much concern for his welfare.

chapter 8

OBEDIENCE AND PUNISHMENT

The emphasis which we have placed on their love of children might lead one to expect that Filipinos are quite permissive and not inclined to punish. Quite on the contrary, they are strict; they are not reluctant to use physical punishment; and they demand obedience. Elsewhere (Guthrie, 1961, pp. 31–46) they have been called loving, controlling parents. Their demands for obedience have at least three aspects. First, since his parents, particularly his mother, brought him into the world, the child owes them a debt of gratitude and submission. Second, each member of the family is expected to obey those older than he. Third, it is believed that misfortune will plague a disobedient and disrespectful child throughout his life. Feelings of gratitude, respect for age, and fears of misfortune are all insistently held before the child to secure his compliance. From the beginning, love, respect, and obedience go together.

In his earliest years the child receives the attention of older people. But as he grows he becomes aware that there are certain things he is expected to do and other things which he must not do. Furthermore, these requirements vary with time and person. Much appears to be dictated by the moods of older people. He is obliged not only to learn certain absolute rules but also to learn to predict what will please or displease in particular situations. With many people exercising some control over him, he faces a formidable task.

Obedience to Family Members

Obedience to parents is, of course, most important. Disobedience results when a child fails to follow his parents' advice, advice which is supposed to be accepted without question. It is commonly believed that failure to do as a parent has advised will lead to a personal disaster. It is taken for granted that God punishes those who do not heed their parents. At the same time parents who fail to inculcate proper attitudes and values are considered very neglectful. Good children indicate good parents and disrespectful, undisciplined children are clear indications of bad parents.

Beyond that, because his mother has borne him, the child owes her a lifelong debt of gratitude. "You would not have been if something had happened to your parents before you were born. You owe the fact of your existence to your parents." This reasoning is felt to be quite compelling by Filipino children with the result that there is very little direct opposition to parental controls. Since the debt is of such a nature, the child does not escape the requirements of obedience on attaining adulthood. As long as they live, parents exercise at least some control over their children.

Some obedience to older siblings is expected of every younger member of the family, but the extent of obedience varies according to the particular dyad involved. Older brothers and sisters may or may not have authority over younger family members depending on the older one's own feelings or on their parents' stand on the matter. Almost three-fourths of our total sample, however, reported some kind of an age hierarchy among siblings enforced by the older children themselves and supported by the parents. In 61 per cent of the families the older siblings were obeyed because the parents demanded it of the younger ones; in 11 per cent of the cases, the older children could expect to be obeyed because they were strong or because they were tactful in demanding obedience.

> Yes, he should obey them [older siblings], but they don't demand too much of him. He answers them back. They don't pressure him, as he is still little and young.

> Her older sister is allowed to threaten her. She obeys her because she is afraid of her.

> He can't refuse them [older siblings] because he knows they'd spank him, too.

> When she refuses to obey her older brothers, I simply remind her that they're older than she, and she complies.

> He does not always obey his brothers and sisters. Sometimes he talks back to them. They ask him to get things, run errands. He obeys, depending on their approach. When he refuses, there is some quarreling.

They can make him obey, but I don't always tolerate their tactics. Sometimes they abuse and ask too much of him.

I insist that she obey them only when their demands are reasonable. Otherwise I let her get away with it.

I tell him, one doesn't hit an older brother. If I [the mother] had died when I bore him, your turn would not have come and you would not have been.

She obeys them all the time, afraid her guardian angel will leave her if she doesn't.

Uncles, aunts, in-laws, and older cousins may also expect obedience from a child. This is usually taught by parents, as noncompliance would be disrespect, a mark not so much against the child as against the parents. More than 30 per cent of the mothers reported that their children obeyed close relatives because the children were on good terms with them or because they recognized age-status. About 15 per cent said their children obeyed their relatives because they knew their parents wanted them to and would punish them if they failed to do so. Even the maid or family helper may request the child to do things and expect obedience. This expectation was reported by 16 per cent of the mothers in the most educated group, who are more likely to have helpers in their households.

Meanings of Obedience

In the Philippines obedience appears to have at least three connotations. It refers first of all to compliance with specific requests. Secondly, it implies compliance with the whole pattern of family expectations with special reference to conduct and interpersonal relationships. An example of obedience in the first sense would be getting water promptly when asked to do so. Being polite and respectful to older neighbors would exemplify the second type of obedience. In addition to these two facets of obedience, Filipinos also include the willingness of the child to observe their warnings about activities which would be dangerous to his health and safety. It would appear that obedience is not necessarily seen as a unitary characteristic. Depending on the issue, a child may be obedient or hardheaded. Depending on the offense he may be ignored, scolded, or physically punished.

In the realm of health and safety, children find many parental expectations restrictive, denying them many experiences which they would like to have. "He should take a nap instead of playing in the sun; he'll catch a fever that way." "She must not run around and play after eating; she'll develop appendicitis." "She shouldn't be out at 'dew-falling' time or dusk; people catch cold that way." No playing with fire, no games by the river or too close to the sea. These are the rules which children find limiting, particularly because they love the sun and cannot understand why their parents do not. The water feels good, while their parents only see the danger of their falling in and drowning. There are seashells and pebbles on the shore and sand that feels good between the toes. Why should one stay in the house and take a nap when one's body calls for movement? The neighborhood fills with other young voices in similar protest.

Nor is the child's health the only area of concern in which the child is kept from doing as he feels. He must also learn appropriate patterns of speech and of relationships with others. To maintain his parents' approval, he must be polite to visitors, deferent to his brothers and sisters and, above all, respectful to his mother and father.

He can be quite a bully. I used to shout at him whenever he bullied the younger children.

If he can't help but quarrel when he plays with them, he simply must stop playing.

He is not to speak any dirty words. If I ever hear him at that . . .

I can't see what is so attractive about visiting with the neighbors. And she is a girl, too!

I tell her that only boys run around like that. She's a girl and she should keep her play in the house or within the yard.

I tell her not to pinch her younger sister when she refuses to obey. She is in the habit of doing that.

Life would be simpler if he obeyed his elder brothers and sisters. They quarrel a lot as he is stubborn and they are too. He talks too much and he gets hit.

She laughs too much and talks too loud. And she forgets and I have to tell her all the time.

As soon as a child is considered old enough to reason, his mother begins to talk to him about how she expects him to behave. Prior to this the child can, within broad limits, do as he pleases with little danger of physical punishment or reprimand. At about the age of six he is pronounced *may isip na* (with a mind now) and is subject to increasing pressure to conform. At this transition point he must begin to observe safety and health precautions, conform to family values, and carry out others' requests. Somewhat different approaches are adopted depending on the category of obedience involved, but Philippine parents emphasize advising as a method of inculcating the values and standards which they want their children to have, as we have already mentioned. The child is the recipient of extended exhortations to which he may not express disagreement in any way. He is expected, and as far as possible forced, to accept parental control. This is not in a punitive sense; it is a part of a nurturing complex in which good advice is as important as good food.

Meanwhile the child is caught between his lack of understanding of what his parents are trying to do and their avowed love and concern for him. "Why can't I hit back when I am hit, simply because he's older and bigger?" "Can we help it if we get angry when we are playing and we quarrel?" "Those little ones are such a nuisance; they're always hanging around and I want to play, too!" "They are supposed to obey me and yet I can't hit them when they don't." "My brothers can run around and play at the neighbors' all the time; why can't I just because I happen to be a girl?" These thoughts run through a child's mind in his confusion at the mounting list of rules. As we have indicated, this stage is made even more difficult by the limits imposed on the extent and manner in which the child may question his elders. There were only three parents who let their children give their reasons without restrictions, many who stipulated that they had better have good reasons and give them in a respectful manner (58 per cent), and some whose children were not allowed to have reasons at all (21 per cent).

> He gives his reasons. And it's okay, just so he's in the right!
> Her answering back does not usually bother me unless I'm in a sour mood. Then she really gets something!
> He answered back. He even went to the extent of shouting back his reasons. When I caught hold of him, I pressed his lips and when he still answered, I spanked him.
> I do not like my children to answer back. If they do, I give them the hardest whip with the belt, because I do not want them to grow up as quarrelsome people.

She gives reasons when we punish her, like telling us it is not her fault. We do not like her to talk back to us.
This reasoning and talking, even when no longer talked to. I show him I am not pleased with it.

The child who does what he is told without any complaints or excuses, pouts or murmurs is considered the good child. The child who has learned to time his complaints and his reasons and phrases them in acceptable language is also good. The child who has not learned and who cannot quite accept all the demands on him is in trouble whether he voices his nonacceptance or keeps it to himself.

Limits and Responsibilities

There are few limits on the amount of noise the child is permitted to make. In large families, conversation and play could become very noisy, but this does not seem to be the case because play and many other activities pour out into the yard. In addition the openness of the house and the acoustical properties of the building materials make high noise levels less irritating. It is not unusual to have the radio playing loud music and still have a conversation going on. Thus, the few times when children are expected to be quiet are when somebody is sick or at siesta (63 per cent), or when other people are in the house (about 10 per cent). A few mothers (6 per cent) said they ask their children to be quiet at certain times but were not specific; two mothers said they didn't tolerate noise while they worked; and only one said she couldn't stand any noise at all.

Aside from demands on his conduct for safety's sake and for family convenience, there is the whole area of responsibility into which the child is gradually initiated. Depending on the particular family situation and the age he has reached, there are always errands to run, household jobs to do, and younger siblings to be cared for. There are chickens and pigs to feed, goats or a carabao to pasture, yard corners to weed, dead leaves to sweep up and burn, and water and firewood to carry to the house. All of these tasks seem to face the child when the noise of other children at play is at its height, when the cool river water beckons, when the suspense in the comic book grips him. And then his mother calls or his grandmother or an uncle, people he loves or people he fears, or simply people whose good graces matter to him.

Her job is to play with her younger brothers and sisters, and she's busy listening to a radio program.

Going to the store, back and forth really gets him. And picking up soiled diapers, too.

Washing and wiping her brother clean after a BM . . .

Looking after his younger brother. He sneaks and goes out to play outside the yard with other children.

It's difficult to get him to scrub the floor [with a coconut husk]. I explain to him why it is important that we have a clean house.

Sweeping the yard. She complains that the broom is too big for her. Or washing dishes. She only reasons, anyway. She can still be made to do it.

She hates to be told to sweep but when others start to do it and she sees this, she does her part.

He hates to be sent on an errand to the store when he is occupied with *Liwayway* [a weekly magazine].

Fewer than a fourth of the mothers reported that their children were quite pleasant about everything and needed no pressure to carry out requests and usual household responsibilities. In the greater part of our sample, however, the parent invariably had to make some kind of bid for obedience. Their comments give insight into the mothers' attitudes toward compliance ranging from acceptance of the child's inability or unwillingness to irritation and determination that the child comply.

There are requests he obeys and requests he does not obey. But he often obeys. At times he is not forced to obey, as he is still small.

I do not have to say anything to make him obey because he usually does if he is not busy with his play.

Caring for the baby. He complains and grunts every time I ask him to. I pretend to be angry and I get him to do it.

She is very obedient and never does anything against my will. She also obeys my two sisters and my father who lives with us.

Very slow in complying with orders. She hates setting and clearing the table and washing dishes most. She'd pout. I can make her do it when I start scolding and when her father is around. She's so afraid of him.

When told to run errands she complains she is tired. When promised money though, she complies.

He'd say when stopped that he's only playing. If "my head is hot," I spank him.

Of all my sons, he is the most obedient. To make him even more obedient, I often give him money.

She is obedient, especially when she sees me tired.

She is obedient; I praise her a lot for it.

Yes, she obeys, especially if she is threatened, and if she can do the work. If not, she complains. If we see she can't really do it, we do the work ourselves.

She pretends to have a stomachache or pain in her legs.

Enforcement of Rules

Parents' reactions to unwillingness and outright refusal to obey varied from understanding acceptance or indifference to persuasion, advising and explaining, bribing, scolding, firmness, threatening, or spanking. The question came up on three different occasions in the interview—when the matter involved concerned the child's health, when it was about obedience in general, and when it had to do with the child's responsibility in the family.

When the child's health or his training was at stake, a recognized area of parental responsibility, parents admitted spanking, pinching, and ear-pulling (41 per cent), and "parent-talking" which is more like scolding than simply advising (24 per cent). Threats of the whip were reported by 7 per cent. Seventeen per cent of the mothers said they reasoned with their child, explained, and advised. Only about 3 per cent admitted that their reaction depended on their mood. As an indication of the importance that mothers attach to obedience when the child's health is felt to be at stake, only 1 per cent of the mothers said they ignored violations of rules in these cases.

When he disobeys, I tell him that his father will get angry. He does not give reasons when he is told this. I think it is disrespectful for a child to reason with his parents.

She obeys because I say God will be angry if she disobeys.

I quite understand why she continues to play with dogs and cats even after I've told her not to. So to find a substitute I usually ask the child of our neighbor to come and play with her. This solves the problem.

I whip her all right, if she does anything that deserves it. I find it effective, but I seldom use it. Most of the time I just make her understand why she has to obey.

If he disobeys, he gives reasons. It is all right when his excuses are reasonable, but if they are not, I feel bad.

I let her have her way. I talk to her afterwards when we are alone.

On the question of requests and carrying out responsibilities only 18 per cent reported spanking and scolding their children into obeying. Threatening or frightening the child into obedience was employed by 14 per cent of the parents, 7 per cent used bribes, and 20 per cent made their children obey through firmness.

He always obeys. I frighten him with a stick.

Spanking does not do any good so I just don't mind him. Three whips from his father usually works.

I baby him and talk to him in a gentle way. If he still won't obey, I whip him with a belt! He's forced to do it then.

I used to spank him more often when he was younger. But a number of people have told me that it is bad to hit a child too much.

When I tell him to do something and he doesn't do it, or follow, he gets pinches and beatings.

To make her obey, I scold her, or promise her something to persuade her.

Very seldom does he disobey. I make him understand the value of an obedient child. When he disobeys, I say, "Who is to be followed, mother or child?"

She is obedient. I promise her a dress or new shoes or new underthings.

Yes, he's obedient; I beat him with a piece of wood.

With respect to obeying rules made for the child's own good, 29 per cent of the mothers reported that their child was strong-willed or, as the Filipinos put it, hardheaded. A quarter of them were reportedly quiet and obedient, another quarter reasoned and acquiesced. The remaining 20 per cent obeyed largely in response to threats. On the other hand, in response to specific requests from the parents, 43 per cent of the children were called very obedient, and another 41 per cent responded in their own time. Only 4 per cent were called stubborn, while 11 per cent obeyed only when they liked the task they had been asked to do. It is apparent that the mothers were making a distinction between obedience to their teaching and obedience to their requests for help. It is also apparent that, even when the child refused the first time he was asked, he would still be considered obedient if he could be threatened or talked into obeying. The statements of the mothers on how they made their children obey are replete with examples of threats. Some mothers (11 per cent) found that words alone were effective; 42 per cent brought up the subject of the whip, 24 per cent of the *momo* or ghosts, and 5 per cent threatened detention in the house. Smaller numbers threatened loss of love, God's anger, father's anger, and the denial of something the child wanted.

The point to remember is that they thought their children were obedient even when they had to force them to obey. They seemed to accept it as fact that children are unable to obey on their own, that they have to be told and made to do what they are told. Self-direction or conscience comes later. The constant admonition, scolding, the seemingly endless flow of advice, and when all else fails, the threat and the spanking or pinching are to insure that, for one reason or another, the child does as he is told. Obedience, at this point, means doing what is required of him by someone feared or respected. The parents expect that with time the children will come to obey without coercion.

The attitude that some amount of disobedience can be expected of children does not necessarily carry with it the tendency to condone disobedient behavior. Thus the child is not labeled disobedient when he has a lapse of good behavior, but the parent takes steps so that this will not be repeated. Advising, bribing, and threatening are first- or second-offense treatments, but where these fail, physical punishment is an accepted recourse.

Punishment

Fewer than 8 per cent of the total sample denied having to use punishment on their children. These children either gave no occasion for punishment or were too afraid to digress from the known rules. Almost 70 per cent reported some occasion for punishment, from denial of favor or privileges, scolding, pinching, and spanking, to some severe forms of posture punishment such as having to maintain the position of Christ on the cross or having to kneel for a period of time on a floor that has been sprinkled with peas or beans. More than 22 per cent reported having to punish their children frequently and severely.

> Many times. When she teases her brothers, I spank her with my slippers.
>
> I whip him only when he gets so hardheaded that I can stand it no longer.
>
> It is only when she lies or does anything really bad that we punish her.
>
> Entering a conversation I am having with someone, and asking money of nonrelatives—this really makes me angry enough to spank her.
>
> We make her kneel down for hours, and lock her up in her room. Not so often though.
>
> He submits to my spanking with not too much resentment. Maybe because I soothe him afterward. His father very seldom spanks, but when he does it probably hurts more.
>
> I haven't whipped or scolded him yet. I love them so much I don't like them to feel any pain.

Parents differed in the degree to which they considered certain behavior an occasion for punishment. Most frequently reported reasons for spanking were "plain hardheadedness," disregard of play and safety rules, and poor conduct in terms of lying, quarreling, teasing, disrespect of elders, unseemly words, unreasonable demands, refusal to share, and growling and murmuring in performing assigned chores.

Asked what punishment they deemed most effective the parents offered many alternatives which included whipping with a belt, a slipper, or a stick, spanking, pinching, ear-pulling, slapping, locking in a room, tying to a pole, and tying in a sack. Mothers also took away privileges of playing or of accompanying parents to market. More than 10 per cent, however, contended that words alone were sufficient.

> I don't if possible and as long as I can I never lay my hands on her. Since she accepts reason, I make her obey me by explaining how much good it will do her if she obeys.
>
> Most effective in making him repent for what he's done is my telling him I'd leave them.
>
> She is most afraid of being whipped with her father's belt and being made to stand in the corner for a long time.

Threatening her that if she repeats the mischief again she'll stop going to school is effective enough.

I sometimes whip him but not to the extent of hurting him.

When she disobeys and I get mad, I put her in the cabinet. That really frightens her.

We do not whip her often but we do scold her a lot. She is most afraid of being left alone in the dark storeroom at night.

Sometimes I threaten to tie him to a pole or put him in a sack.

Having her kneel or locking her up in a room.

Whenever he makes a mistake he either gets pinched or spanked. He is told to get a fresh switch, and he lies down and takes his beating.

Punishers

Since authority lines are age-graded, we might have assumed that anyone in authority could punish the child when there was call for it. Among our mothers, however, only 16 per cent reported that other family elders took a hand in the child's discipline, and only in 18 per cent of the families was there any punishment by older siblings. Generally, the right and responsibility to punish the child lodged with the father and mother. Older siblings and family elders did punish misdemeanors, but only when they knew they had the parent's sanction.

Grandparents and other relatives do not take it upon themselves to punish the youngster unless they feel sure that they are close to the child and to the child's parents, a closeness that the parents would define as *"para na ring ako"* (almost me, with my prerogative as parent). A parent's disapproval of a relative's punishment of his child may not be verbally expressed, but there are subtle ways of making this disapproval felt.

When older siblings punish him, the child can still appeal to his parents, which insures that older siblings do not abuse this prerogative. Stoodley, in a paper on Tagalog family structure (1957), mentioned that the older sibling who makes demands and may punish must be a few steps ahead in the age-ladder, that not necessarily any older sibling may exercise this right. Hurting for the sake of discipline is sharply distinct from simple sibling aggression. The former is allowed, and the intent and meaning is more convincing to the child where there is some age and size difference. Aggression, on the other hand, is resented. The older sibling loses the respect of the younger and subjects himself to reprimand or punishment by his elders.

> He gets whipped with the hand or with a folded magazine when he is naughty. He gets this from me, or his father, or from any of his older brothers and sisters.
>
> Any adult in the house whom he disobeys may punish him.
>
> His older sister and brother slap him or box or kick him in the back when he makes them angry.
>
> My husband and I do the punishing. We may whip him or send him to his room.
>
> Father punishes. He whips her, and she just stays in one corner and cries. Then her father pities her and takes her from the corner and advises her that he won't whip her any more if she tries to be good.
>
> Grandmother uses her slippers to whip him.
>
> Her eldest sister punishes her, too. She's afraid of her.

The Child's Reaction to Punishment

Children take punishment in different ways. There are parents who spank their children more when they cry aloud or when they show any form of resentment. And there are parents who stop when they see that they've hurt the child enough. The children are sensitive to the ways of their parents, and usually have learned to temper their expressions of protest or resentment. But this does not totally account for the variation. There are differences in temperament among children. Some are quiet and submissive. There are others to whom any pressure or blocking, especially when not accepted as justified, is cause for boiling over in tears in an unintelligible mixture of sobs and words or in tantrums of pounding and kicking.

Since Philippine parents expect that their children will be penitent after they have been punished, the children learn to accept punishment rather stoically. The youngster is often required to fetch the instrument of punishment and to bend over to receive the treatment. After the punishment and the tears, he may sit quietly saying with his eyes and his posture what he dare not say with his mouth. In a one-room house the mother and her child are not able to get away from one another. The mother often takes this as an opportunity for advising and in the process relieves herself of her anger and proclaims her adherence to family values. The child, meanwhile, is denied an opportunity to retaliate and is more or less compelled to suppress his anger and bitterness.

The reactions to punishment most often reported were crying, quiet acceptance, crying and sulking, and quiet resentment, in that order. A few children seek to ward off future contact with the stick by promising not to do it again; a few others show no definite-pattern—they cry sometimes and they take it quietly at other times; a few more seek refuge at their grandmother's house. It does not take long for children to learn that any form of resistance can only lead to more lashings, to more angry words, or to longer periods of uneasiness.

He mopes in a corner of the room.

He doesn't resent his father's spanking. Probably because right afterward, he takes him in his arms, soothes him, and gives him money.

If he knows he's at fault, he doesn't answer back.

If punished, she cries in bed and goes to sleep immediately.

He accepts punishment from his mother and father. When he is punished, he cries. He resents being scolded.

If he is to be whipped with the belt or whip, he runs away if he's given the chance. He goes to Grandma's house.

Expectations of obedience and punishment for failure to meet them fit very well into the patterns of interpersonal relations within the family. Everyone older feels responsible for everyone younger. Parents particularly and older siblings as well are convinced that they know what is best for the child. Noncompliance of the child is interpreted as a lack of faith in, and respect for, the older person. The punishment which may follow is usually inflicted with much moralizing rather than in a spirit of retaliation or anger. The purpose of a punishment is not achieved if during and afterward a child expresses resentment and disrespect. Given a show of penitence, the parents are quick to forgive; for they find most painful a protracted period of ill will with the child.

Because there may be many individuals who may and do punish the child, he learns for his own protection to avoid slighting any of his older relatives. He watches their daily moods and judges how many liberties he can take. In a situation in which there are many to please, he avoids extremes and learns to agree out loud and keep any reservations he may have to himself. With all of the advice he receives, he learns to be ready with some explanation for all of his activities. With his family name constantly being invoked as a reason for conformity, he in turn develops an intense sensitivity to any aspersion cast on his family and responds as strongly as, or more strongly than, if he had been attacked himself.

Comparison with the Findings of Sears, Maccoby, and Levin

In contrast to the Filipinos who emphasize not only the health, safety, and training of the child but also the reflection of the child's actions and personality on the family name, the American parents in the Sears study base their demands for obedience on the importance of directing the child's behavior to insure social as well as biological survival and on the necessity of integrating him as a cooperative, nondestructive member of the family. One seldom hears among Americans that the child owes unquestioning obedience to his parents and grandparents because they brought him into the world, but in the Philippines the child is usually expected to accept parental control for this reason without question, although in some cases he may ask questions and express complaints if he does so in a respectful manner. The emphasis for the young child in both America and the Philippines is on health and safety, but the Philippine parents are concerned that the child be good, not only for his own sake, but also because his actions reflect on them and on his other relatives. Thus they make a constant appeal to the child's sense of family responsibility in demanding his obedience, even in matters of his own safety.

Because of the differences in environment, matters which require obedience-training in one society are not necessarily important in the other. Aside from health and safety, American mothers list noise, neatness in the home, and care for property as major problem areas, but the Philippine mother with a house that is easy to care for and a climate which allows outdoor play most of the year faces fewer such difficulties. Likewise, since they rarely have television, Philippine mothers are not concerned about placing restrictions on watching television as are 92 per cent of the mothers in the Sears study. Philippine mothers' major problems concern health and safety (42 per cent) and social values (34 per cent).

Children of both cultures begin chores by about the age of five or six. The Philippine child, for training purposes and for family convenience, is gradually initiated into running errands, caring for younger siblings, doing household chores and feeding domestic animals. On the other hand, American children of five or six are rarely expected to perform tasks regularly. Those who are, are given small chores such as emptying ash trays or picking up toys (35 per cent), although they are encouraged to do more difficult tasks when they show interest. Mothers' reasons for not demanding work range from simplifying housekeeping to sympathizing with the child.

In rewarding and punishing behavior, Philippine mothers seldom or never give praise or tangible rewards for performance although they do use bribes extensively. Sixty-eight per cent of American mothers use rewards at least sometimes, although there is a recurrent feeling that there is something bad or manipulative in giving material rewards which interfere with spontaneous behavior. In the American survey 51 per cent of the mothers use physical punishment, slaps and spankings, at least fairly frequently. Fifty-eight per cent of the Philippine parents use physical punishment, pinching, beating, ear-pulling, fairly frequently and 15 per cent more use it very often. Scolding and haranguing, which is often reported as "parent-talks," is also common (24 per cent). Only 3 per cent of the Philippine mothers report using deprivation of privileges, while American mothers resort to deprivation of television (45 per cent), desserts (19 per cent), toys (11 per cent), and playmates (7 per cent). Forty-eight per cent of the American mothers used withdrawal of love at least occasionally. The Philippine mothers do not use this technique, perhaps because it is ineffective since the child can seek nurturance and comfort from many other individuals in the nuclear or extended family. In short, American mothers use denial of privileges, threats of loss of love, and physical punishment to enforce obedience, while their Philippine opposite numbers are more likely to punish physically, scold, or bribe.

There are three other important differences in obedience and punishment in the two cultures which merit consideration. The Philippine child must obey many other people, his older siblings and relatives, as well as his parents. The American child is usually only required to obey his parents and occasionally an older sibling. Secondly, parents in the Philippines allow the child time to obey. Because he is thought to be unable to act properly without guidance and direction, the child may still be considered obedient when he is slow in complying or when he must be forced to obey. In comparison, among American parents 23 per cent want and expect obedience on the first or second demand, 54 per cent expect obedience with some delay, and 22 per cent expect some obedience but will tolerate noncompliance. A third important factor is the role of teasing in the Philippines. Parents use teasing to shame or wheedle the child into obeying and the child uses teasing conveniently to measure how much he can get away with in shirking duties and disobeying. "Oh, I'll feed the chickens; I was only teasing when I didn't do it before."

Children of both studies were adept at discerning the mood of their parents and reacting to the best advantage in order to shirk their chores and to minimize punishment.

chapter 9

HEALTH AND CLEANLINESS

We have dealt with health and cleanliness in the same chapter because they are seen as connected to one another in the minds of Americans. Cleanliness is more an aesthetic matter to the Filipino. We have not entitled a chapter "toilet training" because the acquisition of bowel control is not an issue about which many matters revolve as is the case in the American home. Philippine homes often do not provide for, and Filipinos place a different emphasis on, privacy in activities having to do with elimination. Since they are not issues of great concern or of excessive secretiveness, urination and defecation do not lead to the same interpersonal events in the Philippines that they may lead to elsewhere.

Wala pang isip, literally "no mind yet" but actually meaning "still lacking in judgment and control," is the excuse that mothers grant the baby when he cannot keep himself clean, when he cannot behave, when he does anything that would be punishable if he were older. The young child is patiently taught but seldom if ever punished or even pushed. It is not so much indulgence of the child as it is an estimate of what he can understand at a given stage which causes certain aspects of his socialization to appear so casual. The Filipino mother has a set of expectations concerning the optimum rate of development of her child. Accepting responsibility for keeping clean is not expected of the child as early as in many other societies.

Each mother is under strong social pressure to keep her house clean, but these demands are not difficult to meet. Her house is especially easy to maintain, more child-proof in terms of design than homes in a temperate climate. The yard takes care of much that might otherwise take place in the house. Children can play their games outside. Major cooking is done in the yard as is cleaning of pots and pans and washing of clothes and diapers. The climate does not limit these arrangements to only four months of the year; it is summer the year round. Even during the four to six months of rainy days, awnings of *nipa* (palm leaf) shingles and the open space under the house permit continuance of these activities.

The House

The materials and the style of construction of the house determine the amount of cleaning which must be done. If the floors are of bamboo, there is enough space between each piece to permit debris to sift through, and the floor can be cleaned with water and dry banana leaves. If floors are of wood, they are waxed and then polished with coconut brushes. Children accept responsibility for phases of this work as soon as they are able to do so. Where living does not stop at the doorstep, the yard must also be swept and kept free of weeds. Older children are assigned the responsibility of keeping the house clean and the yard swept, and they keep younger siblings from adding to their work.

There is a minimum of stress and anxiety surrounding the matter of keeping the house tidy. Since children share the responsibility for the upkeep of the home, the mother literally has as many pairs of hands as she has children over three. In addition she may have sisters or relatives living with her or a paid helper or two. And when children have a part in maintaining order and cleanliness in the household, they tend to supervise one another's activities. Rules observed come to mean less work to do and more time for play. Shoes are left at the foot of the stairs; feet are washed or wiped before going into the house. Watching the young children to make sure they actually do take off their shoes and wash their feet is the concern of the older daughters. The girls are most careful about these preventive measures because if a small muddy-footed brother slips unnoticed into the house, the girls must fetch water and clean the floor. Only the child under three or four has no qualms about coming and going; he is too small to know what he does, but he will learn!

Two-thirds of the mothers reported that their children are careful around the house, that they are active but pick up after play, that there are strict rules and their children know them. Several recall that their children were not always this way but that at around the time of the interview they learned to be more careful or, as the mothers phrased it, more thoughtful.

When he was a bit younger, he used to come in the house with dirty shoes or muddy feet. He no longer does this.

When she makes the house dirty, I ask her to clean the part she's made dirty or pick up things she scattered.

When he gets the house dirty, I ask him to stop playing. Together he and I put the house back in order.

When they start gaining in understanding, it takes only a little reminding to get them to do things or be careful.

Clothing

But a clean home is not enough. The people who live in it have to be clean, too. Next to the time spent for food preparation, care of clothing probably takes up most of the Philippine mother's time. Clothing is light because of the climate, but the heat and humidity necessitate frequent bathing, and clothes have to be washed before they can be worn again. Washing, ironing, and mending are all done by hand. One can imagine the bulk of the wash in an average-size family of six. A few families send their wash to laundresses. Members of the family old enough to do the wash often take turns during the week. As a rule caring for the clothes is an accepted chore; it is part of being wife and mother.

He gets his clothes dirty from playing with mud, climbing up and down trees, clambering over fences or rocks. But a boy will be a boy.

I tell him and I tell him to change to his house clothes before doing anything after school. He has begun to mind this now that he is a little older.

Her clothes get dirty from rolling in the yard, but a child needs play, and we can take care.

She is very neat and changes herself quite often, especially on hot days. It's hard on our housekeeper.

He gets his clothes dirty very quickly. Perhaps this is because he wipes his hands on them.

She changes clothes two to three times a day. It is a little hard on me, but I can't see her walking the neighborhood in dirty sticky clothes.

Personal Cleanliness

Physical cleanliness is another matter of great concern. Someone with clean clothing but neglectful of his person is disparagingly compared to the *kapak*, a small, fresh-water fish whose beautiful, shining scales are a striking contrast to the muddy and dirty viscera it hides inside. Children are bathed because they cannot take care of their necks, their elbows, the back of their ears, or because they will not use soap, and the smell of dirt and sweat remains after a careless bath. With girls there is an added concern. They grow long hair, and the heat makes it an attractive breeding place for lice. These creatures and their eggs that stick to the hair brand a girl dirty and lazy, and her mother equally so. Siesta time is sometimes spent in lice hunting, and the young child who does not see why she has to sit through this ordeal is kept still by threats: "If they are not destroyed, in time they'll become plentiful and grow wings, and they'll pull you by the hair and fly you over the bamboo tops and just drop you." Sooner or later she sees the point in combing the tangles out of her hair and in washing it frequently enough. Hair used to be washed with bark shampoo; now plain soap or commercial shampoos are used. At this stage the children are not as concerned with the clean look or the clean smell as they are when they approach puberty. Throughout childhood they are taught by precept and example the importance of personal cleanliness and of caring for their clothing.

Cleanliness Values and the Infant

The baby's layette includes tiny white shirts, mostly of soft percale with a few of flannel for the cold nights, mittens and socks, bands (*babat*) to bind his middle (a protection for the navel?), and as many diapers as the mother and interested relatives have had time to prepare. This set of baby clothing is usually handed down from the eldest child to the youngest, additions being made every now and then or given by relatives who have only a few children and are not expecting any more.

The *babat* is used on the child for some time beyond the two weeks that it usually takes for what remains of the umbilical cord to dry and fall off. Apparently the spot is considered as delicate as the fontanel, and the use of the *babat* is continued for protection. Mittens and socks are used on particularly cool December nights and during the rainy season. A blanket keeps the baby warm, his own or his mother's which he shares.

In infancy the baby is given sponge baths, except for an occasional immersion. Later the child, with the help of his sisters and brothers, learns to bathe himself in the family shower or a nearby stream. In parts of the Tagalog region prebath preparations involve rubbing manzanilla oil on the child's joints and around his navel. The oiling is to protect him from colic and from getting a cold from the water. The child is then lowered into a shallow basin of lukewarm water and soaped with a soft washcloth. The water is changed and the soap is rinsed off. He is then dried and rubbed with baby powder to protect his skin from the chafing of clothing and diapers; manzanilla or some other kind of oil is rubbed on, and he is diapered and dressed.

The mothers differed widely concerning the age to which they had their children wear diapers. About half the mothers discontinued them before their child was a year old. Around 20 per cent kept their children in diapers until after the eighteenth month with almost half of these continuing until after the second year. Baby pants took the place of diapers in the majority of cases except for 12 per cent in the first group who left off the diaper at the toddling age and permitted the child to go about with only a shirt on.

> She stopped wearing diapers at the age of one and a half. I dressed her in panties and baby dresses.

> He stopped wearing diapers at one year old. He wore pants then.

> He stopped wearing diapers at one year. I used to put him in long trousers at night.

> At four months he was off diapers. It was only at night that he needed to be wrapped in a little sheet or a blanket. In the daytime he only went with his shirt. Now, of course, he does not do that any more.

There appear to be two reasons for early discontinuance of the use of diapers. Some mothers find panties more convenient for babies; they don't slip off as easily as loosely pinned diapers, and they are easier to launder. And in some cases mothers have come to know their babies well enough to be able to interpret the signals of impending elimination, so that they can hold the babies away from them, seat them on their special chairs, or just let them go because they can easily clean up afterward. A very common subject of laughter is an overeager friend or relative who asks to carry a baby. She is warned, "Watch out, he might pay you for it," and more often than not he does. But this is all considered part of his being a baby, *wala pang isip*, so that he is simply washed and dried, and his victim is helped to clean up, all the while warding off the parents' apologies with, "It doesn't really matter."

Accidents such as this do not happen too often when the baby is held by members of his family who have become familiar with his ways. There is interaction between the baby and older members of the family. They hold him, sing and talk to him while he laughs and gurgles or cries, and they even watch him while he sleeps, so that certain body movements, expressions on the face, a manner of crying, or other noises he makes all carry meaning, allowing them to take appropriate precautions before he does anything.

Toilet Training

Questioned on their attempts to teach the child to use the pot or the toilet or whatever is the approved family way for its members, 55 per cent of the mothers reported that they started the child at around one and a half years or later, 26 per cent actually waited until the child was three or older, and around 7 per cent did not make any attempt at all, allowing the child to learn with age. Similar to her attitude toward the child's getting dirty and having to change clothes often, the mother takes the child's wetting or eliminating in his diapers or on the bed or floor as the childish way of doing things, and she patiently cleans up and collects the diapers for the morning's wash. She senses when the child has grown enough to understand or when the child is "big enough to know better." Only then does she attempt to teach him. It is in what they consider old enough that mothers tend to differ from one another. Usually, however, the age at which the child starts to eat adult food becomes the turning point; his feces then can no longer be treated as a baby's since it is harder to wash the smell off diapers and clothing.

No differences showed among the groups in the way the use of the pot or of the toilet was introduced to the child. About 50 per cent of the mothers reported that they put the child on the chair or on the toilet seat at a hint from the child or every time they sensed that the child needed to go. Only about 18 per cent reported following some sort of a time schedule, seating the child every morning, or every morning and night, or after the siesta. About 25 per cent said they taught the child at a certain age but did not specify just how they did it. As many as twenty mothers did not bother to do anything, and with age their children learned.

We trained him to sit on a special chair from nine months on. By two and a half he didn't ask to go; he would just go there himself.

She could tell us that she needed to go, even before she had learned to speak.

She did not use up too many diapers when she was a baby. And afterward she just knew where to go—at around one and a half when she had learned to walk.

We never trained him. At around two he just told us. By then, or around two and a half, he would just go to the potty. By three he could take care of himself, wash himself and his hands. Perhaps he could see what we all did and just learned that way.

He was messy as a baby, but what could one do? Babies have no sense about these things and one can only wait. The chair was always in one corner, and we could tell when he needed to go. We started sitting him on it at around ten months. By two he knew enough to go to the chair. By three he was on his own.

He used to do it everywhere when he was a year old. But at around two, when he could understand a little, we started sitting him on the toilet seat. By three he could take care of himself.

When she started to crawl, there were ways of telling that she needed to go. You could almost read it on her face. We'd get her to the chair, *servicio*, in a hurry. By two and a half to almost three, she could use the regular bowl by herself.

We started sitting her on the *orinola* (potty) at one year. By two and a half we could trust her to ask to go or to go to it on her own.

She had her BM every morning right after waking up. When she learned to sit up, I'd put her on the *servicio*, until it became a habit—where to go and what to do when. I trained her for a month. At two she could go alone, except that somebody had to wash her afterward.

It appeared that mothers were not thinking of simply teaching the use of the pot or toilet when they talked of toilet training. They also meant teaching the child what to do afterward—to have himself washed with water and dried, and later to do it himself. In the **Tagalog** areas children are taught to wash themselves after eliminating since toilet paper is not widely available. Washing accomplishes the same purpose and it does not compound the problem of disposing of paper. Since the child becomes subject to teasing when he goes about carrying the smell of urine or feces, he acquires quickly the family value of looking and smelling clean. This "washing relationship" is an occasion for closeness between the child and certain family members who respond to his call for help. A few mothers recalled that their older children considered this responsibility to the younger sibling their chief aversion. The younger sibling, on the other hand, feels a certain closeness to the sibling, parent, or relative who ministers willingly to this need.

Thus the child may be trained to go to the toilet whenever he needs to go, but he is not considered completely toilet-trained unless he can take care of getting cleaned afterward. This accounts for the reported lateness of completion of toilet training. Thirty-eight per cent in the first group were reportedly not trained until after three, the majority of them not until after they were four or five. The middle and most educated groups reported relatively fewer cases, only 16 per cent and 25 per cent respectively, who were not trained by the age of three.

We may have missed more marked differences between groups in their treatment of this aspect of child teaching, either because some mothers may have felt their family practices were inferior to others and consequently were not candid about them, or because the area from which our sample was drawn did not allow the extreme practices of the country. There are still a few communities in the Philippines where toilets are not a necessary part of living, where a section is marked off for an activity preferably timed for after dark—a hill or a little-used alley or a strip of shore, where pigs are purposely let loose and not fed.

Particularly in the rural areas sanitation does not appear to be a concern, but sightliness is. So long as they are out of the way and the air is not particularly made unpleasant by them, there are no qualms about feces being out in the open. In these areas we might see children squatting anywhere in the yards, perhaps being admonished to move farther away from the house or told, "It is all right; the pig will take care of it." Here, too, we might find children not being taught what to do with themselves afterward, using sticks or leaves instead of water, depending on frequent baths in the stream or at the village artesian well to keep them clean.

This poor state of sanitation may contribute to a high state of infection, particularly intestinal parasites and amoebic dysentery. It appears however that this cost in physical health is offset to an unknown degree by the relative freedom from anxiety over bodily functions. It may also be that careful habits of personal cleanliness reduce the hazards of this poor environmental sanitation.

There is a tendency to lump attitudes toward bowel and bladder activities together when toilet training is discussed. But urine is not considered as unsightly as are feces, and at least in communities where it is not labeled a waste product, only the smell and for adults the modesty factor are matters of concern. One finds the little boys playing in the yard, engaged in a contest of who can urinate the farthest or the highest, openly or covertly, depending on the social standing of the family. Similarly one sees men relieving themselves, their backs turned to the road, facing concrete walls or high bushes, or older women holding their skirts out and urinating standing. Those scenes are particularly common along provincial highways where bus stations are far between and gas stations have not yet been charged with providing comfort facilities for the traveler. Interestingly enough one does not see young women thus engaged or, for that matter, any girl past four.

In the home the facilities for urination range from the *batalan* to a toilet, either outdoors or part of the bathroom facilities in the house. The *batalan* is usually a small extension of the kitchen, open, or topped with a *nipa* awning, with wood or bamboo slats for a floor, under which is often a pit filled with rocks and sand to absorb the water. Where a house has a *batalan,* the back steps usually lead up to it, and this is where family members wash the dirt off their feet before going into the main part of the house. It is also where the girls of the house bathe, dipping water from big earthen jars and pouring it over themselves. It is where pots and pans are washed, where rice washings and dish water are disposed of, and where the less sociable housewife does her laundry. Boys do not usually use the *batalan,* since they can and do urinate anywhere.

In homes where there are toilet facilities, particularly if these are outdoors, there is a pot (*orinola* or *arinola*) where both boys and girls go. This is emptied and washed out periodically or after each use. Even if the bathroom is part of the house, little children still use the pot, since the toilet seat is considered to be too big for them. An *orinola* in the house is a sign that the family cares where their children go, and even the boys are expected to use it. Children are washed afterward with the *orinola* underneath; girls are washed even after urinating. At night one finds an *orinola* outside the mosquito nets under which the family members sleep or in some familiar corner where the children find it even when half asleep.

Sleeping Arrangements and Bed-wetting

Small houses and large families are almost irreconcilable to people who would call a home crowded where more than two have to share a bedroom. But there are a large number of homes in the rural areas where living room, dining room, and bedroom are one with maybe an enclosed space, walled in or screened, where the mats, blankets, pillows, and mosquito nets are folded and stored during the day and where older members of the family dress or change. The above average home has a living room, a dining area as part of the kitchen, and two bedrooms at most. Even these homes will appear crowded, considering that family sizes can run to twelve or more.

Families usually sleep on mats woven out of coarse local fibres which in cool or rainy weather are topped with cotton flannel blankets. Their heads rest on pillows stuffed with kapok (tree cotton). In many areas mosquito nets are necessary. With six to twelve people sleeping in the same room there are many possible sleeping arrangements. Commonly father and mother and the very young children sleep side by side on a mat under one mosquito net. Preadolescent siblings sleep on other mats. After adolescence the girls share one mat and net and the boys another. There are many variations, including one in which a single large net covers all family members.

Of the children who were subjects of the interview, between 55 and 60 per cent reportedly sleep with their parents or with their parents and siblings. Around a third in the first two groups sleep with siblings and only about an eighth in the most educated group. Of the twenty subjects who allegedly sleep by themselves, half had mothers in the most educated group. Some children do sleep with other adults in the family, although fewer than 5 per cent were reported to do so in this particular sample.

Bed-wetting seen in relation to sleeping arrangements provides another illustration of nurturance of the young child. A difficulty we face in interpreting the information we have is the probability that mothers were talking about present sleeping arrangements while viewing bed-wetting historically. We have reason to assume that, if the interviewers had probed further, they would have found that up to age three or four the majority of these children slept with their parents except during the brief period of separation at weaning. The mother who sleeps through the night with her child wet by her side would be called a lazy mother. Mothers, and fathers too, are known to get up in the middle of the night to check through their brood to change them if they are wet, to get them up to prevent the possibility of later inundation, to pull the blankets over cold feet, or to check the shutters for a bad draft. An older sibling, a sister more often than a brother, feels this is her responsibility for the younger siblings who sleep with her.

About 15 per cent of the children reportedly were still bed-wetting at six or up to the time of the interview. The majority, over two-thirds of all the subjects, stopped bed-wetting as late as four or five. A few mothers maintained that bed-wetting is a condition that afflicts some children and cannot be helped. The more common reasons offered for the persistence of bed-wetting to a late age are: getting over-tired or over-excited from play, cold weather, having had too much to drink before bedtime, dreaming, or being afraid of the dark or too lazy to get up.

> He bed-wet when he was small. But when he got a little bigger his father would get him up at around midnight and that was it. We've not had wet mats and blankets since. Also we see to it that they don't drink too much water or any liquids before going to bed.
>
> If parents see to it that their children go to the bathroom before going to bed, they won't bed-wet.
>
> She sleeps with me and I do get mad when she wets the blankets at night. But you can't let her sleep on like that. I just get up and change her.
>
> She stopped bed-wetting at three. Certain nights she'd had too much play during the day.
>
> None of my children bed-wet after around one and a half or two. I believe that bed-wetting is some kind of an illness . . . children who do it after they're babies will continue to do it much later.
>
> The four of them [siblings] sleep together, but they are not bothered when he bed-wets because they sleep very soundly. I change him when I discover it as I check them periodically at night.

It can be irritating to wake up in the middle of the night with half the mat and yourself wet when one of them has an accident. I just get up and change myself, also put a dry blanket over the mat and change the child.

Children are teased and scolded for chronic bed-wetting, especially if it persists beyond four or five. Often a family owns only one set of bedding, and during the rainy season particularly this is difficult to dry in a day's time. Moreover, getting wet almost every night is especially hard on the mats. By and large, bed-wetting is accepted as part of early childhood, and one overhears parents say they are not buying any good mats or sheets until their children have grown beyond the bed-wetting stage.

Concerns about Sleep

Where it is dark at six o'clock at night and light at six in the morning, we would expect both bedtime and waking time to be fairly early. Between 40 per cent and 54 per cent of the Philippine children were reported as regularly asleep by seven or eight o'clock in the evening and from 33 per cent to about 40 per cent as usually asleep by then except on occasions when there were fiestas, celebrations, special movies, a favorite radio program, or if the next day was not a school day. More children in the third group than in the other two kept regular sleeping hours, and slightly fewer in this group than in the other two were allowed an excuse to stay up late. Twenty-five per cent, 16 per cent, and 12 per cent of the mothers in the first, second, and most educated groups, respectively, reported that they were not concerned about their children's bedtime, that they could go to sleep when they got sleepy, some as late as nine or ten o'clock regularly. It is possible that most of these children go to sleep early anyway except in neighborhoods where children form a tightly knit play group or on particularly bright moonlit nights.

The Infant's Health

His size and his softness give every newborn infant an appearance of delicacy and vulnerability. This inspires some kind of awe in the other members of the family. They handle him as gently as possible. He is shielded not only from the well-meaning roughness of the little children in the family but also from the elements to which the older members have become accustomed but which are still somewhat too strong for this young creature.

Brothers and sisters under six, hence *wala pang isip,* are allowed to play with the infant's toes and fingers, if they are gentle enough, but never to touch him around the middle where the umbilical cord is still fresh or on the head where the parietal bones have not sufficiently grown over the fontanel. They may talk to the baby from the side or facing him but not from the back of his head. He would strain his eyes to see who is there, and if this happened frequently he would become cross-eyed.

Especially cute babies are kept away from people who are known to be *usog,* that is, from strangers and pregnant women whose intent attention and fondling are believed to cause the child to become ill. There was incidence of this belief in all three groups of mothers. Certain winds or draughts of air are also believed to cause illness. *Taon* is believed to be caused by the wind. This is a condition in which the infant shows blue or purple under the skin, regular rash-like blotches all over, and in some cases high fever. It is actually one of the forms of acute beriberi, but the mothers with less education felt it was caused by an ill wind. No mother in the most educated group even mentioned the condition; it is most likely that it is unknown in the children of this group.

Concern for the young child's delicate digestive system has been mentioned in the section on feeding. Symptoms of digestive disturbances are treated with mild laxatives, castor oil, castoria, etc., supplemented by baby enemas. Colic is also a cause for concern. When colic occurs, mothers resort to cradling to comfort the child and to rubbing various oils around the child's navel. Accidental swallowing of seeds, buttons, coins, and even pins is often fatal; the sibling caretaker is admonished to be ever watchful on this account.

The baby's skin is another matter of concern. The climate, especially in March and April, is conducive to the development of a kind of rash or prickly heat. This usually occurs where the skin folds around the neck and around the leg and arm joints. Adults are also susceptible to this, but infants are especially pitiful when afflicted. Scabies, a skin infection that spreads by touch, is a much dreaded condition, and mothers are careful to keep their children away from others who are infected and to instruct the older siblings not to keep playmates who show the sores of the infection.

In the Philippines, as in most of the world, colds and fever are the most common afflictions of the young child. As a preventive measure the shutters or windows at the head of the bed should be shut to protect the child from drafts, expecially after he has bathed. He could also catch cold from the dew at dusk. Because of this the baby is rarely taken out after six o'clock at night, and if he is, he is very well wrapped. He is also not to be taken out in the open air just after awakening, no matter what the time of day. Even little children are admonished to stay in for a while after a nap before they rush out to the yard to play.

Fevers are believed to be symptomatic of various conditions. In the case of ordinary fevers, the child is treated with a hot sponge bath and wrapped with warm blankets to cause perspiration. If his fever is accompanied by a headache, a piece of cloth is dipped in strong vinegar and spread on his forehead. However, mothers regard a persisting or a recurring fever as an occasion for more treatment. Some mothers reported that they first take the child to a *hilot* (here meaning one believed to be skilled in putting bones back in place by massage) to make sure that it is not a bone fracture causing the fever.

Not one in our group of mothers mentioned that her child had been *namatanda* (afflicted by little old men of the earth) or that a fever had been induced by extreme fright. These beliefs about fevers still persist in the rural areas, and elaborate rituals are performed by special persons in the community to trace the cause of the illness. A very common practice involves the use of *tawas* (a form of alum). A piece of *tawas* is burned, and the form the piece takes after it has melted and cooled is carefully examined in the belief that it will reveal the cause of the illness. Hearing "It is the face of a kitten," or "It shows a wrinkled old woman," the family looks back to recall incidents just before the illness that might have involved the child and a kitten or the child and an old woman. Fevers could also be an indication that the child was *anusog* (an object of influence), in which case the person suspected of causing the illness is asked to do things to help cure the child. He may be asked to have his saliva mixed with the child's drink or rubbed on the child's forehead.

Of course, a rise in temperature can mark the onset of a children's disease. The Filipino mother recognizes the symptoms of mumps, measles, and chicken pox, but she attributes the initial stages of these illnesses to overexposure to the sun. There is, therefore, a blend of scientific and traditional beliefs about the causes of illness and an associated combining of old and new methods of treatment.

Treatment Practices

There is a wide variety of methods of treatment for illness. What is done for a sick child will depend on his family's beliefs, on the perceived nature of the illness, and on the availability of help. Puericulture centers and rural health units are slowly bringing the acceptance of innoculations and of professional medical attention. Traditional healers, *hilot* and *herbolario,* still play an important role. They may offer treatments which involve herbs, medicines, and massages without any particular magic involved, or they may execute rituals designed to ward off the sorcery or the malevolent spirits which are felt to be the cause of an illness.

When illness struck, approximately a quarter of the first two groups and half of the most educated group would consult a physician at once. About one quarter of each group would try home remedies first and then turn to other sources of help. The group who would confine their treatment to home remedies without recourse to other agents constituted 41 per cent, 31 per cent, and 23 per cent of the three groups respectively.

Traditional methods of treatment continue to play an important role for a number of reasons. Medical attention is expensive, and even where it is free, the physician often prescribes medications which are obtainable only at great cost and in a distant city. The rate of spontaneous recovery from children's illnesses is high enough that there is not much evidence to these practical people that modern medicine cures significantly more than traditional methods. The physician is further handicapped because he often does not see the child until the illness has reached an advanced stage after traditional treatments have been tried without success. Finally, there is still a lively belief in sorcery, in the actions of spirits of the dead, and in ghosts and other similar creatures. Many people believe that such agents play an important role in illness. Since modern medicine does nothing to placate the spirits, the people turn to those who do. If we look at the world as they do for a moment, it becomes quite clear that those who use both *hilot* and physician are simply playing it safe, or in modern phrasing, treating the whole child.

We strongly suspect that the concepts of health and cleanliness indigenous to the culture are subtly different from these concepts as used and viewed in Western societies, and that reported attitudes and practices concerning these matters are not directly comparable. The stress Filipinos place on physical cleanliness, the primary importance of being clean-looking and clean-smelling—in their bodies, their clothing, and their homes—is certainly different from a health-oriented view of cleanliness since they are concerned with appearance and smell. The concepts of microbes and germs, contamination and infection are relatively new, introduced by the schools and reinforced by access to doctors and hospitals. The association of these with dirt is easily acceptable because it is compatible with the aesthetic value people place on cleanliness. The young child cannot differentiate between clean and dirty. Cleanliness values are communicated to him from the start, and the standards of privacy within the family (discussed in the following chapter) permit more room for him to learn by imitation.

If we look to the language for clues, health means a strong body (*malakas ang katawan*), not sickly (*dimasasaktin*). Good appetite, good coloring, and limber stride are the more obvious measures of good health; eating and sleeping are the recognized main ingredients. Illness is usually attributed to poor eating, poor habits of rest and sleep, to undue exposure to the extremes of temperature, to getting wet, to taking a bath on a Friday, to extreme fear or over-excitement, or to some kind of incompatibility with certain people (*usog, lihi*) or certain spirits (*namatanda*). Parents take the responsibility for shielding the child, and as he grows he learns from their admonitions. Many of these ideas are admittedly without scientific basis, but a number of them do make medical sense and the traditional and the scientific are not necessarily poles apart.

Comparison with the Findings of Sears, Maccoby, and Levin

Contrasting the modern bathroom facilities of America and the easy-to-clean home of the Philippine family, we see that mothers in the two societies face different problems in insuring the health and cleanliness of their children. Although the Sears report does not deal with illness, we can use his data to compare the handling of bowel and bladder control, bed-wetting, and rules for sleep in the two societies.

The American home necessitates a more strict routine than the toilet-training practices we have encountered in the Philippine home, and the mother quickly learns when the child is about to relieve himself so that she can put him on the toilet immediately. Many mothers feel that the young child is not responsible for accidents, but by a certain age when the child is considered old enough to control his elimination, accidents are interpreted as willful disobedience. The majority of the American mothers used no pressure or moderate pressure to train their children, although 16 per cent scolded and 2 per cent punished severely. These data indicate that the mothers are not significantly more severe than Philippine mothers, but they do begin toilet training considerably earlier. The average American mother starts training her child by eleven months. Eighty-seven per cent start before twenty months. In contrast, only 37 per cent of Philippine mothers have begun training by the time the child is eighteen months old. Having started later, the Philippine mother also takes longer to complete the process. Bladder control is taught later in the life of the child in both societies.

Fifteen per cent of the Philippine children as compared to 20 per cent of the American children bed-wet, but most parents of both societies were sympathetic and felt that the child could not help himself. Philippine parents get up at night to check their children and to change them, while American parents often check and put the child on the toilet at night without wakening him. Although we have no information on the handling of the problem in older American children, Philippine children are teased and scolded for chronic bet-wetting especially beyond the age of four or five.

Teaching the child to be neat and clean and to develop healthy habits is an important aspect of socialization for both the American and the Philippine mother. It would appear, however, that American mothers surround the acquisition of sphincter control with a good deal more concern than do their Philippine counterparts.

chapter 10

CURIOSITIES
AND THE LEARNING OF
SEX ROLES

Curiosity about one's person is probably one of the earliest aspects of curiosity. His own person is one of the first stimuli that face the newborn; one of the few, too, that remain available to him throughout life. We do not know how long it takes the child to realize that the wiggling toes he can see and touch and the sounds he makes, sometimes a coo and sometimes a cry, are as much himself as the hands with which he touches the toes and the lips and throat that produce those sounds. But we do know that they catch his attention, and as he extends his skills, he manages to explore them further. Later he gets an idea of what his body is, and depending on the opportunities for comparison open to him, he starts to know how much he is like others and how much he is not like them.

But there are complications in learning in this domain. The particular group into which one is born has ideas about how certain aspects of this learning should come about. Certain fears which had their origins in the history of the group have given rise to dos and don'ts. Societies differ in their ideas of what constitutes sufficient clothing, what is appropriate behavior toward one's person, and what language is appropriate. Related are ideas that vary in subtlety, governing physical contact with others and suggesting what is appropriate among girls or among boys or between boys and girls. An added consideration, too, is the line the group draws between family and nonfamily and how this enters into what is appropriate.

The general subject of this chapter deals with the section in the interview with which the most care was exercised in the formulation of the questions. Sex is generally not a topic of nonintimate and nonfamily conversation. It is a delicate subject and a private concern. The questions, therefore, had to be chosen and phrased with two considerations in mind—to enable the interviewers to be comfortable in asking the questions and to avoid the serious possibility of their being judged as indiscreet or indelicate by the interviewees. Even with all these precautions there is a noticeable frequency of skipping the questions in the interview or of having them evaded or not answered at all. Also it became apparent as we analyzed our data that we had not clearly differentiated a number of questions. These include knowledge about physical differences between the sexes, the process of gestation and birth, and the act of sexual intercourse and its relation to conception. These are completely separate topics for the Filipino child.

The Interpersonal Setting within the Family

Certain pictures of the family living situation presented in the earlier chapters raise questions pertinent to this area of the child's interest. Babies being born in the home with young children around or within hearing distance, the openness with which babies are nursed, children sleeping together with their parents under one mosquito net, toilet activities treated very openly, all have implications for the development of attitudes and behavior toward one's own person and toward that of others. The difference between groups in these practices is only a matter of degree whether the family lives in a one-room *bahay-kubo* or in a larger house with many rooms. The child sees a baby sister or brother being bathed. Later he bathes or is bathed with siblings close to his age. He is dressed openly or helped by an older sibling. He is washed after using the pot, or if he is big enough, he washes a younger brother or sister. Only the older siblings are careful about toilet activities, about rubbing and rinsing themselves under their clothing in an open bath, or about changing into dry clothes. Then the young child wonders and sometimes satisfies his curiosity by surreptitious peeping, later teasing the older children, or by direct questions which may be either answered or evaded.

A line, *malaki na* (big or old enough), is clearly drawn when the sibling concerned has started to show signs of puberty. From this point on exposure is defined as shameful and not in good taste. The world of the older sibling now becomes different from the young child's. The other members of the family leave the room or look away when an older sister or brother changes his clothes. More care is taken so that the older children suffer no unnecessary exposure. Adults talk about things the small child does not understand, and when he asks, he is told he is still very young. "You will find out when you get older" is the usual answer. The older sister joins other women talking about monthly periods. The older brother joins a group of boys in an old man's yard and then for about two weeks afterwards keeps mostly to himself with mother and father looking like they were sharing a secret with him. This, unknown to the young child, is the time of his brother's circumcision. The young child is kept out of this; "He is still innocent." And the children do keep out of the affairs of the older people, some of them in fear of censure and some in obedience. Other children are indifferent; they do not notice because they have so many current interests. There will be time enough for these adult secrets when they reach the proper age.

We have no data showing how many parents explain the physical changes that take place with age when the younger children start to get curious, or how many keep quiet, leaving the children to satisfy their curiosity on their own. We do not know how many parents reprimand the child for his curiosity, nor do we know to what extent the children become curious and ask about sexual matters and to what extent they talk and tease about them. But we do know that some children are curious and ask questions:

> He asks why I am somewhat indisposed during the first day of my menstrual period. He also asks why mothers have menstruation. I tell him that without menstruation children will not be born.

> He asks me about myself but he does not show curiosity about the other sex.

> He thinks that a woman has an organ like his.

> My child is not inquisitive. She is too shy.

> He never asks me why girls and boys are different. He does not show curiosity about the other sex.

> He asks and I tell him that by nature girls and boys are different. That is how God made them.

> One time she asked me why she is a girl and her brother a boy. Children of this generation are wise and broad-minded in the sense that they happened to learn things very early, like my child who was not taught but learned from hearsay and sayings. She does not ask about boys. She is quite shy in front of them.

I told him God likes one to be a girl and the other to be a boy.

I told her it was God's will to have boys and girls different.

He asked me why girls have menstruation period. I told him that it is one sign of womanhood.

He often asks why he is different from his girl playmates, and I tell him that the girls' appearance is different and also their sex organs.

Although the most typical comments were "He is not interested in sex" and "He does not ask such questions" (61 per cent), the above quotations indicate that a substantial minority of the children do ask their parents questions and/or discuss sex with siblings or peers.

Accepted Language

Another line besides that marked by age is the boundary between family and nonfamily. There is a language that comes easily when one speaks within the family which one may not use with nonfamily. Certain parts of the body may be mentioned as one would name the nose, eyes, or ears; one may use real names or substitute the word *kuwan*, a noun catchall, but one does not mention them or talk about them in the company of other people. Here again age enters in, for very young children are exempt from the rule on the basis of that age-old excuse, *wala pang isip* (no mind yet). Parents even teach their children to recite or sing doggerel verses that use some of the forbidden terms, and up to a certain age the little ones get away with it; "They are cute."

Young children learn early the difference between boys and girls, that boys are like their fathers and girls like their mothers. There is little mysterious about being male or being female. They can distinguish male from female in kittens, puppies, and other animals around the house; they have no qualms about looking to find out when they choose their pets. Only when they come to a certain age, and this age is dictated by the family *delicadeza*, are they taught that for reasons of good taste certain things are no longer mentioned. From this point on, the deliberate use of these terms is met with censure. They are classified words, just as the word meaning bad mother or flirt are objectionable terms which no well-bred child may use, which parents would claim their children had picked up from the streets or from their playmates if they were to use them.

The children in our sample had already passed the age when they could be excused on the basis of *wala pang isip*. When the mothers were asked how they reacted when their children used words that they would be ashamed for other people to hear, mothers typically replied in the following manner:

> Sometimes she uses bad words and I spank her.
>
> She never uses improper language, but she shouts at me at times, and I explain to her that that is not proper.
>
> She doesn't speak embarrassing words because I give her heavy punishments.
>
> Being an *Iglesia ni Cristo* [a small Protestant sect], he doesn't say any embarrassing words.
>
> When I hear a bad word, I tell him not to say it again. He never repeats it, at least not in front of me.
>
> There are times when children say things they don't understand. She is no exception. I tell her never to say them again.
>
> I tell him it is bad and God does not like it or else he will be punished by God. When I tell him this, he stops but then he forgets again.
>
> She used to say *loko* to her brother and sister when she was angry. I think she learned it from reading comics.
>
> He picks up *loko, demonyo* from his playmates. I pinch him and he stops.
>
> I slap her mouth.
>
> She learned bad words from her playmates. I scold her with pinching, or sometimes I forbid her to play. That stops her.
>
> Sometimes he says something about sex organs, and I divert him to other topics.
>
> She does not use words that are not good. Her grandmother takes her to church.
>
> He does not utter bad words since he does not hear bad words from his parents or from his cousins.
>
> She said *lintik*. I whipped her and she stopped saying it.

Play Activities

Until they are about five years old, boys and girls are treated very much alike. When the children reach school age, the boys start venturing out into the groves or open fields, climbing fences, aiming sling shots, playing war with bamboo pellet guns, and flying kites. Meanwhile the girls stay close to the house, continuing to play house and store, games that leave a few roles open for the boys when they get tired of running about. Venturing out, as boys do, is not encouraged for girls; a girl who would rather play boys' games with boys is called *tomboy* (the native term *binalaki* [boyish] has only been coined recently, as far as we know). There are other restrictions on girls, expectations that they start to act feminine by five or six years of age. Little girls may still take refuge in that license, *wala pang isip*, but they are gently reminded with a touch of censure: "A girl sits with her skirt pulled down in front." "A girl should be at home, not out on the streets or in some neighbor's home." "Nice girls don't talk or laugh that loud."

No question was asked in the interview to obtain information on the concern of parents about boys and girls playing together. There is none as far as the writers know considering that play groups include sibling groups and that parents even help set up the play house or store. "Neighboring" is discouraged in girls only in the fear that the habit may persist to a point where she would prefer visiting and gossiping to doing her household chores.

We have reason to believe that masturbation exists, although the question was not asked of the mothers. There is a term for it in the language, one of those words not used in polite company. But it seems to be accepted as a stage that little boys go through in the same way that their running around half-dressed is accepted up to a point. A little boy's performance sometimes generates amusement in adults and playmates who happen to take notice. But if the child continues to masturbate after reaching a certain age, he will probably be teased until he stops.

Growing into the Next Stage

While in many other societies elaborate rites of passage initiate the child into adulthood, the Filipino child undergoes nothing so complex. There is recognition of growth as parents and relatives comment on the change in a boy's voice or the fact that his eyes are starting to wander toward girls, on his attention to appearance, his frequent baths, his demand for long pants, and timely visits to the barber shop. A boy in his preteens, some as early as nine if his friends are older than he is, starts to think of having himself circumcised. Sometimes the father makes arrangements, but usually there is a man in the village who does this as a favor for the boys in his neighborhood. The boy does not tell his younger siblings because they would not understand and would only tease him; however, his parents and older siblings usually know. His chores in the household are made lighter while he heals. The older members of the family recognize circumcision as his first step toward manhood. The boy begins to be called *binatilyo* (little man) instead of *bata* (child), and usually at seventeen, or even earlier depending upon his evident maturity, he graduates into being *binata* (young man).

The physical changes at puberty also necessitate certain behavior changes in the girl. Her behavior becomes more inhibited and controlled. She is expected to be more careful about her person. If she is teased by the younger ones because they have noticed changes in her, she has been careless, and it is her fault. She no longer bathes with the younger siblings or in public baths; she learns to bathe in a loose fitting long dress. Developing breasts are nothing to be proud of; they embarrass the young girl, and she usually hides herself in loose dresses. The *dalagita* (little maiden), as she is called at this stage, may continue to play with children her age or younger, but she does this less frequently because of her increased household duties and the awareness of her developing body. She begins to shy away from physical contact with boys her age or older, although she continues to be demonstrative of her affections within the family.

Menstruation marks the young girl as *dalaga na* (already a young woman). Conversations among the women in the family from which she was formerly excluded are now open to her. She learns what she should do and what she should not do during her periods. She is not to eat guavas and other sour fruits, which like ice cream, turnips, and cold foods in general cause pain; and she should not take a bath or, in some families, get her head wet since this might make her insane. She is to use warm water, not *tubig na buhay* (fresh, "live" water), for washing. The first time she menstruates she is instructed to take only three steps forward and then one back (in other areas they do other things three times), so that the periods will be no longer than three days. There is so much whispering and secrecy in connection with menstruation that young children become curious. The term for it is taboo and not to be spoken aloud. When little children do hear the word or see something connected with it, they use it to tease their older sisters. They are admonished not to say the word and are told they will know about it when they are older. Little boys are told that this is no concern of theirs, only of older girls and mothers. The curiosity wears off; the child has so many other things to concern him.

Usually growing up in Philippine families is a step-by-step arrangement; the child will learn the next step when he gets there. Meanwhile he pays attention to his current concerns. There are stages, and certain things are appropriate at one stage and not appropriate at another. When the child grows into a new stage, he outgrows and lays aside the things of the prior stage. Thus play and companionship between boys and girls is part of early childhood. At puberty boys band with boys or they are teased as *bakla* or *binabae* (sissy), and girls pick the companionship of girls or they are labeled "flirts." These groups do not mix again until about fourteen or fifteen. Changes are observable not only in the play groups but also in the household arrangements, for the boy now sleeps alone or with the younger boys and the girl sleeps alone or with the younger children. There are few specific rules. Sleeping arrangements appear to be dictated by some kind of sensitivity to what is stage-appropriate and what is not.

Learning about Pregnancy and Birth

In a society which does not seem to surround birth with secrecy where many more births occur at home than in the hospital, and where children hear their mother's labor moans as well as the baby's first cry, how curious will children be about life and how it comes to be? How do adults look at the matter, and how do they react to the expression of a child's interest in it? This interest will depend on prevalent adult attitudes toward the birth process. A matter-of-fact attitude generates little curiosity, and subtle rules about what is appropriate to ask and what is not determine the extent to which children do express this interest.

If we examine the language referring to the birth process, *nanganganak/ang inay ko* (giving birth to a child/my mother) and we realize that the event being described normally occurs within hearing distance of the child, it is almost superfluous to ask if children question where babies come from. They do not have to ask; they know that babies come from mothers. What the child would really be asking is how did the baby happen to be there? And the mothers interpreted our questions that way.

Almost two-thirds of the mothers responding said their children asked no questions about the matter. They said that the child was too young to have that question in mind, or too young to even be curious, or so good and quiet he would not think to ask those questions, or that they, the parents, are "careful" so the child will have nothing to ask. Around 10 per cent said the child probably knows although he has not asked, that he has seen the mother pregnant and has seen younger siblings being born. About 20 per cent said the child did express interest in this, and the answers most often given by the mothers were "You came from mother's tummy," or "through the anus," "God made you there." Only about 6 per cent said they evaded the question and directed their children's interest elsewhere. The few (about 5 per cent) who said they told their children the truth referred to baby animals having both father and mother or went as far as saying, "Father and mother sleep together and that way they have children." More typical answers to questions on the children's curiosity about reproduction were:

He is such a quiet child. He doesn't ask those kinds of questions.

I tell her she comes from the stomach. At her age you can't tell her the truth yet.

I tell him that God puts them there. No, he will not really know how conception takes place until he is old enough to fully understand.

One time he asked how come he became a child. I told him God gave him to us.

I told him that I made him, and he continued to ask—how! So I told him to ask his father. I really don't know if he knows.

She has asked me about that a few times, when she was about five or six. One time I changed the conversation. At another time I told her a story.

I give him an indirect answer, such as "a baby comes from the stomach of the mother." He seems to be satisfied with this kind of answer.

She never asks. The others did, and I told them they came from the guava—we have a guava tree in our yard.

I told him when he was old enough he would know the answer. He found out how he became a person when I was pregnant with my second child.

I told him he was given to us by an American.

Sometimes he asks questions about these things, but I just laugh at him and say God gave him to us. I don't think he knows about these things.

I told him the truth: I tell him that he will know all of it when he grows up to study of it. He was very curious.

I told her that we found her in carabao manure.

I told him babies come when no menstrual flow takes place. When he asked about it, I told him to observe the dog, cat, or pig. He knows where babies come from.

When he asked, I showed him a woman in the family way and told him a child is inside it. He found it out when my sister-in-law gave birth.

I said that God gave them to us. It's good if they're brought up knowing about this so that they will not be so much interested about it when they grow up.

The attitudes of the parents themselves toward these questions clearly pervade the responses they made to their children's inquiries. The mothers sensed what their children wanted to know, but they felt the children were not ripe for the knowledge at that stage. They believed there would be time enough for their children to find out when they were older. The partial answers given were within the children's ability to understand, although they knew them not to be complete. The mothers who evaded the questions probably could not decide what part of the information they could comfortably and appropriately relay.

Learning about Intercourse and Conception

We do have some information on how the mothers themselves found out about reproduction and the parents' roles in it, although in 52 per cent of the cases our young women interviewers simply skipped the question. This is understandable considering that young women are not generally supposed to discuss the subject with nonfamily elders. The 134 mothers who were asked the question showed clear group differences. Seventy-eight per cent in the most educated group, 53 per cent in the second group, and only 15 per cent in the first group said they learned about it in school and from books. Sixteen per cent in the first group, only one mother in the second group, and no mothers in the most educated group said they were told by friends or by other people in the community. Approximately a third in the two less educated groups and only 15 per cent in the most educated group said their mothers told them, a number of them shortly before marriage. A third of the mothers in the first group but only one or two in the other groups said they did not know until they got married, a few of them saying they came to their conclusions when they started having children. We feel that many of these answers are frankly evasive. It is also possible that the embarrassed interviewer distorted her question. We report the material without much confidence in it.

> She probably knows children come from me—from the number of my children born after her. I did not know about this until I was married.

> I think our young people should know about those things when they are of age—at eighteen, let's say. I did not know a thing about it until I got married.

> When I was nearing maidenhood my grandmother told me.

> Our youngsters today probably know about it from books, from school, or perhaps from the movies even. For my part, I didn't know until I got married.

> My parents would never tell me those things. I learned about it from my teacher in high school. Our youngsters are probably told in grade six or high school.

> I was probably seven when I first heard it from the old people. You know how it is in the *barrios*.

> I had an older sister who married before me, and she told me.

> Young people begin to know conception at their high school days since they are studying that in general science. I cannot remember, but I think as you grow older even if you did not study you'd know it.

> Young people should know how conception takes place at the age of fifteen. I found out also at fifteen. I asked my mother about it.

> Through stories I myself learned it when I was in second year high school.

We find it difficult to understand how the information could have arrived this late in the lives of these women, particularly considering the physical design of the homes in which they grew up. In a way it illustrates that privacy is not alone a matter of walls or the number of rooms but a matter of personal responsibility, of carefulness in one's ways dictated by a learned sense of *delicadeza*. It illustrates, too, as has been emphasized in this discussion, the parents' concern that their children know about the next stage only at the appropriate time.

The study did not attempt to find out how the fathers would have responded to the question, but there is reason to believe that men learn about reproduction much earlier than women. Apparently there is greater opportunity for boys to discuss the subject among themselves; they are not equally bound by the rules of propriety and modesty that apply to women. It is possible, too, that they are not equally susceptible to the greatly romanticized and idealized versions of love and marriage in the culture.

Comparison with the Findings of Sears, Maccoby, and Levin

As we compare the conclusions of Sears et al. on the handling of children's sexual curiosities and activities with our findings in the Philippines, we note the striking contrast between the restrictions and preventive measures of American mothers and the "You will learn when you are old enough" attitude of Filipinos. American mothers go to great lengths to minimize sexual stimulations and thinking. They place boys and girls in different rooms, stop bathing them together when they show undue curiosity, keep them clothed at all times, give them loose fitting clothes, distract them when they stimulate the genital area, and avoid mentioning sex as part of the general pattern of de-emphasis. Mothers also use sanctions such as "Put your clothes on so that you don't catch cold," tell the child he will hurt himself or that it is dirty when he touches his genitals, avoid labels by not giving names to the sex organs, and control information about sex and birth to prevent the child from thinking, talking, or knowing about sex.

In contrast, in the Philippines the child cares for, bathes, and toilet trains his younger siblings, and physical functions are openly accepted. Although the families often sleep together in the same room, the parents try to prevent the children from observing sexual intercourse. Children are often present or nearby when their mothers give birth to their younger siblings. In this frank atmosphere the inquisitive child is simply told that he will know all about these things when he is old enough or is given an amused, evasive answer. In addition, he has the opportunity to satisfy many questions simply by observation.

Modesty, which is progressively a problem in dressing, bathing, and toilet training for the American mother who exerts mild but firm pressure on the child, is also important in the Philippines. Especially by puberty, the laxness and casualness of childish behavior is replaced by new skills in dressing and bathing which are considered proper for the young emerging adult. Modesty rather than repression would appear to be the best characterization of the attitude developed by the Filipino child toward sexual and other bodily functions.

Masturbation in children, which Sears et al. found to be considered a problem by American mothers (25 per cent were not permissive, 50 per cent were slightly or moderately permissive), is probably an accepted stage that little boys go through in the Philippines. The little boy's performance sometimes amuses adults and playmates; but if the child continues after a certain age, he is teased until he stops.

Half the American mothers reported having witnessed their children participating in "show it" games, urinating contests, and other sex play. The mothers who did encounter this in general tried not to make it appear serious, although most felt that it definitely should be prevented if possible. The curiosities of Philippine children may not be so strongly aroused. Philippine mothers encourage boys and girls to play together, relying largely on teasing to control disapproved behavior.

It would appear that the Philippine attitudes in this area are characterized by less absolute rules. Precocious sexual activities are not so much forbidden as they are considered premature. There is a good deal of reliance on the control exerted by the presence of others in addition to the internalized standards of the family. Our research does not answer the very significant question of whether these childhood differences result in different anxiety patterns among adults.

There are also probably fewer absolute rules concerning relationships between members of the same sex. Although it was not an item in our research nor in the Sears research, we can add that Philippine psychiatrists report that Filipinos are not particularly concerned about homosexual manifestations. As is the case in many other parts of the world, Filipino males hold hands or grasp each other's arms as a gesture of friendship and acceptance. In some of the larger cities, especially Manila, males who dress as women and solicit the attentions of men are regarded with amusement or only mild annoyance. Our information in this area is limited, but we are led to believe that the generally tolerant attitude permits some males to move rather freely from masculine to feminine sexual roles and then back to masculine roles again. However, with respect to all aspects of sexual behavior, we must caution that our data are limited.

chapter 11

HANDLING HURT
AND ANGER

Since life is filled with situations in which one is made uncomfortable or is prevented from doing what one wants to do, the pattern of reactions to frustration is an exceedingly important aspect of one's personality. The processes of learning in this domain probably begin very early in life, long before the individual has acquired much language facility. The critical periods of learning various aspects of the hostile reaction remain a matter of conjecture. Certainly patterns are not universal. Since some unusual patterns of reaction can be seen in Philippine children, it should prove quite fruitful to examine some of the circumstances in which the patterns were acquired.

Discomforts during infancy are, as far as we can be sure, largely physical. The baby's sense of "I" is still largely visceral and tactile. He cries when he is hungry or wet to express physical distress. Since he is hardly in a position to help himself, his attempts are largely calls for aid. Philippine parents interpret these reactions as anger, persistent demanding, despair, or patient waiting; and they label the infants *iyakin* (tending to cry much), *mabait* (good), or *tahimik* (quiet). A good, quiet baby is appreciated, but the more demanding infant is tolerated because "He does not know what he is doing; he is still a baby." This tolerance may be tinged with irritation, particularly when the mother or caretaker is faced with other tasks, but the baby eventually gets the attention he wants, because the mother who lets her baby cry is criticized as neglectful.

As the baby grows older he begins to perceive the order of things in the family and his place in the scheme. As his skills increase he ceases to be a helpless infant, but he does not easily outgrow the feeling of omnipotence acquired in infancy when his summons was law. Consequently he now becomes susceptible to other discomforts—the pain of being denied his way, the pain of being ignored, and the pain of not understanding or not being understood. He must recognize the rights of other people in the family, older siblings and perhaps a younger sibling, and of the parents themselves. He soon learns not only that he cannot dictate what others may or may not do, but also that he must abide by family rules which he may or may not understand. Sometimes he accepts a rule at face value and abides by it, but sometimes a rule seems so unreasonable that it infuriates him. There are times when rules are so contradictory that he becomes confused and does not know what to expect. Reactions to all these situations differ from child to child.

The Filipino child is not taught to look out for himself or to care for his own concerns first but is encouraged to consider every member of the family. From his earliest childhood, he learns through gentle reminding and mild to severe reproof that, although he has his wants, others as important as he is have their wants too. If there is conflict and he is old enough to understand, he is made to see that he should give way. If he is not old enough, he is told repeatedly that this is the way of the good individual. Parental advice runs on the constant theme that he cannot always have his way because there are others who want their way too. If his is a big family, he must give in more often. He learns early that resistance and self-assertion are rarely successful. Yet, although a child may see his place in the scheme of things, he goes through a long and trying period before he is able to accept this place and live happily with it. He learns not to show when he is angry, to smile when he would rather not smile, and to preserve goodwill when his impulses are to destroy.

One of the most important things a child learns is that the temperaments of individuals around him differ. He can be at ease with a sweet-tempered, mild-mannered person. But it is difficult to smile when he is with those who are irritable, sour-tempered, and hard to get along with. Other persons are easily angered, but always for a cause. He must be careful not to rouse their anger. The child also learns to discern the temperament of the usually mild-mannered person who is subject to infrequent but violent outbursts, *nasaloob ang kulo* (inside is boiling or seething). All of these distinctions are important, for he must adjust his behavior to the different temperaments in the group in order to be successful in interpersonal relationships.

Frequency and Causes of Anger

Four questions in the interview sought related information: on the incidence of anger in children, the circumstances that tend to rouse these anger reactions, how the mothers recognized anger in its various forms, and parental handling of outbursts. Fewer than 6 per cent of the mothers claimed that their children were so even-tempered that they never got angry. Almost 75 per cent admitted that their children did get angry but not too often. Twenty per cent reported that the children who were subjects of the interview were hotheaded and *magagalitin* (tending to be angry very easily).

The most frequent precipitants of anger in these children were being crossed, not being given what they had asked for, having their possessions interfered with, and being teased. Anger also arose when the child was not given the attention he sought, when he was bothered while at work or at play, when he was called to run errands when he did not feel like it, or when he was punished and did not feel he deserved it.

> He seldom gets angry unless he is disturbed or called names. Whenever he is angry, he cries by himself and says not a word.

> When he can't get things done the proper way or anyone has meddled with his playthings he gets angry. But this does not happen often. When he is angry with me or with an older person he just sulks or murmurs. I do not like this but I just ignore him.

> When she's told she is dull in class, she really gets very angry.

> When her older brother nicknames her *Duhat* [a dark berry], she gets very angry.

> I know he gets angry when I do not buy him what he asks for. He sits down, head hanging, and remains silent a long time.

> She can't stand being paired off with her boy playmates. She gets so angry she hurls stones at her teasers.

> She gets very angry when she is defeated in a quarrel with her brother. This does not happen too often, though. She's a very bad sport.

> He gets angry very often whenever anything he owns is taken by other children. He wants to hurt the other children when

he is angry. When he notices that he is the topic of conversation among the elders, he gets angry. I advise the elders to stop looking at him or talking about him.

His head is a little bit big, and he is sensitive about it. When he overhears people talking about it he cries. This started when he was about seven.

He is so fond of playing with the goats and chickens that his brothers call him goat spouse or chicken spouse. This makes him very angry.

Expressions of Anger

Mothers recognized anger and hurt feelings in various forms ranging from silent withdrawal and crying, murmuring and pouting, refusal to eat or come home, to loud sobbing, hitting others, and beating against walls or floors. More than two-thirds of the children reportedly had temper tantrums—38 per cent had mild ones occasionally, 21 per cent had severe ones infrequently, 9 per cent had mild tantrums quite frequently, and only about 7 per cent had severe tantrums rather frequently. On the other hand, 22 per cent were reported not to have had any temper tantrums. They were described as good-natured, and seven (3 per cent) were afraid to throw tantrums because "They knew what they'd get from their father if they did!"

If ever she gets angry, she goes to the room and cries there.

She pinches her younger brothers and sisters when she's angry with them. She cries, too, when she's really angry.

He gets angry very easily, especially when he is not obeyed or he cannot get what he wants. When he is angry with me because I've hurt his feelings, he refuses to eat and at times refuses to do his part in the house chores.

She hates for anybody to interfere with her things or if anybody taunts her when she is in a bad mood to start with. We keep out of her way when she is angry. I talk to her afterward, when she's in a better mood.

When she's angry, she wants to hurt her sister and throw anything she gets hold of.

He'd wear a dark pout, muss up his hair, and just sit there.

He rolls on the floor and cries and howls when he is not allowed what he wants. I ignore him, and he cools off, gets over it.

You can see it on his face when he is angry. He refuses to eat, and at times, when really very angry, he sits on the ground, kicking his heels, tears running down his nose and cheeks.

There has never been any time that she got angry. She's gentle even with dogs and cats. And she's quite close to our maid. When she tells me she wants something and I don't think she should have it, I explain to her and she does not insist. She accepts reasons.

No, she does not get angry often. When angry, she speaks out her wishes very loud. Sometimes she murmurs or cries in the corner and will not answer us when we talk to her. I do not allow her to answer me back. If she does, I whip her. This makes me very angry with her if she insists on answering me back as if she were quarreling with me. I do not like this done by my children.

He throws his toys all over the place when he is angry. I let him do this to release his anger. He picks them up afterward.

She gets angry when her brothers and sisters meddle with her work. She can get so loud when she's angry. She tears up her dress and cries. I scold her when she does this.

He's the silent type. He's never angry. He's gentle and silent. He won't talk with anybody, goes to his room and locks himself up; after a while he comes out as if nothing had happened. He just keeps silent. We've made him believe that God loves those who are gentle and good.

Parents' Reactions to Anger

Outbursts of temper can be irritating and inconvenient in a household, but they appear to be expected of children. Although parents often punish these displays, we see instances where parents feel ambivalent, almost as if they remember their own childhood emotions. More than a third of the parents felt that it was best to ignore the child at the height of his anger. Nine mothers (4 per cent) admitted that their handling of the situation varied according to their own mood, that they did scold and even spanked when they were particularly irritated. More than a fourth of the mothers tried humoring the child or advising him after he had cooled off. About 11 per cent scolded the child as a rule. Of the twenty-two mothers (9 per cent) who said they spanked their children every time they showed anger, only two were from the two more educated groups. Fifteen mothers (6 per cent) said they used spanking as a last resort when neither soothing nor ignoring helped. Three mothers, who felt it necessary to spank or scold lest the tantrums become habitual, made a point to comfort their children afterwards.

There are times when I humor her and times when I hit her with the back of my slippers.

I stop her murmuring by telling her that God does not like children who are naughty. She behaves better whenever God is mentioned.

I give her what she likes, when I see that she is really feeling bad.

When she is angry, we all just leave her alone.

I ask him to stop and if he still does not, I promise to buy him playthings or new clothes, and cuddle him, and his anger subsides.

Sometimes I divert his attention with funny stories, and sometimes I just let him go his own way.

I let him cry. He stops when he sees that no one is paying him any attention.

I appease him and promise him something.

I just stare him straight in the eye. One look and it is sufficient to stop him. That tells him his place.

When angry, he'd get a pillow and a blanket and sleep in one corner of the house. One time we could not find him. It had gotten dark, and he still had not come home. Somebody said he was at my sister's home. I was ironing then, but I went out into the cold air to get him. His father gave him a big whipping.

She's afraid to show any anger toward me because I'd whip her.

He does not throw tantrums and he keeps his anger to himself anyway, so I just let it pass. I don't speak to him either.

I ask him what the matter is, and if he still will not speak and I begin to lose patience, I spank him in anger till he stops crying.

I have him lie prone on the floor, and I beat him once but hard!

It appears that anger in itself is not considered bad. What seems to be decried is the manner of expressing anger, or the harboring of it against one's parents, or against anyone for that matter. To get angry is inevitable, but to express it disrespectfully or to harbor it is strongly disapproved and punished. Directing anger at one's parents constitutes a form of irreverence and ingratitude, and venting one's anger on others, or nursing it inside, marks one as hard and unforgiving. Parents recognize that children do get angry with them when parents don't let them have their way or when they discover that the parents are not being fair or truthful with them and do not understand them. Children are expected to take this in stride. They may cry, they may be hurt. But they may not nurse anger, nor murmur and curse under their breath, nor lash out in a torrent of angry words, nor throw a tantrum. Very few of the mothers, fewer than 10 per cent, could be considered more than moderately permissive about letting a child show his anger.

Quarrels with Siblings and Peers

Disapproval of expressions of anger extends to the child's activities with his siblings and peers. In the parent-supported age-hierarchy among siblings the child should respect and obey his older siblings and protect and care for those younger. Nevertheless, 56 per cent of the children reportedly have quarreled with siblings, the majority only with younger siblings, about a fourth only with older siblings, and more than a third with both younger and older siblings. These quarrels ranged from mild verbal arguments to hitting, pinching, and even hair-pulling.

> He spanks the little ones and they fight back. When I see them quarreling I tell them to stop. When they don't I spank them all.

> Quarrels are more often among the younger ones. They pinch, and they hit one another. I only interfere when I notice that someone is getting hurt or they're being too rough.

> I scold all of them. They cannot tell me it is one or the other's fault. A fault or not, they were both parties to the quarrel, so they both need talking to.

> He just talks and talks. He is the smaller one so he knows he cannot fight the bigger brother but this does not stop him from lashing out with his tongue.

> He teases his older brothers and makes them very angry. He also hits them sometimes. When I find this out, I make him stay in a corner.

> She often quarrels with her elder sister. She talks back to her sister. She utters unpleasant words and makes faces. She seldom strikes or pinches. I stop her at once, for she should not behave that way to her older sisters.

They shout at one another. They never draw their fists. I usually stop them and say that brothers do not quarrel.

He quarrels with his sister. He pulls her hair till she cries.

These family quarrels are largely products of ordinary play frictions, shirking of responsibility, attempting to get the other to do the task, refusal of a younger to obey an older sibling, interference with staked property ("picking fruits from my tree when his tree has as much fruit" or "playing with my marbles after he was not careful about his"), or mild, good-natured teasing which develops into taunting. Thus a mother could say, "They'd be playing very quietly and smoothly out there in the yard, and pretty soon you'd hear voices raised in anger, crying, and actual hitting." Since all involved are her children she usually reacts by scolding or spanking all of them, or she invokes the age sanction, "You should know better than that; you are older," or "You should have more respect for age; he is your older brother," or the family sanction, "Brothers and sisters do not quarrel."

About 20 per cent of the children reportedly never quarreled in their play. Forty-three of these were described as quiet and good-natured, five were simply cowardly and would run away from quarrels, and five were so strong that none dared provoke them into a quarrel. Twenty-five per cent were labeled quarrelsome; they would initiate the quarrel situation and see it through. A small 4 per cent would strike in anger and run home before getting more seriously involved; and about 8 per cent would get hit and run home crying, afraid to hit back. Twenty per cent were reported to be not really quarrelsome but would hit back in retaliation. Twenty-three per cent of the children were involved only in verbal quarrels or were not on speaking terms with the person with whom they had quarreled, which marks the distinction between *makipagkagalit* (be in an anger or enemy relationship) and *makipag-away* (quarreling more in terms of coming to blows).

No, she does not quarrel; she comes and tells me what happened, crying as she does.

He often engages in fistfights and stone duels.

He does not quarrel too much. But when they make him angry he retaliates. He hits his playmates with his fists.

She always wants to be leader of the group. She has not learned to accept defeat. When she is displeased she takes all her toys home and the other children are left with nothing to play with.

You know it when she has quarreled with her playmates. She does not go out to play and she does not talk with them when she meets them.

Quarrels with Neighbors' Children

In an earlier section of the interview when we asked the mothers what they did when their child was involved in a quarrel or fight with neighbors' children, we noted the strong tendency to discourage fighting, the admonition to stay away from quarrel situations, to avoid any cause for quarrel, and to come straight home rather than get further involved. We assessed the response to the question "What do you do when he quarrels?" in terms of the parents' rules concerning quarreling. Only nine mothers said they told their children they could fight back, that they should not come home from a fight crying. Eight of these mothers were from the least educated group and one from the most educated group. Eighteen mothers (10 per cent) allowed verbal quarrels feeling that these are inevitable but told the child not to get involved in physical bouts. The rest of the mothers advocated no quarreling whatsoever and told their children to stay at home to avoid playmates they couldn't get along with rather than to fight with them. If they were challenged, they were to come home and tell their mother or tell the other child's mother; and if they couldn't stand to be teased, they were to avoid it by refraining from teasing others.

It would be interesting to compare this parental code concerning conflict situations with the code of the peer group. We do not have specific information on the latter, unfortunately, but we wonder how much counterpressure the peer group exerts to stir the child away from his parents' admonitions. The child who runs home to mother, who cries, or simply retreats from a fight is branded with certain names that in themselves goad him to self-defense. He is called *iyakin* (crybaby), *sumbungera* (tattletale), *duwag* (cowardly), and these taunts not only follow him as he runs home but also greet him when he once again ventures out. If the child faces his mother with this problem, she comforts him saying that it is better to be branded *duwag* (coward) than *basagulero* (literally, head-breaker). Adult values are always held up to him as more important. There is more honor in patience and control than in winning a fight.

These adult attitudes toward violence and open anger force the child to seek other ways of expressing his feelings. He learns the value of waiting until his adversary has cooled off. He learns indirect ways of expressing hurt and ill feeling in the same way that he learns indirect ways of expressing fondness in order to minimize the likelihood of rebuff and to avoid occasion for open unpleasantness.

Teasing in the Child's World

We found many forms of teasing prevalent not only in the child's world but in the adult world as well. Teasing serves many functions. It is a way to sound out how far one may go. If rebuffed one can counter with "I was only teasing." It permits one to express some tender feelings without the risk of ridicule since the affection was offered only half seriously. It is a way of offering criticism without the uncomfortable feeling of openly standing in judgment or finding fault. Adults tease children about certain behavior instead of openly or directly dissuading them. Teasing is one way for the child to express himself with his elders without risking their displeasure; "He is not talking back; it is only a joke." Among his peers teasing is a way of asserting himself and of getting back at his playmates. If he cannot hit with his fists and run or face the consequences of retribution or parental censure, he can certainly tease. All in all, teasing is a convenient instrument of social interaction which allows the expression of individual feelings within a group that places a premium on pleasantness in interpersonal relationships.

Only 8 per cent of the children were reported by their mothers to be nonteasers, and a small 3 per cent do not initiate teasing but do tease back. Ten per cent tease only a little, and about 80 per cent tease a great deal. Of these, more than half are "great teasers"; they tease even their elders. About a third of them tease only younger siblings, and about an eighth tease only older siblings.

Children's teasing ranges from name-calling to annoying imitating behavior, pairing off the other with a boy (if a girl) or with a girl (if a boy), making fun of the other's defeat or punishment, making faces, mimicking characteristics that the other is sensitive about, and many other little cruelties that can be created by a child's imagination. However, teasing need not have any particular content, since the playfulness and the tone of words or actions determine the fine line between joking and teasing.

> He sticks his tongue out or opens his eyes wide at him. He knows his brother gets very angry at this.
>
> He knows how to tease his brothers and sisters—he grabs their toys and waits till they protest in anger, or he pairs them off with their boy or girl playmates till they cry.
>
> He calls his brothers and sisters all sorts of names—*kalbo* [bald], *mabaho* [smelly], *bingi* [deaf].
>
> Yes, he teases his cousins by adding words that rhyme with their names as *Juan-pakwan* [Juan watermelon] or *Hulya-tulya* [Julia-clam], etc.
>
> She would make faces at her older sister or hide her things and refuse to tell her where to find them.
>
> He teases even his elders, talks to them playfully.

Different children react to teasing in different ways partly because they may be in different stages of developing the approved reaction of teasing back. In our sample only about a third tease back, about a fourth cry, an additional tenth cry and run to someone for shelter. Twenty per cent of the children are so angered that they fight, and a small 7 per cent simply "seethe and boil inside." Only three children were reported to enjoy being teased, and five children simply leave the situation, ignoring the teasing. A handful, probably the few strong ones who nevertheless "have shallow tear wells" cannot keep from crying but manage to tease back.

> This teasing generally leads to quarreling because she can never take it.
>
> She has a tiny growth on the side of her ear, and they call her *kuntil* because of that. She fends off this teasing by making out as if she will hit them or she makes funny faces at them or calls them funny names.
>
> When he felt bad about his elders calling him names—*malaking ulo* [big head], etc.—he'd come and tell me and I'd comfort him that it is not really that bad.
>
> If she's told she is *dalaga na* [a lady already] she gets very angry; she cries and throws anything she can put her hands on.
>
> The teasing which makes her most angry is *Napulot ka lamang ng nanay mo* [You were only found somewhere by your mother, you're not really her child].

They pair him off with his girl classmates, but he can take this teasing. He usually teases back.

The moment they call him black he gets in a fighting mood and no one can stop him. He is so sensitive about his skin.

She seems to enjoy teasing if she started the teasing herself. But once it gets too thick that she finds herself in the middle she gets angry; she can't really stand to be teased, *bungi* [lacking one or a few teeth], shortie, bamboo legs.

He teases back. But he backs down when he is called *Romeong bungi*. He hates to be called that especially in front of other people.

She sometimes loses her temper when she is teased, and she comes out with unprintable words. I slap her on the mouth when I hear her at this.

Duling [cross-eyed] really sends her into a fit of anger.

Sensitiveness

Whether teasing produces a child's sensitivity or his sensitivity invites teasing cannot be determined here; but one is teased about something about which one is known to be vulnerable, about which one is believed to be touchy. A child with dark skin might be teased about it or about the lighter skin of his siblings and told that he probably was just found somewhere and raised by his parents because he couldn't possibly be their own with that skin of his! Or he has tried so hard to "straighten his tongue but it simply won't obey his efforts" and the name *utal* thus makes him furious. Or he bed-wets and has been told it is shameful for his age. Or he may be particularly careful about his possessions, the few things he can call his own, and his siblings are so careless that interference with his things even in jest is not amusing to him. Or others imitate his particular walk or tell him he is some little girl's or some old woman's boyfriend or call him a boast or a flirt (for a girl) or some other vaguely understood negative term. According to our mothers' reports only 18 per cent of the children were not sensitive about anything.

In connection with our discussion of teasing and sensitiveness, we would like to introduce *hiya,* a concept of central importance in the patterning of a Filipino child's behavior. It is difficult to understand *hiya* in English because it involves two opposing concepts, one of shame and one of pride. It is further complicated by the fact that not only is the child himself involved in this constellation of feelings, but his family is also. To fail, to fall short, to be accused of wrongdoing is experienced as personally distressing and as a reflection on one's family name. By the processes of learning the child develops the capacity to experience intense feelings of inferiority, humiliation, and loss of self-esteem. *Hiya* refers to the capacity for this painful experience and to the pattern of defenses which the child develops to avoid its occurrence. It is a mixture of pride, dignity, self-control, and shame. To be *walang hiya* (without *hiya*) is to be without modesty or character and is as negative a statement as one can make about a child.

Although we have not included this phenomenon in our research, it would appear that the sensitiveness to criticism which is often attributed to the adult Filipino is in part a residual of the childhood training which gives rise to *hiya*. Throughout life he is more or less discouraged from giving spontaneous, full expression to negative feelings. By the same token he has little opportunity to develop skills for handling criticism and insult which may come in his direction. It is almost as if he had signed a nonaggression pact and had disarmed.

The interplay of sensitivity, *hiya*, and teasing may be of great significance in determining important aspects of the Filipino child's individual personality. Our data shed little light on the topic. Observation techniques and extended individual histories would clarify some of the issues. Nevertheless, we feel that *hiya* is an important personality process that must be introduced because it makes some order of observations which are otherwise confusing.

Expression of Feelings and Interpersonal Values

There is an almost compulsive avoidance of the term *aggression* in this chapter. This is deliberate because in our preliminary discussions on this particular aspect of child behavior and the attendant socialization practices we realized that we could not use the concept and still be specific and descriptive. We also wanted to stay away from the assumptions that underlie the frustration-aggression hypothesis and concentrate instead on parental handling of the child's initial lack of skill in social interaction.

There is a tendency to think that anger, hurt, or thwarting necessarily induces a person to strike out, to retaliate, or, where the outlet is blocked, to repress but retain the angry impulses. If the emotion is expressed in a socially desirable form, the original impulse is said to have been redirected or sublimated. It is possible, however, that there are few aggressive habits in Filipino children, that the situation in which the child grows does not lead to his learning aggressive responses to the cues that occasion aggressive responses in children of another society. We therefore avoided interpreting our information in terms of aggression, overt and displaced. Instead we reported the child's hurt and anger reactions in his relationships with children and adults within the family and outside of it, including material concerning which reactions are sanctioned and which are not, the actual sanctions parents use, and the purpose for which they use them.

We noted a strong tendency to emphasize the value of smooth interpersonal relationships, of knowing when to speak, how to speak, and what to say in consideration of another person's feelings. In the Philippines nothing is more serious than to be considered *walang kapwa tao* (without fellowship, not knowing how to interact with people in good fellowship). The approved pattern is to take care that the other person's feelings are not hurt. There are ways of approaching a situation without creating unpleasantness, and there is always time enough to do so when goodwill is at stake.

A child is enjoined not to make a parent angry. He is admonished not to quarrel and to avoid occasions that might lead to fights and arguments. Losing control of himself, talking loud in anger, and quarrelsomeness are represented as immature, marks of poor upbringing, of a family lacking in taste. When he is angered, he does not talk back or fight back or harbor ill-feelings. He is expected to strive to get back as quickly as possible to a state of goodwill, to be forgiving and understanding of others. He may cry or express his hurt in a good-natured manner hoping to make the other understand. Winning an argument does not bring comfort; it is more important to gain the antagonist's goodwill.

If he has no opportunity to unburden himself graciously of aggrieved feelings directly to the person concerned, he can always communicate his feelings through a sympathetic third party; and if the latter is tactful, the original good relationship may be restored. Siblings and aunts serve as intermediaries when a child wants his parents to know that he has been hurt or angered by some of their actions. Peers angry with one another may also make use of go-betweens, an arrangement that carries into adult interpersonal relationships.

This does not mean that there are no actual anger outbursts in the society. They are not approved, but they do occur; for the society's values and standards are not necessarily backed up by foolproof and systematic controls. A child may be told time and again that uncontrolled anger exposes a person to censure, that noncontrol of emotions which shows up in quarreling is gross and indelicate; but in a fit of anger the parents may be unable to control themselves. Even if the parents are good models of what they profess, there are people in the community who are not. Opportunities for developing skill in the handling of one's emotions are not available to every individual to an equal degree within the same community or even within the same family. Still, according to the ideals of the society, whatever the circumstances, losing one's temper, saying harsh words, wounding the sensitive feelings of another person are all to be avoided at almost any cost.

There is another interpersonal phenomenon which belongs in this realm. In the rural areas particularly, but in the cities as well, persons from time to time go *amok*. Such an individual begins without warning to assault anyone in his presence, friend or stranger. His weapon is most frequently a bolo or a gun. He may kill or wound a half dozen people before he is subdued or killed himself. The *amok* phenomenon occurs primarily in the Philippines and in adjacent Malay areas of Indonesia and Malaysia. It should not be equated with the psychotic outbursts of someone who goes berserk in Western countries. The *amok* who survives is not able to give a very coherent account of what happened. It usually turns out that he has been harboring some resentment for a long time and was no longer able to control himself. He has probably been the object of a good deal of gossip and teasing. His behavior may be an indication of his inability to make a modulated expression of negative feelings. In many ways this is the parallel in the adult of the tantrum of the child.

We do not wish to leave the impression that we regard the Filipino emphasis on good relationships as a reaction formation against unrecognized hostility. He is aware that he is angry. At the same time the emphasis does in effect deny or curtail the overt expression of anger. But it is an end in its own right as well, just as achievement or power may be important goals in the lives of others. We must also keep in mind that most Filipinos live most of their lives in the presence of others. Since in a one-room house a mother and her children cannot easily get away from one another, it is of utmost importance that they learn to get along with a minimum of stress. Filipinos do not adopt the alternative solution of outright suppression of children's spontaneity but encourage children to avoid situations which may precipitate friction. Having developed skill in sensing others' sensitivities, they can continue to live together in apparent harmony even after the dependent years of childhood have passed.

It appears that the handling of hostile and angry feelings by members of this society has led to a series of defensive operations which are not so much in evidence in Western societies. These differences spring in part from the realities of the extended family which result in a sort of extended self, in which it is not one person alone who hates or is attacked but his whole family. The members of each group accordingly encourage behavior which will keep them out of trouble. It is this formulation which leads us to avoid the application of psychodynamic principles developed in societies where there is a much greater emphasis on the individual's responsibility for his own behavior.

Comparison with the Findings of Sears, Maccoby, and Levin

There are major differences between our findings in the Philippines and those of Sears in the United States. Although outright aggression against parents, siblings, and peers is punished, the American mother considers some successful aggression against peers not only useful but essential. More than half the American mothers believed that the child should defend himself. To the extent that the child did not fight to his parent's satisfaction, he was actually trained and encouraged. This is a marked contrast to the Philippine ideal of smooth interpersonal relationships at any cost.

Ninety-five per cent of the American mothers reported at least some instances of aggression against the parents themselves. Mothers observed also that children learned ingenious ways to annoy and gain revenge while channeling their aggression into more acceptable behavior. In the Philippines, however, hurt and anger are expressed mainly through silence, pouting, crying, occasional temper tantrums, and extensive teasing, as well as by the indirect method of using a third party as a go-between; but they are seldom manifested in direct aggression. The greatest differences appear when the issue involves fighting with children who are not part of the family. Sixty per cent of Philippine mothers in contrast to 13 per cent of American mothers insist that their children should not fight (Sears, 1957, p. 246).

Aggressive behavior, both physical and verbal, is clearly less tolerated in the Philippines. The Filipinos have, however, evolved an intricate set of interpersonal processes to reduce the sources of irritation without dangerous confrontations of antagonists. The American family gives, superficially at least, an opportunity for less inhibited expression of anger. In addition to differences in degree there are differences in the configuration of expectations and of response habits. The Filipino child is trained to make use of others when he faces a hostile situation. The American child is more often encouraged to settle his own difficulties. In the Philippines it is not possible for children from two families to harbor great resentment while their parents remain good friends or for children to remain friends when their parents are feuding, although this is frequently the case in the United States.

Neither Philippine nor American mothers are permissive when it comes to aggressive action toward either parents or siblings. The American child is encouraged to stand up for his rights, while the Filipino child is encouraged to associate with those who are required to respect his rights. Teasing, *hiya,* and sensitivity are key concepts to the syndrome of characteristics by which the Filipino child deals with angry impulses.

chapter 12

THE CHILD'S FEARS

In our preliminary interviewing we found that Filipino children have several fears which play a considerable role in their lives. Parents use the threat of unseen creatures and of strange people to enforce many of their rules. In addition to a world of elders and siblings whose authority must be reckoned with, there exists a world of fairies, ghosts, spirits of the dead, and gnomes whose goodwill the child must try to maintain. Animals, too, are used as threats, especially on occasions when the animal is felt to be a disguised malevolent sorcerer. Adults, particularly those who are different by reason of physical features or race, may also become threats to disobedient children. Many of these beliefs persist into adulthood and become socially disruptive when a community comes to believe that one of its members is a sorcerer and is responsible for someone's illness or misfortune.

These beliefs are of great antiquity and have persisted side by side with the Catholic religion for several hundred years. In fact, some people use Catholic sacred objects such as crucifixes to ward off the effects of pre-Christian spirits. The beliefs are maintained from one generation to the next partly because they conveniently supplement other methods of controlling children. In the rural Philippines the adjustment a child makes to these phenomenologically real objects may constitute a factor in personality development without an obvious parallel in more secular societies.

In our interviews we tried to find out what the mothers recalled as the early fears and the current fears of their children. So that we might be able to trace the possible origins of these fears, we also asked them if they ever frightened their children into obeying and what techniques they used. Since we know that the parents are not the sole socializing agents in the child's life, we asked them if other people had also used these techniques on their children. We suspected, too, that the mothers' childhood fears would have something to do with the fears of their children and with the threats used, so we asked them to recall the fear threats they received as children.

The Child's Early Fears

Having established through our first interviews that fears appeared when the child was very young, we asked what he was afraid of as a baby. Animals such as pigs, dogs, and cats were reported as being frequent fear objects for 38 per cent of the children. Twenty-four per cent were reportedly afraid of ghosts and the dark. Eight children (3 per cent) were reported as being afraid of cockroaches and two of centipedes and worms. Eight per cent (twenty children) were said to have been afraid of real people, frequently those with big voices and large stomachs. Other fear objects reported were knives and heights. Some children feared being left alone in a room. About 13 per cent of the children, however, were reportedly not afraid of anything when they were babies. Some of the mothers' replies were:

> As a baby she was most afraid of the toy dog which had very big ears. Only when she grew a little older did she show fear of the dark.
> The lizard makes a weird sound with its tail. Even I get the shivers when I hear it. He was most afraid of that as a baby.
> We used to make the sound of the *aswang* [Filipino vampire] and then say *"momo"* [ghosts], and he would be afraid.
> He was afraid of cats and puppies, especially when they got near him.
> As a baby he was afraid of everybody except his father and me. When he was bigger he was afraid of his uncle, whose voice sounds like thunder.

It should be borne in mind that mothers were recalling this information six or seven years after the event, so that it was possible that certain information was not recalled because the present situation offered no reminders. It is probable also that the present situation favored selective recall. The babies' fear of ghosts and of knives, fears that develop only after a certain degree of perceptual development, may be current rather than characteristic of earlier childhood. There was no mention of the startle reaction com-

monly observed in babies at loud noises, sudden confrontation, or
on being dropped or thrown up in the air. There were very few
reports of the turning away reaction (*pangingilala*) often accompanied by crying, common to babies from about the sixth month
whenever they are approached by unfamiliar persons or even by
familiar persons other than the mother. Either *pangingilala* is not
considered a fear reaction, or more specific and adult-oriented fears
suppress its recall.

The Child's Current Fears

We expected and found some modification in the reported fears of
children as they grew older. The differences would have been greater
had recall of early fears been more accurate or had the two sets
of information been solicited more independently. Fear of animals
dropped in frequency from 38 per cent to 12 per cent; fear of ghosts
and of the dark rose from 24 per cent to 48 per cent. Twelve per
cent were reported to be afraid of real people, particularly those
with fear labels such as the afternoon peddler with his bundle on
his head or on his back, or even worse, the bearded, turbanned
Indian peddler, locally named the *Bombay*. Six per cent were afraid
of cockroaches, snakes, worms, and centipedes; 2 per cent of thunder and lightning; and a very few of knives and spears, of heights,
and of being locked up.

> Up to now he is afraid of stout people with big tummies, and
> of drunkards. When he was younger we used to frighten him
> with these, saying that a man's big tummy is full of all the
> naughty children he's eaten.
>
> He doesn't like to be injected because he's afraid of the needle.
> He's also afraid when someone tells him about ghosts.
>
> He is afraid of mad dogs, sometimes of any strange dog, espe-
> cially if the dog has a tail that curls back between the legs
> and is very thin. I guess he's heard enough about all the injec-
> tions he'll have to take if he gets bitten.
>
> He is not afraid of the dark but he is afraid of stories that
> feature the *aswang* [vampire] and *multo* [spirits of the dead].
>
> He did not used to be afraid of anything when he was younger.
> Now that he's grown older he is scared even by the mere men-
> tion of *multo* or *aswang*.

She must have heard from somewhere that the stout janitor eats children. She is very much afraid of him, would go out of her way to avoid him.

She's not afraid of anything her other siblings are afraid of—no *aswang* or *multo* or any frightening story makes her afraid. But in a thunderstorm you can't get her to leave your side or anybody else's side.

She is very much afraid of the dark. As soon as it gets dark you can't send her out or to a different room for anything. Especially when her aunt, who was my sister, died.

Now he says there are no such things as *aswang*, but still he continues to believe that there are ghosts. Also, now he is most afraid of the belt of his father.

He is afraid of nothing but the whip. This is because we do not frighten him with vampires and spirits. I do not want my children to believe any of those things.

Now he is afraid of moving insects, especially the spider.

These quotations give some indication of the change in the children's fears, the overcoming or forgetting of old fears and the learning of new ones. Of the thirty-two children who were not afraid of anything when they were younger, two-thirds continued to have no particular fears, and a third developed fears of insects and crawling things, of animals, of certain people, of spirits, and of the dark. Only half of the ten originally afraid of insects and worms retained fear of them, four are now afraid of ghosts, and one of somebody who eats people. Of the ninety-two children who were originally afraid of dogs, cats, and other animals, only twenty-two remained afraid of them, thirteen have overcome their fear and are now allegedly not afraid of anything. Two-thirds of them have developed some other fear—of insects and snakes, of corpses and live people—and one-third of spirits and of the dark which the spirits supposedly inhabit. Only six of the original twenty who were afraid of certain people have continued to be afraid. Four of them now fear nothing, three have developed fear of insects and the weird mewing of cats at night, six are afraid of ghosts and one has become afraid of lightning. More than 80 per cent of those who were afraid of the dark and of ghosts are still afraid of ghosts, two are afraid of nothing and the rest fear other people, cats, and corpses. Of the twenty-four who were afraid of thunder and lightning, only four have continued to be. Nine of them are now afraid of ghosts, six of corpses and of real people. Fears may shift from one object to another, but they have not disappeared by the age of seven.

Tracing the Origins of Fears

Since it is hardly conceivable that children's fears are spontaneous and unlearned, certain aspects of the child's world in his first six or seven years must have influenced their development. Something had conditioned them to fear certain objects more than others and ghosts and spirits more than objective dangers.

It appears that supernatural beings serve a useful purpose as threats against disobedience. Although the young child is much indulged and older members of the family help in caring for him, large families and the concern of providing for so many members make it necessary that the child learn to temper his demands and the expression of his impulses. The mother has things to do, older siblings have their work and play interests, and older members of the family want quiet, especially at siesta time or at the end of a tiring day. Indulged children will tend to cry. They are active and love to wander about when parents think they should not be out in the hot sun or exposed to the cold night air. Parents cannot watch their children all the time nor can they persuade the children that they see all they do and will therefore be able to punish them when they behave contrary to their parents' rules. To enhance their control they create in their children's minds personages of even greater authority—all-powerful and all-seeing, and sometimes even cruel.

To the question "What do you threaten him with when you want him to obey or to stop crying?" about 50 per cent of the mothers said they used threats of whipping, detention, or denial of wants; about 25 per cent reported that they used fear threats: *momo*, thunder, the cat; and 4 per cent said Jesus or God or the guardian angel would get angry.

"*Ayan na ang pusa . . . mi . . . i . . . yaw!*" (Here comes the cat, meow!) very quickly gets the two-year-old to stop screaming or to close his eyes for sleep, fluttering lids notwithstanding. The peddler with his bundle of wares, a turban on his head, a dagger on his waist used for cutting strings and cloth, is out to kidnap little children who wander out in mid-afternoon. Or the little old man with a long beard who lives in the earth mound by the river (*nuno sa punso*) or the little man (*tiyanak*) in the bamboo clump will take you to his home or make you lose your way, and you will never find your way back home. Or at night that big dark giant (*kapre*) in the big rain tree by the old school house will grab

you and play with you, and you will just die of fright. These creatures and many more (see Guthrie, 1961, pp. 47–58) certainly keep
children home for their naps or for early bedtime and keep them
playing in their own backyards or in the immediate neighborhood.

Sometimes the threats capitalize on the child's earlier fears of
strange or frightening men with "booming voices" and "huge tum-
mies." The child is made to believe that these people will break
their bones or eat them alive if they don't stop crying. There are
also the spirits of dead relatives or neighbors who will visit you
and show themselves to you if you are not good; they have skull
faces, cold hands, and no bodies.

> She wouldn't let me inspect her hair for lice. So she would
> stay for it and keep still, I'd tell her that if I did not catch
> them on time they would multiply so fast and grow wings and
> they'd fly with her over the sea and drop her right in the
> middle.

> He is afraid when I apply tincture of iodine or mercurochrome
> to his bruises. So he'll let me, I say the sting of the medicine
> is better than having a whole carabao come out of that little
> cut, or even grains of rice.

> When I want her to stop doing something I tell her that if
> she does not stop, I'm going to lock her up alone in the dark
> storeroom. We frighten her also with a certain legendary man
> whom children in this place think eats naughty children.

> I'll give you to that blind beggar who comes by our house at
> noon.

> I'll call the witch who lives by the field and get her to eat
> you.

> Somebody goes about getting children, putting them in a sack,
> and dumping them into the river.

> Watch out! The *pusang lampong* [prowler cat] will get you.

> Worms will smell your tears or hear you crying, and they will
> enter your eyes and ears.

> I'll give you to that man who's always here looking for little
> children to take with him.

> I'll get the *Bombay* to eat you.

> Our neighbor is big, stout, and has a long beard. It used to
> be that when I couldn't make her stop crying I'd pretend to
> call for him to come. She'd stop immediately.

> At night I used to tell her that the cat was around so she
> would stop crying. Then somebody would imitate the cat's cry.

> I used to say there's a big man outside. He has very big eyes,
> big teeth, and he will get you if you will not stop crying. Some-
> times I hide myself. Then he will stop.

Her brothers and sisters frighten her when she's hardheaded and won't obey them.

When I can't make her stop crying, I tell her that the thunder hates children's crying, and she stops then.

We don't use any stories or anything that will produce fear. We just tell him that, if he won't stop crying, his guardian angel will go away and will no longer protect him.

We used to frighten her with kittens and dogs. Their cries are especially frightening and sometimes somebody would imitate them. Then she would stop.

I threaten her in order to stop her from doing something I don't want her to do. I say, "If you do it, God will get angry." She stops.

We sometimes threaten him that the *aswang* will come if he does not stop. Or else, we show him the big rod for whipping or his father's belt.

To stop him from doing something we scare him with "The *momo* will eat you" or "There is *Mang Panong* [a huge man whom children believe to eat babies]."

Only slightly more than 10 per cent of the group were not threatened with any fear object at all, and nine of these children (a third of this group) reportedly have no fears. The rest, except for five whose mothers gave no information, somehow did develop certain fears—of an insect, of the cat, of certain people, and of ghosts.

Parents are not the only source of this training in fear. Playmates and siblings like to play pranks on one another, older children on younger children; and frightened squeals and scared giggles can liven up a hot and humid, unexciting afternoon. Of course, we do not know that children's fears start this way; for like teasing, pranks intended to frighten are not played on those who show no fear. Frequently, too, pranksters and victim alike end up being scared.

Her sisters frighten her by telling her "There's a ghost in the dark," but she is not afraid.

Besides the mother, his father, his sister, and grandfather also frighten him by showing him a stick for whipping and telling him he'll not be given any food.

Father used to frighten her with cats when he couldn't get her to stop crying. The maid frightens her too.

When she stays with her uncles and aunts, they frighten her with the legendary man who eats naughty children near their house.

His sister and auntie frighten him. His father, however, does not like our frightening him. He says this sort of thing is not good for children; they will grow up to be nervous.

His auntie frightens him when he goes to her house. They frighten him with the *pugot*, a big, headless man who lives in a big tree, who is believed by the children to kill naughty children. He reports to me that his auntie frightened him. I tell him there is really no such thing as a *pugot*.

In the community children are not barred from wakes and vigils, and they are not deaf to the stories that are most popular on these occasions, accounts of the *multo* (ghosts), the souls of the dead, or of other spirits that fly about at midnight. If they are dubious, they do not have to go far for verification; their grandparents, if not their parents, still believe in these spirits. What youngster has not gone home from one of these gatherings and on his way passed a tree alight with fireflies, believed to be the torches of ghosts, without feeling that a pair of eyeless sockets are staring a hole into the back of his head, or that some soundless, footless thing is following at his heels!

Mothers Recall Their Own Childhood Fears

Almost 40 per cent of the mothers said they were made afraid of ghosts and spirits and of the dark when they were children. Nine per cent were afraid of strange people: the *Bombay* or Indian peddler; the Chinaman speaking a strange tongue, shoulder bent under the load of two balanced sacks heavy with empty bottles and other junk; or some insane woman unkempt and wandering the streets, her laugh shrill, her speech unintelligible, her mien empty or forbidding. About 21 per cent of the mothers could not remember their childhood fears. Eighteen mothers (7 per cent) remembered being threatened with being tied up in a sack as punishment for wrongdoing. Nineteen mothers remembered being afraid of lizards, earthworms, tiny mice, and frogs. Three mothers recalled threats that the crow or the monkey or hair lice would carry them away.

> I used not to be able to sleep when somebody just died. They used to tell me that the dead make visits, especially on the third day, and they touch your feet or your hands and sometimes even your face with cold hands. I used to sleep with the sheet pulled over my face in fear.

They used to frighten me about the *Aetas* [Negritos]. *"Ayan na ang Aeta* [Here comes the *Aeta*]*,"* they'd say.

My mother used to frighten me by saying "The *kapre* is coming. He hears you from that acacia tree."

Their ghost stories were frequent and really frightening. Until now I feared ghosts, although I have learned they don't exist.

1 used to stop making foolishness as soon as they put me inside the sack. I hated to be in there.

They used to frighten me with a certain ghost that wears all white and who walks to town every evening to visit children he hears crying.

They used to frighten me with a *momo,* especially when somebody died.

When I was a child they used to frighten me with weird sounds, the sound that the *aswang* made most especially.

They used to tell me that if I did not strive to be good, they'd get the *Bombay* to carry me away.

The children's fears reported by the mothers examined in relation to the childhood fears recalled by the mothers show one interesting point. Of the 119 children who now fear ghosts and the dark including the fifty-eight who reportedly had these fears even much earlier, 50 per cent were reported by mothers who had the same fears as children. It is interesting, too, that while the recalled childhood fears of mothers showed no difference between groups, more mothers in the first and second groups (52 per cent and 48 per cent) than in the most educated group (35 per cent) reported fear of ghosts and of the dark in their children. The reverse trend shows in fears reported of real, live people. More mothers in the most educated group (25 per cent) than in the second and first groups (15 per cent and 8 per cent) reported this kind of fear in their children. It is possible that higher education has taken the mothers a little farther away from the more traditional belief in spirits and has led them to use different sanctions and point out more real dangers.

A Critical Inspection of Children's Fears

Since Sears, Maccoby, and Levin did not examine American children's fears, we will consider our information in the light of Philippine culture itself. As early as the first century of the Spanish occupation of the country, a number of people commented that the Filipino lives in a crowded world, peopled with two kinds of beings—creatures like himself and beings with other than human qualities but, like him, imbued with feelings and with as much capacity for being pleased or angered. The picture may have changed a little now. The content of these beliefs may have become modified from contact with the world of other peoples—dragons from China and, from the West, Dracula, Frankenstein, steel robots, and Martians. In urban centers particularly, the original picture may even be completely blurred by movies, television, and comic books. Here also people with access to scientific information scoff at the old beliefs, but we do not know how much reversal we would get and how immediate this reversal would be if they were faced with situations that defy available explanations. Perhaps a more accurate description of the situation would be that people fall along a belief-unbelief continuum in this regard. In the rural areas people mass more toward the traditional belief end of the continuum and in the urban areas the massing is more toward unbelief or rational rejection. But even urban children have heard the stories.

Belief in the magical spirits is, to a considerable degree, shared. The *momo* and *multo* are not sole properties of the child's world; they inhabit the greater world of the adult as well. Earlier in the child's life they are convenient instruments for obtaining the child's compliance, whether the adult citing them believes or denies their existence himself. Our information here is not definite, but we suspect that fear threats are used more often when the child is much younger than at the time he is of school age—a practice congruent with the *wala pang isip* concept of the young child. Since one cannot reason with a young child, frightening him into obeying is more convenient. Later when compliance has become habitual or when the child has grown enough to understand, this technique is used less often, although in community myth and legend and in every day pranks these spirits live on.

Lest this discussion of fear threats as an instrument of discipline leave the impression that parents are not concerned at all about children's being afraid, we should recall that extreme fears are believed by some parents to be causes of childhood illness. Some parents admonish their older children not to frighten younger ones, particularly when they know that the child is especially vulnerable in that regard. We know, too, that parents are irritated when the child's fear of the dark or of an anthill on the way interferes with his ability or willingness to go on a necessary errand.

Many questions remain. Is there actual parental concern that children outgrow their fears? How many parents actually try to explain away fears to a child? Or are fears accepted as natural, the child being expected to outgrow immature displays of fear although not necessarily to outgrow fear itself? He may have frequent nightmares from the fears of his waking hours; but as in the handling of the child's dependency, the parent or someone else is there to comfort him, the warmth of a familiar hand to assure him that the cold touch of that strange hand is not real. He will learn to handle his fears for himself as he grows and as he comes to understand more and more society's expectations of him at each stage. He will come to know when he may cry out in fright and run and cling, when he may cower and not be taunted, and when he should conceal his fears.

We do not know the fate of these fears which have been learned very early in childhood. We can find evidence that some are retained throughout life. It would be interesting to speculate about the personality residuals of those fears which the individual says he no longer holds, but our evidence is scanty. It could be that many of these fears assert themselves again when the individual is ill or is in grief or danger. As a threat of punishment for wrongdoing, childhood fears may operate as vaguely experienced admonitions, continuing their social control function without being experienced as vividly as in childhood. It is reasonably certain that childhood fears are not often completely overcome. They were acquired at a stage of learning which tends to produce reactions not readily extinguished or changed with new learning. However, we do not have the evidence which would enable us to infer how many of the security operations of the adult arise out of a need to reduce some of the fears that were learned in childhood.

chapter 13

PARENTAL VALUES
AND CHILD REARING

The child bears his family's name and his family's honor. This custom is not only a matter of tradition or law; it is supported by
a strong and close-knit pattern of relationships among kin. It is
actually a complex system, but it can be expressed in the simple
statement, "The child is an extension of his parents." His parents
are in turn extensions of their parents, continuous with, and representative of, their own families. Had the custom of surnaming not
taken root, a Filipino would be referred to as the child of his parents, grandchild of their parents, nephew of their siblings and
cousins, sibling of their other children, and cousin of their nephews
and nieces. If he is a good man, he does honor to the whole family;
if he commits wrong, the misdeed soils the family name.

The family, thus, has something at stake in each of its members. The child reflects his whole family in all that he is and in
all that he does. From his earliest years he moves in the family
circle, consciously and unconsciously, willingly and unwillingly. He
is trained in their ways; he absorbs their values. Certain behavior
earns praise, and he can read approval in special favors, special
permissions, and in casual parental remarks about him in conversation with other people. Behavior that leads to disapproval is even
easier to identify since scolding and punishment for misdemeanors are prompt and obvious. There is a difference, however;
disapproved matters are discussed only within the family, while
achievements are made public. In their attempts to advise their
children, parents invoke models of good and bad from within the
family itself or from outside. They know what kind of children
they want, and they are provided with a socially sanctioned set
of techniques calculated to produce children who have the qualities
desired. The two central elements in this relationship are a loving,

controlling attitude and an emphasis on the involvement of the whole family.

Our purpose in the terminal portion of the interview was to gain some perspective on the values which parents reported as guides in their treatment of their children. We wanted to know their ideas of a good child and their disappointments. We wanted them to compare their methods with those of their own parents and with those of their neighbors. We felt that a statement of the ideals and hopes of parents would give us a more comprehensive perspective on their relationship with their children.

Parental Expectations for the Child

Our information in this area is based on answers to three questions in the interview concerning what the mothers enjoyed or liked most about their children, what made them angriest, and how they might like them to grow up differently from other children.

The valued traits that were mentioned most frequently were expressiveness, alertness, and intelligence (29 per cent); thoughtfulness and maturity, generosity and affectionateness (20 per cent); and obedience, respectfulness, and honesty (17 per cent). More specifically valued in the first group of traits mentioned was a good memory for songs and poems with good ability for learning and for expressive rendition. Ability to learn was desired by a considerably higher percentage in the least educated group than in the other two groups. This difference may indicate an actual higher value placed on overt learning ability by hopeful parents in the first group or a different pattern of response influenced by their connecting the interviewers with the school system.

The traits that parents valued in their children reflect various feelings. Some answers exude simple fondness or joy in the trait itself; others suggest a contribution to parental convenience; still others show a tinge of pride in the trait as an achievement of their child.

> She is a good and quiet child, and she's never given me any cause for worry.
> She is cute and sweet, the prettiest of my children!
> She has never been a crybaby and has therefore never been a bother at all.

He is very kind. I just want him to stay like he is.

He is so studious I think he will get to be a doctor some day. And he is very obedient, too.

He is so alive and comical. I love it when he tells funny stories.

He uses words as if he were an old person. From the age of five he has shown that he can reason wisely.

He is a happy child and has a smile for everyone who comes to our house. He is very respectful, too.

She hears something on the radio and in no time at all she is able to sing it, or if it is a poem, she picks it up in no time at all. She is the same way with dances.

The ability to perform and entertain at an early age is greatly valued. Visitors and relatives, as well as parents and siblings, show great interest when a four-year-old is invited or, if necessary, coerced to sing. They are not particularly patient if the child is too anxious to perform. Parents also encourage children to join in the work of grown-ups, and even though it takes longer, they have the child help them in many phases of the daily chores. Even in cities, working mothers may take their children to the office with them. Finally, the widespread emphasis on responding to the feelings of others is manifested by early training in affectionateness and respect.

Disapproved Behavior

The other side of the coin, what connected with the child makes the mothers angriest, complements the mothers' statements concerning positive traits. Actions that mothers did not like and therefore reprimanded most frequently were: not answering when spoken to, withdrawing when crossed on unreasonable demands, not coming at once when called, and doing work grudgingly. The mothers also disapproved of playing outside the yard or being out on the streets most of the time, because the children were not available when they were needed, or the mother could not keep track of what was happening to them. Also disapproved were making siblings cry, being noisy, disorderly, quarrelsome, lying, and using unseemly words. More specific statements of behavior that parents considered undesirable are the following:

She won't leave her elder siblings' things alone, and reminding her over and over does not seem to help.

She's asking for money all the time—five centavos for this, five centavos for that. She's quite a spendthrift, that child.

He cannot seem to control himself when other people are visiting. Sometimes, even in the presence of other people, I am forced to punish him.

Showing off when there are visitors in the house makes me most angry. Sometimes I can't help pinching her.

I get irritated when I have to repeat myself to her several times. I tell her she should pay more attention.

She forgets to wash her hands sometimes, when she eats. And sometimes she is very noisy. But I really get angry with her when she shows any sign of disobedience.

When there are visitors at home, we do not want her to be staying around, because it is not good manners for children to mingle with older people. They disturb the conversation, particularly when they are noisy.

Ideal Behavior

Asked what they disliked in their particular child, the mothers tended to be preoccupied with concerns of the moment, with very specific behavior that they were finding inconvenient or irritating at the time. The question, "How would you like your child to be different from other children?" demanded that the mothers think in terms of more long range goals. What do they really want to make of their children?

Twenty-three per cent wanted their children to be tractable and unspoiled so that they would be secure in the future and able to take care of themselves. Five per cent added that this is why they believe in being a little strict. A common saying is, "A little 'no' now will go a long way later." About 9 per cent stated the belief that the child needs the parents' understanding, careful surveillance, and constant reminding. Eighteen per cent wanted the child to be obedient and respectful, concerned about parents and siblings; *sino pa kaya ang magtitinginan!* (who else should look after one another!). Parents disliked children who grow up uncaring about the past, *di marunong lumingon sa pinanggalingan* (who do not care to look back). Quiet and contented children were the desire of 9 per cent of the mothers who felt their children should not prefer the company of their friends out on the streets to being at home with their families. A sizeable group (13 per cent) expressed concern over the good health of the children, their being well-fed and well provided for in terms of material comforts. Five per cent wanted their children to grow up alert and intelligent, not nervous and inhibited. They felt that excessive self-consciousness is a result of unreasonable strictness on the part of parents.

> We are trying to inculcate in him those virtues that every good Christian should have. We believe this is the most important of our duties to him.
> I would like to see them grow up and raise their families. I want them to be homebodies, not like those young people who are always out on the streets exchanging gossip.
> I want her to be honest and frank with me—not to just keep sullen when she has a grievance or to murmur.
> I would like her to be well-educated, to be successful afterward, and to be well-mannered.
> I don't want them to be used to the luxuries of living.
> I want my child to be religious and to be diligent in his studies. I don't want my children to be too spirited.
> I would like her to be religious, to go to church not only on Sundays but also on other days of obligation.
> I would like my children to feel that we have duties to them, but they in turn have duties to us, their parents.
> I would like him to feel the value of time—that there should be time for playing, time for work, and time for rest.

These are statements of parents' goals for their children, but they are also a confession of the parents' own values. In stating their expectations for the child, they also define what they expect of themselves as parents. The qualities desired are many of those which preserve family solidarity. To an outsider, these qualities would appear to be docility, subordination to elders, and a suppression of individual ambitions. For participants, it is experienced as respect for the wisdom of older people, gratitude to parents for having been born, and a recognition of the greater good of the family as a whole.

These ideals express the Philippine goal of smooth relationships with others. The individual avoids overt conflict; he makes his parents happy by his cheerfulness; and he shows a pattern of personal pride. Above all, parents want their children to have good dispositions. Interestingly, parents do not express the hope that their children will be ambitious or show great achievements. There is no mention of a child becoming rich or famous. On the contrary, they stress the hope that their child will be attendant to family values. The mother acknowledges that what she does will have much to do with her child's later behavior. She firmly believes that a child's behavior is an expression of his parents' attitudes. She will receive credit if he approaches family and community ideals, and it will be her fault if he fails. There is little escape behind genetic or constitutional factors. These mothers are environmental determinists, whether they know it or not. Not all of them, of course, make explicit their ideas of the responsibilities which parenthood entails, but this may be due to the limitations of the interview situation in which they are led to discuss only immediate matters.

Comparison with Methods of Their Parents

We asked the mothers to recall if there was any difference between the way they were reared and the way they are now rearing their children. Sixty-four per cent of the whole group saw no difference; they were rearing their children now the way they remembered their mothers reared them. But looking at the three groups of mothers separately, we find most mothers making the *no difference* response in the least educated group (71 per cent), and the fewest in the most educated group (41 per cent), while the second group came between (61 per cent). The more frequently cited differences are "My children get better care," and "My parents were very strict; I am more liberal with my children." Five mothers, however, thought their parents had been too lenient, and they were more strict with their children now. Three mothers thought they were as strict and careful as their parents but in different ways. Four mothers said they try to give their children whatever they want because their parents could not afford this for them when they were children. Four mothers said they teach their children certain things that their parents failed to teach them, such as handling money, keeping house, and the need for learning and finishing school.

> I am raising my children the way our parents raised us. I think they did very well by us.
> I am raising them the way I was raised. I think the old ways are better than the new ways. During those days the parents

were really responsible and concerned with their children, but now other parents take children for granted. From my observation they will play *mahjong* or go to a show and leave their children under the guidance of the nursemaid. This is especially true with those well-to-do families like our neighbors. Sometimes even if their children are really at fault they will not even talk to them or beat them.

I am raising my children differently from the way I was raised. I give my children the best comforts of life that my husband and I can afford. I give them the best food and clothes. I give them all the love they need. Why? Because I know now that they need these things, and it is my duty to give them what I know they need. My parents did not know this.

I am raising them a little differently, like seeing to it that they fix their own things, that they eat right, and that they attend school regularly.

I don't want to be too strict with my children because they will not be close to me. I use modern psychology on my children.

We take them to the clinic or to the hospital for any treatment. I never acceded to my old folks' advice that I see an *herbolario* [herb doctor].

My parents were very strict. But I believe in being more liberal and democratic.

My parents were too poor and ignorant to provide me with what I now provide my children.

My mother worked as a seamstress, and my brother and I found ourselves left alone. Now I don't want my children being left alone, and I worry lest anything happen to them.

I grew up with my grandmother and they were very strict with me even when I was still tiny. My children are very free, on the other hand, and by the mercy of God we are still alive to look after them.

In the same way that a significantly lower percentage in the most educated group said that their child-rearing techniques were not any different from those of their mothers, a significantly higher percentage said their children get better care now than they themselves did as children. Better care, according to their statements, appears to mean less use of superstitions and more use of current knowledge about children. Typical examples of the responses made to this effect follow:

I am more modern than my mother, but I still expect my children to be respectful. I don't want them to get in the habit of talking back to their parents.

I still say I learned most of it from my mother. But civilization is a little different now—then we didn't call a doctor for the little things. Now a little warm feel of the palm and the doctor at once.
I learned much more from the doctor. I remember that mother wouldn't give us a bath or trim our nails on days that spell with an *r*, and, of course, those things don't bother me now.
I do what I see produces good results in addition to doing the things I remember mother used to do with her children.
My children go to bed early, bathe daily, and eat a lot of fruits and vegetables. They are more free to mix with their friends, too, and go to children's parties. When we were children we were not allowed to bathe on Fridays, or to eat fruit early in the morning, or to play with the neighbors enough.
I remember how they used to close all the windows at night when a child had a cold. And she was not permitted to take a bath either. I don't follow these old ways. And I see to it, too, that my children do not eat just anything.
My parents did not know then how to keep us from skin infections and all that. I am very careful with my children about those things. I don't let my children handle everything, or sit just anywhere.

Most mothers still go to their own mothers or older relatives when they need advice on child rearing, although about a fourth of the whole group insisted that they had developed their techniques on their own. In the interview the mothers could give only a more general statement, and this largely of attitude, not an incident by incident account of how they handle the day-by-day conflicts that constantly arise between conviction and practice. We know that mothers, the most educated group especially, have drawn more and more from sources other than tradition for advice and suggestions. They gleaned information from books and pamphlets and from doctors and nurses now available even to the rural people through health units and puericulture centers. Half of the mothers in the most educated group reported having drawn from these nonfamily sources, in contrast to 10 per cent and 22 per cent in the first and second groups respectively.

I do what I remember my mother used to do, and in addition I learned quite a few things in school, too.
I have my own way of rearing my children, but once in a while I seek the advice of my parents.
My ways are a mixture of what I learned from older people, from the doctor, and from my readings. I've read Dr. Spock's *Baby and Child Care.*

I learned quite a few things from the physician who attended me at delivery. Also, I obtained information from books and from my married friends.

Comparison with Methods of Other Parents

We felt that we would probably gain more insight into the mothers' definitions of parenthood and its responsibilities if we asked them to comment on the child-rearing practices of people other than themselves and their parents. Thus, we asked the following: What mistakes do other parents make in raising their children? Is there anything your relatives do in raising their children that you would disagree with? What are these? How would you like your child to be different?

Only twenty-one of the mothers (8 per cent) declined to give any criticism, fifteen of them saying that their neighbors' practices were not any different from theirs and six finding justification in "I don't pry into what they do." The greatest concern (38 per cent) appears to be a too permissive policy with children, overindulgence, not setting any limits, and being afraid to exercise authority or use discipline on them. This concern expresses the sentiment of the national epic poet, Balagtas, when he writes:

> He who is raised in relative ease tends to grow up wanting in good counsel and judgment. He is the sorry fruit of mistaken caring, of a parent's pity for the child she so loved.

Fourteen per cent of the mothers were concerned that some parents are negligent and do not take time to teach their child what he should know; they leave the development of the "right" values to chance. Balagtas' poem continues on this same theme:

> What makes for a bad child springs from babying and ill-advised love, and from neglect by the lazy parent whose duty it is to have taught him well.

Another parental characteristic that quite a few mothers deplored is selfish negligence, indulgence of the self and neglect of the children. This is contrary to the Filipino tradition that parents should make sacrifices for their children because they brought them into the world. The parent, in regarding her needs above her child's needs, invites criticism. Other faults of parents cited are overstrictness, overprotectiveness, and superstition. Twenty-one mothers (8 per cent) deplored both extremes—too much parental pressure and too much leniency. About 5 per cent of the mothers denounced unfairness and unreasonableness in some parents. Unwillingness to listen to the child or a tendency to side with her own child indiscriminately were also subjects of criticism.

When they compare themselves with others, the Philippine mothers find little difference between their own and their parents' practices, but they feel that the majority of other parents are neglectful or too permissive. It would appear that the conviction that a child is almost wholly the product of his parents' teaching has led our respondents to be very defensive about their own family traditions. The same belief has led them to be critical of those outside of the family.

I want my child to be good and obedient and not always away with his friends somewhere.

Some parents don't allow their children to play with their neighbor's children. They let them play with dirty things and they let them not take a bath when they don't want to. They tolerate the children's coming home late at night.

It is a mistake to show lavish love to children, to punish them too much, or to give them everything they want.

Kulang sa pangaral [They are lacking in advice]. They don't teach their children to be good Catholics. They are too harsh in punishing their children. They don't let their children help in household chores. Parents themselves are not too harmonious in their dealings with each other.

They try to get obedience and respect from the children by scoldings and whippings which only scare them and make the children curse their parents.

Some parents let their children play morning and afternoon and do not even know who their playmates are.

Some parents are so neglectful and uncaring that their children wander about unkempt and rude, too.

Other parents are too democratic, and their children grow up carefree. I want my children to grow in self-discipline, and I want them to finish their studies.

I do have something against the way they beat their children. I use only my hand when I spank, and I look after what hurt I've done afterward so they know I forgive them.

Some of my relatives do not want their children to continue their studies. They should not have that attitude even though poor. As parents they should find ways of helping their children through school, since education is the best inheritance that parents can give.

Some kind of a Filipino ideology appears to emerge from all these, a mixture of the old and the new; the product of each generation's striving to improve upon its own knowledge yet maintain that which has been instilled by tradition as good. Basically these seem to be the elements of this ideology, particularly among the more literate and articulate:

1) Parents should love their children even above themselves, but this love should not be lavish or blind. There is room in love for control and no room for foolish pity and unwarranted sheltering.

2) Training in the basic values of obedience, respect, and dignity is a prime responsibility. A parent should not be stingy in his advice or sparing in his punishment when the situation demands it.

3) Parents should not be lenient but neither should they be too strict. The children should find them reasonable, friendly, and willing to listen. Children can reason agreeably if they are taught.

4) A mother has the right and responsibility to know a child's private thoughts so that she can guide his thinking and advise him properly.

5) Advice is not enough. Parents should be good models, too.

6) Children are young and they need a parent's constant watching. They should be fed correctly, clothed, kept clean. Parents should keep track of their children's comings and goings and of the company they keep.

7) Children should not be spared from participating in the household chores. They develop skills for later life this way and also learn to be responsible.

8) Schooling is a parent's best legacy to his children. Nothing should be spared to insure them an education.

Parental Values and a Changing Culture

In the past the Philippine culture was one in which there were few choices beyond those sanctioned by the entire society. There was no looking outward or comparison of Filipino values with those of other cultures. The Filipino of the past felt he was living the one possible way in which he could live. If he heard of different ways of life, he dismissed them as unworkable for him.

However, as contact with Western culture and its values has

increased, Filipinos, especially the young and educated, have become more willing to question traditional values and customs. This is not to say that the younger generation in the Philippines has abandoned tradition, for this is far from the actual situation. Today young people are thinking about the ways of their parents in contrast to the new ways. The typical result of this questioning is a mixture of old patterns with elements of newer ones. The expectations for children appear to be the traditional ones; parents still expect respect and obedience from their children. But the foundations of these values, from the child's viewpoint, are no longer the same. In the past children respected and obeyed their parents because of gratitude and acknowledged parental superiority; now respect and obedience are ideally given to the parents out of love. However, there is still a sense of the child's indebtedness to the parents by virtue of their parenthood and merit.

The parents in our study had looked back into their childhood and remembered their parents' ways with them. The majority said they were rearing their children their mother's way, but a growing number are aware that they have started to change. These are largely the younger mothers and usually those who have had some college education. They remembered what they had resented as children and had decided these matters should not be repeated with their own children. Some of these decisions had probably undergone modification as the young adults started to see things from the standpoint of parents and as they found wisdom and reason in what before had appeared unfair and unreasonable. But apparently this early motivation for change did leave them open and more sensitive to the possible conflicts their children face and more cognizant of children's capacities for understanding.

Generally speaking, however, Filipinos are proud of their way of life, regarding with suspicion and contempt those who compromise what they think is important. What change there is has occurred in metropolitan areas. There is probably little questioning of traditional values in rural areas, particularly values which involve the life of the family.

chapter 14

CONCLUSIONS

We began this research with three purposes: to describe the patterns of relationships between Philippine mothers and their children, to compare these data with American findings, and to examine the results to see if they shed any light on the problems of personality formation in both Philippine and American cultures. The descriptive aspect of our research represents a selection from all of the observations that could have been made; as such it is subject to biases and omissions. Almost certainly the similarity of American and Filipino childhood experiences has been exaggerated because the selection of aspects to be considered has been dominated by earlier research done almost without exception in Western cultures. Comparisons suffer for similar reasons. The aspects of dependency, for instance, are considered almost entirely along dimensions of dependency in Western cultural configurations. Finally, when we interpret anything, we use concepts which differ depending on whether we are dealing with an electrical, a physiological, or a political event. As events become less dramatically different there is a temptation to use the same concepts for two sets of events, such as behavior patterns in two different cultures, and in the process to obscure important differences. This may or may not lead to difficulty. There is no difficulty, for instance, in reporting that one man struck another; but we may meet problems in trying to interpret the event because our concepts may not adequately characterize the feelings which prompted the act. The same problem arises if we try to account for an assaultive act by a psychotic person without using concepts from psychopathology.

Our three purposes, of description, comparison, and interpretation, are beset by problems arising out of differences not only in degree but also in the configurations of motives and possibly in the nature of the motives themselves. In this research we have found that there are new factors, such as the extended family, which must be included in our descriptions. Behavior patterns take on new meanings; dependency is approved and interpreted in the framework of respect. Novel patterns, such as *hiya*, have also been taken into account and we have retained their Philippine names to emphasize their more or less untranslatable surplus meaning.

Personality theorists and clinical psychologists have placed a good deal of emphasis on problems in handling sexual, hostile, and dependent impulses. There are other domains of personality conflict, but these are among the most important. The Philippines offers a new perspective on each of these potentially troublesome areas of personality integration. Certainly there are controls on the expression of sexual urges, but the controls would appear to permit a shift of role with circumstances that does not appear possible for those who have been raised in Western society. Homosexuality must be re-evaluated if transvestism and associated homosexual practices can be assumed and put aside as easily as appears to be the case in the Philippines. Dependency becomes a conflictful area only where it is disapproved. In the Philippines taking help from others seems to be a tolerable pattern and is not the matter of conflict that it is in the West. Hostility, however, can become a serious problem in extended families. The dynamics of hostility and its relationship to sensitivity would warrant much careful observation. The instinctual nature of sexuality and hostility which has been postulated on the basis of clinical observations is called into question by our Philippine observations. Both systems of behavior show considerable variation under the impact of Philippine socialization; differences which cast doubt on instinctual formulations.

Philippine Childhood

Even before a child is born in a *nipa* house, with a midwife or *hilot* in attendance, he has been an object of concern to his mother. Believing in maternal impressions, she has sought through diet, mental concentration, and other activities to make sure that she bears a child with the desired physical and personality features. Immediately after birth, the placenta may be disposed of in a way calculated to insure certain qualities of character.

Since the baby is breast-fed on demand for a period of many months, feeding becomes an occasion for close continued contact with the mother. Food remains an important social stimulus throughout life. Continued contact in the feeding situation coincides with the development of an extensive dependency pattern which is encouraged and approved. At the same time obedience is demanded with the threat of stern punishment. This is augmented by prolonged periods of advice giving. Health and cleanliness measures are kept at levels commensurate with the demands of the environment.

The sexual interests and incipient sexual activities of the child are apparently recognized within each family constellation, but outside the family the topic is not discussed. There is a marked double standard as far as adult heterosexuality is concerned which apparently begins in childhood with earlier concern for female children. In a process which we do not fully understand, the child is encouraged to develop controls over sexuality without surrounding the activity with threats that interfere with later sanctioned heterosexual behavior. Hostility and aggression are special problems because of the pressures of an extended family and as an outgrowth of extensive teasing. Modesty, respect, and self-control, accompanied by a sanctioned pattern of insecurity (*hiya*), serve to suppress expression of anger. It would seem that teasing plays a role in the indirect expression of anger and at the same time denies an opportunity for a hostile outburst.

The child's behavior is also modified and controlled by a world of nonhuman creatures, not often seen but usually vividly present, ready to trick or harm careless or disobedient children. Fairies, sorcerers, and gnomes are accepted by many adults who learned of them before an age of critical judgment and who pass these beliefs on to children at the optimum age for lifelong retention.

In the Filipino family, children are wanted, numerous, guided, indulged, teased, and intimidated, but rarely ignored. Children are important, an extension of the family, recipients of the family's fortunes and fate. They are the center of concern of parents, siblings, cousins, and others related only by friendship and ritual bonds. In spite of the fact that many adults are willing to assume responsibility for him, the child's wishes and preferences are taken into account. A parent may seek to persuade a child to change his mind but is loath to use his strength or position to impose his will in a completely arbitrary fashion.

With many others to please and little opportunity or encouragement to be alone, the child's major responsibility lies in keeping good relationships. *Hiya* serves as a threat if he fails to maintain proper respect and obedience patterns. He learns to compromise and defer and to draw some of his satisfaction from the activities of those around him. He has some special privileges if he is the youngest, but none for being male or female. As he grows, the consensus of expectations shifts, and more adult patterns are valued while behavior appropriate to an earlier age is teased without much mercy. The shift is made easy by the fact that there are few activities from which children are excluded.

American Childhood

An American child's birth epitomizes some of the contrasts with the Filipino's experiences. The former is most frequently born in an impersonal environment removed from the home with relatives and siblings excluded. Medications and unseen masked attendants sometimes render the whole delivery process not only impersonal but completely amnesic. Newborn babies are infrequently breast-fed. During these first four or five days of life they are shown only to nuclear family members and are particularly shielded from the spontaneous interest of siblings. Feeding and toilet training become private issues, as much for the convenience of the mother as for the welfare of the child. An American mother does not as a rule share her child-rearing duties with relatives or at times even with her husband. Possibly because she is so predominantly the source of attention, rivalry may develop between siblings, a condition which is less likely where many adults are available to attend to the children. By the same token, all of her children are seeking ways to please her, because she alone offers predictable attention or displeasure.

There are other important contrasts. The American mother is much more concerned with the appropriate sex role. Boys and girls may be treated equally but are expected to be somewhat different. Uniqueness rather than family values may be stressed. Hostility and assertion are not so disruptive where only two or three people are involved. A child is encouraged to be himself, even at the expense of the complete approval of neighbors and friends. Achievement, not enjoyment, is often the first goal for the child. His age level is emphasized to him in many ways, and he is subtly denied opportunities to play with those who are markedly older or younger than he is at the moment. Since he plays outside his family, he can quarrel and change friends; he does not have to learn to live in peace with everyone. He can develop and assert his own interests without upsetting the precarious balance of an extended family which emphasizes interdependence. At the same time he has only a few people who will give him unqualified acceptance; and even they usually expect him to take care of himself. He becomes relatively as insensitive to others' feelings as they are to his. Independence, achievement, and, later, sexual attractiveness become important goals. An individual is encouraged to look to his own resources, to develop the capacity to take care of himself. He is expected to seek the support of his family only when he encounters obstacles which he cannot overcome himself.

Philippine Adult Interpersonal Patterns

We cannot leave our description of child rearing without asking what kind of adult follows from such childhood experiences. This description has been developed more or less independently of the preceding chapters. We do not expect it to agree completely with our research information, because we are not convinced that there is a compelling reason why certain adult patterns must inevitably follow a given childhood experience. There is probably a certain congruity, but on the other hand, no society fails to have role expectations of children different from those of adults. Among adults there are shared expectations in interpersonal patterns; adults share definitions of other adults in the same way that they share definitions of children, definitions which change with age. Looking at things this way we may proceed to an examination of the prevailing interpersonal patterns of adult Filipinos and seek some of the continuities from childhood to adulthood.

We have chosen to begin with a Filipino's description of his own people. D. F. Batacan (1956) in his study of the traits of the Filipinos reports:

> . . . hardly a dissenting voice will be heard in protest should we proclaim our so-called virtues and admirable qualities as a people. In the order of their universal recognition we would gladly enumerate them with the greatest ease, as follows: (1) hospitality, (2) modesty, (3) politeness, (4) bravery and patriotism, (5) patience and ability to bear pain, (6) love of

home and devotion to family ties, (7) high sense of personal dignity, (8) religiousness and love for Christian principles.

Enumerated without regard to the prevalence or gravity of the various ailments, our peculiar traits which I consider undesirable and which need early attention and remedy are: (1) the *mind your own business* attitude . . . , (2) the *keeping up with the Santoses* behavior, (3) the *Bahala na* attitude or fatalism, (4) fondness for fiestas, (5) the siesta habit, (6) overdoses of *amor propio* or extreme sensitiveness, or excessive self-pride, (7) poor sportsmanship and vindictiveness, (8) tendency to engage in gossip, (9) the *Ningas Kugon* behavior or rapid loss of initial enthusiasm for a project, (10) jealousy and envy. (pp. 1–2, 3)

Batacan shows the willingness of Filipinos, referred to in our opening pages, to discuss both what they consider positive and what they consider negative about themselves. It is interesting that Batacan devoted two and one half pages to a discussion of virtues and divided the remaining three hundred pages between a discussion of his list of undesirable traits and an exploration of these traits in teachers, businessmen, politicians, and others. Finally in the last part he invited "the reader to meditate on the teachings of our heroes and martyrs." Filipinos can indeed be very critical of nonfamily members and of their government, but they tend to idealize parents and national heroes.

Batacan's list of virtues has been affirmed by visitors to the Philippines including the earliest Spanish invaders. A stranger is welcomed and made to feel important, often to the stranger's embarrassment if he is not accustomed to such a degree of hospitality. Modesty, dignity, and politeness permeate relationships not only with strangers but within the family as well. Filipinos are patient, letting each person take his own time. They do not complain when things go wrong; rather they react minimally to their own and to others' distress. This is a society which wants people to be happy, and they spare no effort to make others enjoy themselves, for in doing so they feel happy themselves. At the same time they keep smiling when things go wrong, since it is bad taste to show one's unhappiness and annoyance.

But all is not blissful, and inevitable stresses and strains arise. The price Filipinos pay for their contentment includes procrastination, fatalism, a lack of awareness of the needs of people outside their circle of family and friends, a hypersensitivity to the attitudes of others, and a good deal of difficulty handling the feelings that arise when they lose a contest. Dependent as they are on the opinion of others for their own feelings of personal worth, they expend a good deal of effort making sure that they are well regarded and taking precautions that they are not badly regarded. For this reason gossip and criticism become very powerful weapons with which to attack someone. They are the favored methods of expressing annoyance and resentment.

The central role of the family in the life of the Filipino has been asserted by almost everyone who has written about Filipinos. Good discussions have been offered by Stoodley (1957) and Fox (1961). We have discussed the family in our chapter on dependency. Each individual is both dependent on, and depended on by, his extended family. His reference group is his relatives. He finds it is best if his views coincide more or less with theirs. As a result he has little experience with impersonal situations, and he often feels uncomfortable if he is forced to remain long in a situation where he cannot give and receive personalized responses.

The family pattern becomes, in many ways, the prototype of interpersonal patterns. A politician behaves like a benevolent father in many ways; he is expected to use all the means at his disposal to help those who have family and quasi-family relationships with him. Much of the respect and submissiveness expected by parents has its counterpart in the politeness and deference shown by Filipinos toward older and important people. In the Tagalog dialect, for instance, the word *po* is inserted when one addresses any older person to carry with it an expression of respect, something akin to the use of *sir* in English. Similarly, the tranquility and unanimity cherished within the nuclear family is also cherished and idealized in nonfamily contacts. The Filipino seems to have little chance to learn the technique of dealing with persons who do not seek peace. There are few methods short of ostracism to handle someone who complains bitterly. When his complaints are shared, cliques are formed. Peace is difficult to restore and often comes about through the agencies of third parties. The Filipino has more trouble with those relationships which he cannot handle within family patterns.

Rarely is a Filipino by choice on his own or alone in a situation. If we wish to understand him, we must see him where he feels best, in the context of his family. This results in a sort of extension of self so that his successes are those of the family, and the grief of another member is his as well. He works to enhance the position of his family, since he will be evaluated by their reputation and not by his alone. They control him because he can quite literally get them into trouble. In a land where vengeance patterns are still strong, a wrongdoing involving one member, involves all members; dishonor to one is disgrace to all. Within this situation dependability and discretion are to be desired; initiative and innovation are risky. A family member learns to show his agreement with family views and to keep his reservations and disagreements to himself.

In many situations outside the family the Filipino would rather not become involved in long range commitments unless there is a good deal of flexibility in the arrangement. Above all he finds it hard to tolerate prolonged periods of stress between himself and those with whom he is working. If things become uncomfortable, he may quit, even though real hardship may follow while he is out of a job. His security lies more in the goodwill of those with whom he has to deal than in the amount of money he is earning. To achieve this, the Filipinos have developed the fine art of keeping their strongest feelings to themselves and of compromising with others. Lynch (1962) pointed out that Filipinos achieve smooth interpersonal relationships through courtesy in face-to-face contacts, euphemism, and where things are really touchy, the use of an intermediary or go-between.

Another important element in the interpersonal pattern of Filipinos is the pattern obligations or *utang na loob* described by Hollnsteiner (1962). When a Filipino does a favor for another, he expects to receive a favor in return at some later date which the giver of the favor may specify. The relationship is not, however, terminated by the return of a favor; a more extended relationship of obligation is involved in which each may look to the other according to need and according to ability to help. Favors include loans of money, recommendations for jobs, introductions, and almost any form of help. Within the framework of this relationship, one can seek assistance rather freely and not feel uncomfortably indebted. The whole society maintains the effectiveness of this system by disapproving strongly of someone who is *walang utang na loob*, without a sense of his debts.

Still another concept that is of great importance in understanding how Filipinos feel and think is the concept of *hiya* which we have mentioned in connection with teasing and sensitiveness as a mixture of shame, embarrassment, and inferiority feelings. There can be many occasions which give rise to *hiya:* someone fails an examination; a marriage proposal made with others' knowledge is rejected; one does not have money to properly clothe one's children; or one has been scolded by an elder. The experience is deeply painful to a Filipino, and he will go to great lengths to avoid it. It would appear that this is such a distressing experience of such duration that lifelong decisions result from it; at least Filipinos have offered a good many accounts, some autobiographical, of the traumatic nature of this experience.

It is very easy to hurt the feelings of a Filipino. Slight matters appear to cause great distress, and a direct outspoken criticism is catastrophic. This is the *amor propio* to which Batacan refers, an inability to tolerate negative evaluations from others, a trait closely related to *hiya*. School children quit school because teachers criticize them. Employees resign because they have been reprimanded. Foreigners, such as Americans, are feared because they are so blunt.

The dangers arising from excessive sensitivity are avoided by indirect statements, euphemisms, and go-betweens which enable one to thoroughly determine the state of mind of the other before one raises a difficult issue. Coincident with this deliberately tangential approach, a Filipino watches his listener carefully for any postural or intonational cues which would enable him to learn what the other is feeling. One Filipino summed it up by saying he never asked a question before he knew what the answer would be. Filipinos have an almost uncanny skill in determining the feelings of others. The nonverbal communication is enhanced by the use of euphemism and indirect expressions which are facilitated by Philippine languages. The result of all of this is that much more in the way of messages has passed back and forth between the participants than has actually been said.

In addition to avoiding slights, the Filipino is exceedingly anxious to make the other person feel good. For this reason he will show great respect and politeness, and often exaggerate the importance of the other person to his face. Filipinos see this for what it is and enjoy it; for to fail to do it raises risks of painful, blunt conversation. This is not to be equated with the American's urge to be loved. The gist of a Filipino saying is that it doesn't matter if you like me, just so long as you don't shame me. A great deal of the vagueness of Philippine planning springs from this desire to keep everybody happy. In the same spirit the national legislature tends to work toward unanimity on legislation even though the majority party may have the votes to pass any bill it chooses to support. But this would make enemies, and to avoid ill will, politicians engage in a great deal of give and take until legislation moves ahead with virtual unanimity. Debate in this type of society can be hazardous, but surprisingly, one of the popular forms of entertainment is *Balagtasan* or debate in rhyme. In this form it is safe, but in political campaigns where personal attacks reach a very un-Philippine pitch the followers of various politicians become so caught up in the fight that a good deal of civil disorder may ensue. After such an affair it is not sufficient for the politicians to agree to bury the hatchet. They have a reconciliation and emerge smiling happily with arms around one another. Then their followers warily follow suit, for the peace may not last. But for the moment at least, that happy state of affairs in which people feel good about one another exists. And the controversial issues which Westerners keep worrying about are set aside to be dealt with only if they cannot be avoided.

Contrasts between Philippine and American Patterns

At the end of many of our chapters we have offered a comparison of our findings with those of Sears, Maccoby, and Levin (1957). We have discussed in a number of places in this report the difficulties we have encountered in attempting to compare American and Philippine child-rearing practices. The greatest differences between our data and those of Sears occurred in the answers to the first three questions of the second part of the interview (p. 215). Ninety per cent of our sample reported breast-feeding, 85 per cent for more than six months, whereas only 15 per cent of the American mothers breast-fed for more than three months. Weaning, according to our tables, is not greatly different from Sears' findings. However, weaning in America means giving up the bottle, whereas in the Philippines it means giving up breast-feeding and sleeping beside the mother. In the Philippines, weaning is a matter of social separation and in poorer homes probably an occasion for hunger and beginning undernourishment. The constellation of events is much more extensive for the Filipino child, involving a great modification of relationships in addition to a change in mode of obtaining food. The difference is made greater by the fact that the American mother has introduced many baby foods prior to weaning, whereas the

Philippine mother has relied almost entirely on her milk as a food for the child.

Bowel training is not directly comparable because in the Philippines a child must learn a rather difficult skill of washing himself after a bowel movement. Since siblings and adults assist him, his ability to take care of himself, which is the criterion of being trained, is delayed. This difference in task and in definition accounts in part for the observation that only 20 per cent of Philippine children are considered trained by twenty-four months, while 80 per cent of American children are on their own by the same age. Again, the difference between the situations is not a single difference but many differences which make toilet training a very different set of events in the two countries. In America, the mother, who is usually the only other person connected with this activity, is more or less impersonally concerned with the mechanics of elimination. A secretive and somewhat negative aura surrounds the training period. Satisfactory completion is greeted with relief. In contrast, in the Philippines adults and older siblings all watch the child for signs of impending elimination and also participate in washing the child afterwards. In many instances there is no special private place for elimination. Training is prolonged, becoming an occasion for helpfulness and closeness rather than a bitter struggle with overtones of distaste and resentment.

American and Philippine mothers do not differ as much in their attitudes about fighting within the family as they do when the scrap involves peers outside of the family. Filipino children may quarrel with siblings, but they must avoid altercations with neighbors' children. In a pattern that persists in adulthood, the children are encouraged to withdraw from a situation in which tempers might flare. The ideal child is one who lives peacefully with others and does not hurt their feelings. He relies on his family to protect his rights. Instead of the assertion of his own interests with frequent associated aggression, the Filipino child is encouraged to avoid aggressive acts and to attain his personal interests by winning the interest of the larger group.

Finally, possibly in response to the physical environment, the Filipino mothers in our sample reported fewer restrictions on the child's activities. He can move more freely around the neighborhood; he can play more freely in the house; he can go to bed later; and there is less restriction on the amount of noise he can make.

In both societies there are marked individual differences between families. One American mother weans at five months, a second at ten; one teaches her child to go to the bathroom at fourteen months, while others permit their children to wear diapers a year longer. Within one society the differences are differences of preference, convenience, or attitude, but the reasons for the practices are more or less shared. The differences across cultures are more profound, for they involve differences in the meaning of the activity, differences in the persons involved, and differences in the context of relationships in which the practice takes place. Individual differences from one mother to the next do not appear along the same continua in the two cultures. There are significant differences between the cultures in the configuration of attitudes and practices surrounding birth, feeding, weaning, toilet training, dependency, hostility, and sexuality.

Implications for Personality Theory

Linton observed twenty years ago that:

> The most fundamental problem which confronts students of personality today is that of the degree to which the deeper levels of personality are conditioned by environmental factors. This problem cannot be solved by laboratory techniques. It is impossible to create controlled environments comparable to the social-cultural configurations within which all human beings develop. Neither can one appraise the influence of many environmental factors by observations carried on within the frame of our own culture and society. Many of the factors operative here are taken so much for granted that they never enter into the investigator's calculations. The only way in which the Personality Psychologist can get the comparative data which he requires is by the study of individuals reared in different societies and cultures. (1945, p. xvi)

In the intervening years we feel that too frequently cross-cultural studies of personality have assumed that the deeper levels of personality are the same in all societies. One makes this assumption when one uses psychoanalytic concepts to account for behavior in societies far removed from that in which Freud formulated his ideas. It is a tribute either to Freud's genius or to the ambiguity of his concepts that psychoanalytic interpretations are as convincing as they appear to be.

As we stated at the outset, we have adopted an interpersonal point of view which emphasizes the role of learning in social situations in the formation of personality. This is a parsimonious approach, and it appears to yield satisfactory results. In the domains of sexuality, dependency, and aggression, we feel that our observations in the Philippines confirm the importance of social learning.

Philippine children have many opportunities to observe adult models. Surrounded by many people who reinforce his age-appropriate behavior and who, by teasing, punish behavior which falls outside the consensus, the child is aided by many models since he is not excluded from adult activities. Dependency behavior is maintained and slowly modified through childhood. It is not a conflictful area but rather one which is approved by the society and enjoyed at least some of the time by both persons in a dependent relationship.

Our evidence is slight, but we conjecture that heterosexual behavior is similarly influenced by the availability of models. A child is teased for behavior which is either precocious or delayed. He is labeled according to his age as being ready or not ready for certain information; he is not deemed bad at one juncture for behavior which would be expected later on. Since the majority of his contacts are within an extended family, he is surrounded by adults who feel some responsibility for him. Accordingly, he receives a more consistent set of models and rewards than is the case where only a few of the adults around a child have any special interest in him and where markedly conflicting models are offered by outsiders. Even homosexual behavior is treated leniently and is not the object of panic that it is in some other societies. We would argue that sexual role behavior can be understood in a social learning framework without denying its physiological components. Our data and impressions lead us to question the theory that the solution of conflicts in the sexual realm constitutes the keystone of the arch of personality.

The maintenance of smooth relationships and goodwill and the control of anger and hostility constitute an area of much complexity in the life of the Filipino. Again, members of the extended family offer a good deal of reinforcement, shaping skills in this realm. Models of effective behavior are readily available to imitate. The number of adults to be kept happy and the living arrangements dictated by the environment make activities in this domain a continuing matter of concern. Personality patterns are extensively elaborated in this aspect. One who has developed a wide repertoire of responses is approved, while someone who has not learned to live in peace with others is rejected.

What, then, are the factors which are different in the Philippines which may have some significant effect on the deeper levels of personality? Our data permit us only to offer a most tentative response to this question. We are convinced that the Filipino child, from conception on, develops in a matrix of social determinants which is different, and the degree of difference produces different personality processes.

The Filipino child is never alone. In a one-room house with many siblings and other relatives the child may be several years old before he has his first experience of being out of sight of others. In addition he is carried, handled, and touched a great deal, and, of course, he may possibly never sleep alone throughout his whole life span. Since he is in such continuing contact with others, he develops a good many techniques for handling the variety of stresses which inevitably arise. With the fundamental importance to him of activities in this domain, his personality in formation and structure is oriented to his relationships with others.

The child has many models to emulate among the older persons who are important to him and many conflicting expectations to fulfill. Under these circumstances internalization of norms is probably modified, and he develops a pattern of responding to the expectations of others and of shifting as others and their expectations shift. This is, of course, akin to the shame-versus-guilt orientation that has been suggested by others. The single most important implication of this difference is that a single parent, the mother, probably has less to do with personality development and possible personality difficulties than is the case when the mother is almost the only adult figure in the child's life. Superego formation in this setting must be markedly different as attested by differences in social organization and control. There has been a good deal of discussion of shame and guilt in societies, for instance by Spiro (1961, pp. 116–121). The systems of control which the Filipino child develops are designed to placate and please many others or at least to avoid irritating them.

In our interviews and in the data we report, there is little to support the inevitability of sibling rivalry. In the same vein, the encouragement of dependency and physical closeness and the lack of privacy in sleeping arrangements provide excellent conditions for the arousal of oedipal strivings if they are universal and instinctual.

However, our data and our interviews offer little to support the oedipal theory. The indifference of the Filipino to males dressing as women, and to the associated homosexual activity, suggests that the direction of sexual interest is greatly the result of social factors. Instinctually oriented libido theory would probably have been formulated quite differently if it had been based on observations made in the Philippines.

Traditional psychoanalytic theory of personality development has placed a good deal of emphasis on events associated with the acquisition of sphincter control. In a setting where bathrooms are infrequent, this training is quite different and the personality sequelae probably are also. In the Philippines the washing relationship and the easier acceptance of bodily functions reduces the likelihood of toilet training experiences serving as the basis of subsequent anal character traits in the Western sense. If anything, these experiences are likely to make Filipinos more dependent and conscious of others, personality patterns which are not ordinarily considered to be established in connection with the acquisition of sphincter control.

Our data are too limited to permit extended consideration of the problem of psychosexual orientation. Indications of a latency period are not in evidence in this population. Rather there is a clear emphasis on the environmental or social determination of changes in behavior as a function of the age of the individual. The sexual drive is seen as subject to a good deal of direction and social control, as witness the chaperone system and the emphasis on parental advice.

With many people living in a close physical and social relationship, the handling of hostility is of crucial importance. A good deal of emphasis is placed on the ability to avoid potentially angry situations. Sensitivity and shame may be derivatives of conditioning in this domain. In this population handling negative feelings toward others would appear to be the most fundamental problem in personality organization that we have been able to infer.

Concluding Remarks

The Philippines provides a range of environmental determinants of personality which cannot be found or readily simulated in the

American setting. By observing Filipino children we are able to make some inferences concerning the effect of variables over ranges which do not often appear in American settings. The ideal of an experiment in which only one variable is systematically varied is not reached in research of this sort. However, we do gain a situation where certain conditions are consistently different over periods long enough to give us some suggestion of their total effect. Although we cannot assign causal significance with confidence, we can observe the relationship between personality formation and structure on the one hand and patterns of closeness, dependency, a different pattern of bowel training, a different significance of aggression, and a different set of psychosexual patterns. Research with populations such as those in the Philippines should enable us to determine how specific or general are the relationships between the variables we employ in our personality theories.

Finally, much further research, possibly employing factor analytic or other multidimensional techniques, is needed to answer the question of what Sears (1961) has called the equivalence of transcultural variables. We have emphasized the differences by using Tagalog terms for personality configurations and interpersonal processes which we felt were inadequately described by an American concept. Insofar as the two societies emphasize different matters and practice different patterns of relationships between their members, we would argue that members of these societies have different personality formations, and that different concepts are probably necessary.

If one were to develop a theory of personality based on Philippine patterns he would likely emphasize that certain experiences were of crucial significance. It appears to us that there are a half dozen interpersonal skills which a Filipino child must learn at certain more or less specific stages in his development:

1. Recognize subtle cues which reveal the unspoken feelings of others.
2. Cope with angry feelings without striking out at others.
3. Give and receive help; pool his well-being with that of his nuclear and extended family.
4. Ignore activities of others which, although visible, are said to be none of his concern.
5. Tease and be teased without losing his self-control.
6. Recognize his obligations to others for favors received.

We are convinced that it makes a lot of difference whether you develop your personality theory in Vienna or Manila.

This book has been concerned with the description, comparison, and interpretation of the child-rearing behavior of a group of mothers. These women were firmly convinced that they could influence greatly what became of their children. They were articulate concerning their methods and hopes. This made the task of description rather easy. Comparison with American mothers was more difficult because mothers in the two societies did not cope with the same problems, nor were they seeking similar results. Interpretation, at our present state of data collection and of theory construction, is a risky matter. But these data enable us to gain perspective on our theories of personality development, and they suggest possible fruitful directions for new research.

bibliography

Abasolo-Domingo, Maria Fe. Child-rearing practices in barrio Cruz na Ligas. Unpublished masters thesis, Univer. of the Philippines, 1961.

Barton, R. F. *The half-way sun*. New York: Brewer & Warren, 1930.

Batacan, D. F. *Looking at ourselves*. Manila: Philaw Publishing, 1956.

Blair, Emma H., & Robertson, J. A. *The Philippine Islands, 1493–1898*. Cleveland: Clark, 1903.

Carreon, M. L. *Philippine studies in mental measurement*. New York: World Book, 1926.

Clarke, Edith. *My mother who fathered me; a study of the family in three selected communities in Jamaica*. London: Allen & Unwin, 1957.

Cole, F. C. *The peoples of Malaysia*. New York: Van Nostrand, 1945.

Coller, R. W. Barrio Gacao. *University of the Philippines Community Development Research Council, Study Series*, 1960, No. 9.

Conklin, H. C. *Hanunoo agriculture*. Rome: Food and Agriculture Organization, 1957.

Eggan, F. Some social institutions in the Mountain Province and their significance for historical and comparative studies. *J. East Asiatic Stud.*, 1954, 3, 329–335.

Foreman, J. *The Philippine Islands*. New York: Scribners, 1890.

Fox, R. B. Filipino family and kinship. *Philippine Quart.*, 1961, 2, No. 1.

Fox, R. B. The Pinatubo Negritos: Their useful plants and material culture. *Philippine J. of Sci.*, 1953, 81, 173–414.

Geertz, Hildred. *The Javanese family*. New York: Free Press, 1961.

Gironiere, P. P. *Twenty years in the Philippines*. New York: Harper, 1854.

Guthrie, G. M. *The Filipino child and Philippine society*. Manila: Philippine Normal College Press, 1961.

Guthrie, G. M. Structure of maternal attitudes in two cultures. *J. Psychol.*, 1966, 62, 155–165.

Guthrie, Helen A. Infant feeding practices in the Philippines. *Tropical and geographic Med.*, 1962, 14, 164–169.

Harlow, H. Love in infant monkeys. *Scientific Amer.*, 1959, 200 (6), 68–74.

Hart, D. V. The Philippine plaza complex. *Yale University Southeast Asia Studies, Cultural Report Series*, 1955, No. 3.

Hartendorp, A. V. H. *History of industry and trade of the Philippines*. Manila: Philippine Education Co., 1958.

Hollnsteiner, Mary R. Reciprocity in the lowland Philippines. Manila: Ateneo Univer. Press. *IPC Papers*, 1962, No. 2.

Hsu, F. L. K. *Under the ancestors' shadow*. New York: Columbia Univer. Press, 1948.

Hunt, C. L., et al. *Sociology in the Philippine setting*. Manila: Alemar's, 1954.

Kardiner, A. *The psychological frontiers of society*. New York: Columbia Univer. Press, 1945.

Kaut, C. Utang na loob: A system of contractual obligation among Tagalogs. *Southwestern J. Anthrop.*, 1961, 17, 256–272.

Keesing, F. M. *The ethnohistory of northern Luzon*. Stanford: Stanford Univer. Press, 1962.

Lambrecht, F. The Mayawyaw ritual. *Publications of the Catholic Anthropological Conference*, 1932–1941, Vol. IV, Nos. 1–5.

Landy, D. *Tropical childhood*. Chapel Hill: Univer. North Carolina Press, 1959.

Levine, R. A., & Levine, Barbara B. Nyansongo: A Gusii community in Kenya. In Beatrice B. Whiting (Ed.), *Six cultures*. New York: Wiley, 1963. Pp. 19–202.

Lewis, O. *Tepoztlan village in Mexico*. New York: Holt, Rinehart & Winston, 1960.

Linton, R. *The cultural background of personality*. New York: Appleton-Century-Crofts, 1945.

Lynch, F. Lowland Philippine values: Social acceptance. Manila: Ateneo Univer. Press. *IPC Papers*, 1962, No. 2.

Lynch, F. Social class in a Bicol town. *University of Chicago Philippine Studies Program Research Series*, 1959, No. 1.

Maretzki, T. W., & Maretzki, Hatsumi. Taira: An Okinawan village. In Beatrice B. Whiting (Ed.), *Six cultures*. New York: Wiley, 1963. Pp. 367–539.

Minturn, Leigh, & Hitchcock, J. T. The Rajputs of Khalapur, India. In Beatrice B. Whiting (Ed.), *Six cultures*. New York: Wiley, 1963. Pp. 207–361.

Mullahy, P. *Oedipus myth and complex*. New York: Hermitage Press, 1948.

Murray, H. A. *Explorations in personality*. New York: Oxford Univer. Press, 1958.

Nurge, Ethel. *Life in a Leyte Village*. Seattle: Univer. of Washington Press, 1965.

Nydegger, W. F., & Nydegger, Corrine. Tarong: An Ilocos barrio in the Philippines. In Beatrice B. Whiting (Ed.), *Six cultures*. New York: Wiley, 1963. Pp. 697–867.

Oracion, T. An introduction to the culture of the Magahats of the Upper Tayaban River Valley, Tolong, Negros Oriental, Philippines. Unpublished masters thesis, Univer. of Chicago, 1952.

Pal, A. P. The resources, levels of living and aspirations of rural households in Negros Oriental. *University of the Philippines Community Development Research Council*, 1963.

Pecson, Geronima T. *Our Filipino children*. Manila: National Media Production Center, 1962.

Romney, K., & Romney, Romaine. The Mixtecans of Juxtlahuaca, Mexico. In Beatrice B. Whiting (Ed.), *Six cultures*. New York: Wiley, 1963. Pp. 545–691.

Scott, W. H. Boyhood in Sagada. *Anthrop. Quart.*, 1958, 31, 61–72.

Sears, R. R. Transcultural variables and conceptual equivalence. In B. Kaplan (Ed.), *Studying personality cross-culturally*. Evanston: Row, Peterson, 1961. Pp. 445–455.

✓ Sears, R. R., Maccoby, Eleanor E., & Levin, H. *Patterns of child rearing*. Evanston: Row, Peterson, 1957.

Social Welfare Administration. National report of the Philippines on the theme "The child in the family," presented to the Second International Study Conference on Child Welfare, Japan, 1958 (mimeographed).

Solis, Miguela M. *Understanding the Filipino child*. Manila: Bartolome, 1957.

Spiro, M. Social systems, personality, and functional analysis. In B. Kaplan (Ed.), *Studying personality cross-culturally*. Evanston: Row, Peterson, 1961. Pp. 93–127.

Stoodley, B. H. Some aspects of Tagalog family structure. *Amer. Anthrop.*, 1957, 59, 236–249.

Sullivan, H. S. *Collected works*. New York: Norton, 1964.

Tangco, M. The Christian peoples of the Philippines. *Univer. of the Philippines natural and appl. Sci. Bull.*, 1951, 11, 1–115.

Vanoverbergh, M. The Isneg. *Publications of the Catholic Anthropological Conference*, 1932–1941, Vol. III, Nos. 1–4.

✓ Whiting, J. W. M., & Child, I. L. *Child training and personality*. New Haven: Yale Univer. Press, 1953.

Whiting, J. W. M. et al. Field guide for the cross-cultural study of child rearing. New York: Social Science Research Council, 1953.

Whorf, B. L. *Language, thought and reality: Selected writings of Benjamin Lee Whorf*. J. B. Carroll (Ed.). New York: Wiley, 1956.

appendix

Final Form of Interview Schedule (English Version)

I'm a student at the Philippine Normal College and this has been assigned to me as part of my student-teaching. I want to ask you some questions about X.

1. Mother: _____ Age: _____
   Occupation: _____
   Highest grade completed: _____
   From what place: _____
   Dialect: _____Social class: _____

2. Father:_____Age: _____
   Occupation: _____
   Highest grade completed: _____
   From what place: _____
   Dialect: _____Social class: _____

3. Children—List from eldest to youngest, including ages. Encircle the child talked about; underline any dead siblings.

4. Are any of your children adopted?

5. Are any of your children being raised by other people?

6. Other adults in the home—Ages, relationship to the child.

Pregnancy and Birth:

7. How many children did you hope for when you got married? (Try to find out her feelings about having children—if she looked forward to having X especially.)

8. There are couples who don't seem to be able to have children. What do you think they should do?

9. How are your pregnancies?

10. What difficulties did you have when you were pregnant with X?

11. Did you have any particular cravings? What did you do about them? Any particular aversions? What did you do? How about your husband during your pregnancy? Did he have any difficulties?

12. What did you like or hate so much that you think it had an effect on X? (In what way did he take after this?)

13. Where was X born? Who attended you? Describe the circumstances. Any difficulties you remember? (Watch for possible effects of this on parent-attitude toward the child.) (What do they do for long labor?)

    *What kind of a baby was X then as you remember him now? What do you remember most clearly about him?

    * Is there anything you should be careful about in disposing of the placenta? What should you do? Why is that desirable?

Feeding:

14. How was X fed as a baby? If bottle-fed, why? Did somebody breast-feed him besides you? Why? How long did this go on?

    *If you had a choice, which way of feeding would you rather your child had? Why?

15. How often did you feel you had to feed X? Did you have to feed him everytime he cried, or did you have a definite time for feeding?

16. What did you do when he cried and you felt he was not hungry? Did you use any pacifiers? Why? What kind?

17. What food is good for nursing mothers? Which of these did you have more of when you nursed X?

18. How old was X when you stopped breast-feeding him? Why did you stop? How did you wean him? Who helped you wean him? Did you have any difficulties?

19. What did you feed him when you stopped breast-feeding?

20. When did he start drinking from a glass and being fed from a spoon? When did he start feeding himself? Do you remember how he learned?

21. At what age was he given food which required chewing? What was it?

22. Was he difficult to feed? What did you do when he refused any food? (Ask specifically what these were.) Does he still refuse this?

    *What happens when he does not like the food ready at that time?

23. What was the most difficult thing about feeding him, and why was it difficult?

Dependency:

24. How communicative is he with you? Does he tell you everything? When he needs something, or something bothers him, or something has made

* The asterisk refers to items included in final form which were not in preliminary forms.

him so happy, do you always know? (Try to find out at different ages.)
Do you encourage this (let him tell you all he wants to)?

*What do you do when you're so busy you can't stand his talk anymore?
Who else does he talk to?

25. When he comes home crying, what do you do? When you hear a report about him from his playmates or the neighbors, what do you do?

26. Can he hold his own with other children? How is he in his play with others? What children (age, kind, sex) does he usually choose for playmates? (Or does he have no choice?)

27. Does he often come to you for help? What does he ask help for? What things does he ask you to do for him that you think he can do? When do you help him?

*Does it irritate you sometimes especially when you're busy? What do you do?

28. What do you do when he has a fight with a neighbor's child? What usually happens? What do you tell him?

29. There are children who are overtly affectionate and those who are not. How about X? How does he show affection or ask for it? With whom does he usually do this?

30. What help does he ask of his father? How often does he go to his father for help? (How close is X to him?) Who else does he go to for help? To his older siblings? Besides being close to you to whom else is he very close?

31. Why is it that although we believe we should love our children equally, we have one or two who are so good, we can't help being very pleased with them? Have you felt this way about any of your children? Do the children notice this? When usually? What do they say? Does the child know it? How does X feel about it?

Does any of your children sometimes feel that one of them gets more (affection) care from you than he does? When does this usually happen? Do they say it or do you just know it? How? What do you do when this happens?

* When you're going somewhere, what do you do about him? Does he want to tag along often? What happens when you can't take him along and he insists? What do you do? How do you manage to leave him?

32. When he wants something so badly and he is crossed, what does he do (so that you or whoever crossed him could notice his disappointment)? Or does he show it at all? In what things does he hate being crossed? What do you do when you notice?

Obedience, Punishment:

33. What things that you tell him not to do, does he do? How often does this happen?

34. What do you do when he disobeys? Does he give reasons when he does? How do you feel about children's reasoning back?

35. Do you have to punish him very often? How? How often? What punishment does he fear most or is most effective do you think?

36. Does he obey? What do you do or say that makes him obey or to make him obey?

37. What are some things he doesn't want to do? How does he make these known to you? How could he be made to do them?

38. Does he always have to obey his older brothers and sisters? Does he talk back to them? What are some things that they ask him to do? Which does he obey? What happens when he does not obey?

39. Who else does he have to obey at home? In what things? What happens when he does not obey them?

40. Who may punish him? What types of punishment may they give? From whom does he accept punishment? What does he do when he is punished? What punishment (and from whom) does he seem to resent most?

41. What are the things he does that you don't like him to do? What happens or what do you do when he does these?

Health and Cleanliness:

42. Does he get his clothes dirty? How? Is this not very much trouble to you?

43. Parents often complain about how children can get the house so dirty and disorderly. Does X give you any problems in this? What do you do?

44. When did he stop wearing diapers? (Find out if there was any substitute or if the child just went without anything.)

45. Did you have any difficulty with his elimination? How was it when he was a baby? When he started to crawl, sit, and walk a little?

    Did you have to teach him when to do it and where or did he just learn it by himself? How do you think he learned?

    How did you teach him? How old was he when you started teaching him? About how old was he when he learned this (where and when)? About how old was he when he could be left alone in this?

46. What time does he go to sleep? Regularly? Or are there nights when he may stay up later? When?

47. Does he bed-wet? How often was this when he was still a baby? When did it get reduced to how it is now? What makes children bed-wet usually?

48. Who sleeps with him? Is it any trouble for the companion when he bed-wets? What happens? (Find out parent's reaction to this when it happens.)

49. When did he stop bed-wetting? Did you have to do anything to stop it?

Sex, Curiosities:

Does it not usually happen that children say things or ask questions, in all innocence, and we wonder if we should laugh or get angry or be serious about them? For example—

50. Did he ever ask questions about where he came from or where any young child came from? (If yes,) how did you answer him? (If no,) do you think he knows about where babies come from? How do you think he found out?

Would you know when our young people really start knowing about how conception takes place? In your case, when did you find out? (Try to find out how she found out.)

51. Does he ever ask about you, or his father, or about himself/herself? Or why girls are that way and boys are different? What do you say to him?

If he has any curiosity about boys/girls or about himself/herself do you think he would be afraid to ask you? Who might he ask?

52. Can he take a bath alone? Change his clothes alone? (Find out where they bathe and change clothes.) How old was he when he started doing these alone? Who used to help him with these before? Why did you (or anybody) stop? (Find out if it was the parent's idea to stop or the child's refusal to be helped—and why.)

How does the child react to bathing or to being bathed—any difficulty, or does he enjoy it?

53. Does he use words which you do not like, words which you would be ashamed about if other people would hear? Where could he have picked these up? What did you do to stop him? What happens?

Aggression:

54. Does he get angry often? What does he get angry about? Does he ever get angry with you? With any older person? Does he speak it out loud, murmur, take it out on something else? Do you allow this?

What does he do when he is angry with you? What do you do? What do others do?

55. What does he do when he gets angry?

56. Does he have temper tantrums? In what forms? What usually brings these about?

57. What do you do when he is angry or has a tantrum?

58. With whom does he quarrel most often? How does he quarrel? (What does he do?) What should he do?

59. What does he do when he quarrels with his older brothers and sisters? When they quarrel with him? When he quarrels with his younger brothers and sisters? (Does he strike, pinch, etc. . . ?) What do you do?

60. When he wants something he cannot have, what does he do?

61. Does he tease? Whom does he tease often? How does he tease? Does he call names? What names does he use?

62. What does he do when he is teased? What teasing makes him most angry?
*What are the things about him that he doesn't like you to talk to other people about? What does he do when he overhears? When did he start being sensitive about this?
*What are the things he does not like to be teased about? When do you think this (sensitivity) started?
*What are the things he is proud to tell you about?
*What are the things you cannot make him do when other people are around? Why?

63. What makes you most angry with him? What do you do when he really gets you very angry?

Fears:

64. What was he most afraid of as a baby? When he was bigger? Now?

65. What do you use or say to frighten him when you want him to stop doing something or when you don't want him to do something? What happens?

66. Who else frightens him? With what? What does X do?

67. What stories make him most afraid?

68. Do you remember what they used to frighten you about when you were a child?

69. What ailments did you guard X against? What methods did you use? From whom did you learn these methods? (Try to get at practices based on belief and on mothers' or old folk advice especially.)

Parental Values:

70. What did you like best in him as a young child? What is the thing that you would like him most to be? Do you let him know this? How?

71. From whom did you learn your way of rearing your children? Are you raising your children differently from the way you were raised? In what ways? Was there anything in their way of raising you that you would not want to apply to your own children? What are these? Why?

72. What mistakes do other parents make in raising their children? Is there anything your relatives do in raising their children that you would disagree with? What are these? How would you like your child to be different?

Ratings for Specific Comparison with Sears

1. How many months did you breast-feed? _____

2. At what age did you begin to wean and at what age did you complete it?
   Began: _____ Completed: _____

3. There has been a lot of talk about whether it is better to have a regular feeding schedule for a baby, or to feed him whenever he is hungry. How do you feel about this? How did you handle this with X?
   Check the letter below which is closest to the mother's answer:
   _____ a. Complete self-demand: child always fed when he cried (was hungry). Child permitted to eat as much, and as long, or as little as he wanted at a feeding.
   _____ b. Schedule set by child himself: fairly regular, but no evidence that mother exerted any pressure to bring this about.
   _____ c. Vague attempts at scheduling, but mother would never wake child for a feeding and would feed as much as an hour early if it seemed necessary.
   _____ d. Rough schedule, which mother would modify by as much as half hour if the child seemed hungry.
   _____ e. Fairly rigid schedule, which would not be modified by more than fifteen minutes.
   _____ f. Rigid feeding schedule: child fed by clock, wakened for feedings.

4. Have you had any problems about X eating enough, or eating the kinds of food he needs?
   Check the letter below which is closest to the mother's answer:
   _____ a. No feeding problems: child has hearty appetite, eats what is given to him, enjoys food.
   _____ b. Mild problems: one or two brief incidents. In general, good appetite.

———— c. "Finicky" about food. Some loss of appetite, periods not prolonged.

———— d. Considerable feeding problems: loss of appetite, many fads in eating.

———— e. Severe problems: child would gag or vomit, refuse to eat. Resistance to eating prolonged.

5. At what age did you begin bowel training?
   At what age was it completed?
   Began: ——————————— Completed: ———————————

6. How did you train him to control his bowel movements?
   Check the letter below which is closest to the mother's answer:

———— a. Not at all severe. Child more or less trained himself. Not his fault when he has accidents; they are considered natural. No punishment or scolding.

———— b. Slight pressure. Mild disapproval for some late accidents; mother makes some efforts to show child where, when, and how to go toilet.

———— c. Moderate pressure. Scolding for some late deviations; fairly frequent toileting.

———— d. Fairly severe training. Child scolded fairly often; mother clearly shows disapproval. Child may be left on toilet for fairly lengthy periods.

———— e. Very severe training. Child punished severely for deviations; mother angry and emotional over them.

7. Does he still bed-wet? ———————
   How often? If not any more when did he stop? ———————

8. What did you do when he cried when he was a baby?
   Check the letter below which is closest to the mother's answer:

———— a. Extremely unresponsive. Believed child must not be spoiled; didn't want to "give in" to crying.

———— b. Mother relatively unresponsive. Child generally picked up only when mother believed something was wrong; allowed to cry for extended periods.

———— c. "It depends." Picked up if mother thought child was hungry; allowed to cry if mother thought it was simply "fretful." Would allow to cry for a while, but not too long.

———— d. Relatively responsive. Usually picked child up, although occasionally allowed it to cry for brief periods.

———— e. Highly responsive to infant's crying; always picked it up immediately.

9. What do you do when he gets angry at you and shows his anger?

Check the letter below which is closest to the mother's answer:

_____ a. Not at all permissive. Believes this is something one should not permit under any circumstances. Always attempts to stop child immediately; neither verbal nor physical aggression permitted.

_____ b. Slightly permissive.

_____ c. Moderately permissive. Feels that one must expect a certain amount of this, but that it should be discouraged rather firmly. May permit some "sassing" but no hitting.

_____ d. Quite permissive.

_____ e. Completely permissive. Does not attempt to stop child from hitting parent or shouting angrily at him. May express belief that child has right to hit parent if parent has right to hit child.

10. What do you do when he quarrels and fights with his brothers and sisters?

Check the letter below which is closest to the mother's answer:

_____ a. Not at all permissive. Parents try to stop quarreling and fighting immediately. Punish severely.

_____ b. Slightly permissive.

_____ c. Moderately permissive. Stop if somebody getting hurt; may allow verbal battles if they don't go on too long. Scolding given but not severe punishment.

_____ d. Quite permissive.

_____ e. Entirely permissive. Mother never interferes in children's quarrels; they are allowed to fight it out. Parents do not try to stop or prevent this.

11. What do you do when he quarrels and fights with other children.

Check the letter below which is closest to the mother's answer:

_____ a. Not at all permissive. Parent always tries to stop or prevent fights. Child severely punished for fighting.

_____ b. Slightly permissive.

_____ c. Moderately permissive. Parent will not interfere unless someone is getting hurt. Child may be scolded for fighting; but not severely punished. Mother will let quite a bit of it go on.

_____ d. Quite permissive.

_____ e. Entirely permissive. Mother never interferes, never tells child she does not want him to fight. Considers it natural, part of growing up.

12. What must X do when other children fight with him?

_____ a. None whatsoever. Parent explicitly says she does not want child to fight with other children—ever. Child encouraged to come home if going gets rough.

_____ b. No demands to fight, but no statement that it should always be discouraged.

_____ c. Slight demands for fighting. If child is really being bullied, he should defend self but in general should not fight.

_____ d. Moderate demands for fighting. Should defend self, but never start fights and not hit back if other child is smaller.

_____ e. High demands for fighting. Child should never take anything from other children; important to hold up one's own end, not come asking for help.

13. How much do you let him go away from the house?

_____ a. No restrictions. Child permitted to go wherever he wishes—across streets, to other children's yards, etc.

_____ b. A few restrictions. Child may go several streets away, visit other children by self, but must let mother know where he is.

_____ c. Quite a bit of restriction. Child can go to school by self but otherwise not across street or off street or across boundaries (boundaries in this case larger than own yard).

_____ d. Restricted to front of house and own yard but allowed to go to school alone.

_____ e. Child restricted to own yard and not allowed to go to school alone.

14. How much do you have to control him in the house?

_____ a. No restrictions. Child may jump on furniture, mark on walls, put feet up, play with other people's things.

_____ b. Few restrictions

_____ c. Moderate restrictions. May jump on some things, not others. Possibly certain parts of the house set aside for careful treatment.

_____ d. Considerable restriction. Important for child to be careful of household furnishings.

_____ e. Many restrictions. Very important for child to be careful about marking and jumping. Must take off shoes before putting feet up. All furniture, all parts of the house to be treated carefully. Not allowed to touch a large number of objects.

15. When does he go to bed? How much do you insist that he go at that time?

_____ a. Not at all strict—no particular rules. Child goes to bed when sleepy; may have lights on and door open if he wishes.

_____ b. A few limitations. Parents have bedtime in mind, but allow deviations fairly often; consider child's special needs at time.

_____ c. Some limitations. Child supposed to be in bed at a certain time, but parents allow some leeway. Mild scolding for not conforming.

_____ d. Fairly strict. Will not stretch bedtime very much or very often; considerable pressure for conformity.

_____ e. Very strict—no leeway. Child must be in bed on dot, lights out, door closed; no getting up for company. Punishment for deviation.

16. How much do you try to control the noise he makes?

_____ a. Not at all strict. Child may yell, run, bang—without reprimand. Rough loud games permitted. "After all, you expect noise from children."

_____ b. A few restrictions on noise.

_____ c. Moderately strict. Children must not shout, must avoid banging and loudest games, but quite a bit of leeway allowed.

_____ d. Quite strict about noise.

_____ e. Very strict. Children may never run in house, shout or yell, or bang doors. Punishment for noise-making.

17. Some parents expect their children to obey immediately when they tell them to be quiet or pick something up and so on. Others don't think it is terribly important for a child to obey right away. How do you feel about this?

_____ a. Does not expect obedience. May say one should not expect it of a child this young, or that parents can be wrong, too, and do not have the right to expect children to snap to attention.

_____ b. Expects some obedience, but will speak several times; tolerant attitude toward noncompliance.

_____ c. Wants child to obey, but expects some delay. Whether tolerates delay depends on what the situation is. Some scolding or other pressure for not obeying.

_____ d. Wants and expects obedience. Generally expects child to obey on first or second demand; considerable pressure for conformity.

_____ e. Expects instant obedience; does not tolerate any delay. Punishment for deviation—very strict.

index